You Gotta Eat Here!

JOHN CATUCCI
AND MICHAEL VLESSIDES

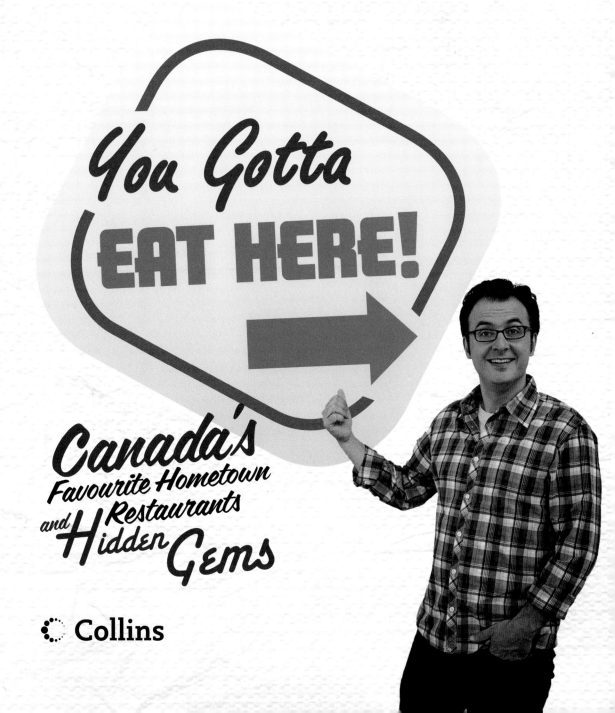

You Gotta
EAT HERE!

Canada's Favourite Hometown Restaurants and Hidden Gems

Collins

HarperCollins Publishers Ltd
2 Bloor Street East, 20th Floor
Toronto, Ontario, Canada
M4W 1A8

www.harpercollins.ca

Library and Archives Canada Cataloguing in Publication
information is available upon request.

ISBN 978-1-44341-615-3

Printed and bound in Canada
TC 9 8 7 6 5 4 3 2 1

Contents

INTRODUCTION 1

EASTERN CANADA

The Armview Restaurant & Lounge, Halifax, NS 6

Boneheads BBQ, Halifax, NS 10

Charlene's Bayside Restaurant & Cafe, Whycocomagh, NS 14

Ches's Famous Fish & Chips, St. John's, NL. 18

Coastal Waters Restaurant & Pub, Ingonish, NS. 22

Déjà BU!, Caraquet, NB. 26

Landmark Cafe, Victoria by the Sea, PEI 30

Magnolia's Grill, Lunenburg, NS. 34

New Glasgow Lobster Suppers, New Glasgow, PEI 38

Rick's Fish 'N' Chips & Seafood House, St. Peter's Bay, PEI 44

Saint John Ale House, Saint John, NB 48

Salvatore's Pizzaiolo Trattoria, Halifax, NS. 54

Tide & Boar Gastropub, Moncton, NB 58

Urban Deli, Saint John, NB 62

Water-Prince Corner Shop and Lobster Pound, Charlottetown, PEI 66

CENTRAL CANADA

Baffo's Pizza & Pasta, Bolton, ON 74

Boomers Gourmet Fries, Stratford, ON 80

Bubi's Awesome Eats, Windsor, ON 84

Busters Barbeque, Vermilion Bay, ON 88

Café Polonez, Toronto, ON 92

Cardinal Rule, Toronto, ON 98

Chez Claudette, Montreal, QC 102

Chicago Style Pizza Shack, Hamilton, ON. 106

The Dam Pub Gastropub, Thornbury, ON 112

D&S Southern Comfort B.B.Q., Carlsbad Springs, ON. 116

Dangerous Dan's Diner, Toronto, ON 120

Elgin Street Diner, Ottawa, ON 124

The Grilled Cheese, Toronto, ON 128

Hadley's, Toronto, ON 132

The Harbour Diner, Hamilton, ON 138

Haugen's Chicken & Ribs Barbeque, Port Perry, ON 142

Hoito Restaurant, Thunder Bay, ON 146

Joe Feta's Greek Village, St. Catharines, ON 152

The Main Deli Steak House, Montreal, QC 156

The Musket Restaurant, Toronto, ON 160

Philadelphia Kitchen, Orangeville, ON 164

Phil's Original BBQ, Toronto, ON 168

Pizzeria Napoletana, Montreal, QC 172

Prince Albert's Diner, London, ON 176

Reggie's Hot Grill, Peterborough, ON 180

Relish the Best in Burgers, London, ON 184

Schwartz's Deli, Montreal, QC 188

Shish-Kabob Hut Greek Restaurant, Peterborough, ON 192

Stoneface Dolly's, Ottawa, ON 196

Stoney's Bread Company, Oakville, ON 200

That Little Place by the Lights, Huntsville, ON 204

Tre Sorelle, Orillia, ON 208

Tunnel Bar-B-Q, Windsor, ON 212

Uncle Betty's Diner, Toronto, ON 216

WESTERN CANADA

Argo Café, Vancouver, BC 222

Bistro Dansk, Winnipeg, MB 228

Blondies, Winnipeg, MB 232

Boon Burger Café, Winnipeg, MB 236

Chuckwagon Cafe & Cattle Company, Turner Valley, AB 240

Deja Vu Cafe, Moose Jaw, SK 244

Diner Deluxe, Calgary, AB 248

Evelyn's Memory Lane Cafe, High River, AB 252

Fat City Franks, Calgary, AB 256

Floyd's Diner, Victoria, BC 260

Fraser Park Restaurant, Burnaby, BC 266

Highlands Kitchen, Edmonton, AB 268

Jelly Modern Doughnuts, Calgary, AB 272

John's Place Restaurant, Victoria, BC 278

Mrs. Riches Restaurant, Nanaimo, BC 284

Neighbour's Restaurant, Vancouver, BC 288

Pagliacci's, Victoria, BC 292

Pfanntastic Pannenkoek Haus, Calgary, AB 296

Red Top Drive-Inn Restaurant, Winnipeg, MB 300

Rock Cod Café, Cowichan Bay, BC 304

SugarBowl, Edmonton, AB 308

The Tallest Poppy, Winnipeg, MB 312

The Tomahawk Barbecue, North Vancouver, BC 318

Topanga Cafe, Vancouver, BC 322

Tres Carnales Taquería, Edmonton, AB 328

Tubby Dog, Calgary, AB 332

Urban Diner, Edmonton, AB 336

ACKNOWLEDGEMENTS 341

RECIPE INDEX 345

YOU GOTTA EAT HERE! CHECKLIST 347

PHOTO CREDITS 355

I eat for a living.

THAT'S WHAT I TELL PEOPLE WHEN THEY ASK ME WHAT I DO. I TRAVEL THE COUNTRY AND EAT FOR A LIVING.

Along the way I have the distinct pleasure of cooking with some of Canada's best chefs. Best chefs, you ask? At joints that sell hotdogs with wasabi, macaroni and cheese as sushi, and clams on poutine? Yes, my friends, *best chefs*. These folks may not be whipping up exotic cuisine in fancy five-star restaurants, but each one of them is imaginative and daring, and so passionate about what they do that they'll even let an Italian-Canadian comedian stick his nose—and a bunch of TV cameras— into their very livelihood.

I talk to them about their lives, find out what makes them tick, ask them the secrets to their incredible food. And no matter what part of this huge country I find myself in, they all say the same thing: the best food always comes from the heart. And OK, so the ingredients make a difference, too. But when it comes to whipping up food that warms the heart, the primary ingredient is love.

This comes as no surprise to me, though. I grew up with the notion of food-as-affection. Family homestyle cooking, memories forged around the dinner table . . . these were the same lessons passed down to me by my dad. Antonio Catucci may have been a tailor by trade, but he was a chef at heart.

My dad didn't take vacations. He didn't make a lot of money. He worked three jobs my entire life. But my dad loved food. He lived to eat. He was the kind of guy who thrived on feeding people, who ached when you were already full and he couldn't possibly tempt you with another course or two.

When Sundays finally rolled around, Dad couldn't wait to get into the kitchen. He'd wake up early (he woke up early *every* morning; he was everyone else's alarm clock) and start his ragu. He'd use *sotto spalla* (beef shoulder) and slow cook it in the most delicious tomato sauce I ever tasted. Six hours later the ragu was ready and the beef so tender you could cut it with

a spoon. Then he'd come into my room with a fresh panino from the bakery across the street and a bowl of the sauce. He'd pass it over, and with a wink that meant "don't tell anyone else I brought you this," he'd go and crash on the couch for an afternoon nap until it was time for dinner.

My dad passed away on August 18, 2009. He was seventy-two, and I miss him every day. He never got to see the show, but I know he'd be proud to tell his friends that his son eats for a living.

Who cares if it's been more burgers than lasagna and more poutine than marinara sauce? Dad would understand that no matter what you're putting on the table in front of someone—even if it's a nine-pound burger—if it's made with love, it's worth eating.

So lay those napkins across your laps and dig in, amigos! What follows is a lighthearted look at some of the places I've been privileged enough to visit these past few years. But this book is about more than just food, as a good meal always is. You'll also grab a glimpse of the personalities, the environment, and the clientele that make these places special.

Just save a spot at the table for me, OK?

The Armview Restaurant & Lounge

EST. 1951
7156 CHEBUCTO ROAD
HALIFAX · NS · B3L 1N4
WWW.THEARMVIEW.COM

There's something special about a place that undergoes a change in ownership but still celebrates its heritage. That's the Armview Restaurant & Lounge, a Halifax gem that for more than sixty years has been serving up the freshest seafood money can buy. Maybe that's why the three childhood friends who own the Armview—George Kapetanakis, Peter Tsuluhas, and Billy Nikolaou—have adopted the motto "Straight from the shore to our door!"

When George, Peter, and Billy took over the Armview, they shut its doors and extensively renovated the Halifax landmark, but not in the name of modernization. Instead, the trio embraced its history, lovingly restoring the interior to echo the original diner's flair. The result is a retro-chic atmosphere that combines yesterday with today.

The Armview's menu does the same thing, offering happy customers everything from old-school comfort foods to international delicacies. But what really sets the Armview apart is its selection of fresh fish and the many ways it's used in their menu.

One of my favourites is the Mango Halibut Salad, where two skewers of locally caught halibut are grilled on the charbroiler and perched on top of a bed of arugula, baby tomatoes, mangoes, and red onions, then topped with a homemade lime vinaigrette. After eating more burgers than my arteries care to remember, I won't soon forget that peppery yet tangy change.

Local haddock is also a big part of the Armview's menu, and it's served with delicious simplicity. You can get it pan-seared, poached, or baked, but the lightly breaded pan-seared

When you've been serving up diner fare for more than sixty years, you're doing it right. On some nights the Armview's lounge hosts live music for its food-craving clientele.

The three childhood friends who own the Armview have adopted the motto "Straight from the shore to our door!"

The Mango Halibut Salad is a refreshingly light and delicious meal that speaks to the Armview's commitment to local ingredients with an international twist.

piece I had—served with mashed potatoes and peas and drizzled with a squeeze of fresh lemon juice—was so tender it melted in my mouth. The Haddock Burger is also breaded, then deep-fried ever so slightly. Served with homemade tartar sauce, it was a gorgeous thing to behold, crispy on the outside but still moist and tender on the inside. Oh, and in case you were wondering: yes, they do serve fish and chips!

But please don't think the menu at the Armview begins and ends with fish. That would not do justice to this place at all. On the contrary, amigos, this place offers virtually anything your mouth desires, no matter what time of day or night you wander in. Their breakfast and brunch menu serves everything from a Pear and Brie Panini to Lobster Eggs Benedict.

Those looking for more traditional fare can feast on a wide selection of burgers, sandwiches, and pasta. The Dingle Tower Burger—named after a local monument that stands within eyeshot of the Armview—is a massive mouthful that combines two mouth-watering beef patties covered with double orders of bacon and Cheddar and topped with pickles and garlic mayo. There's also a wide selection of Greek dishes like horiatiki (traditional Greek salad), kalamari, souvlaki, and even baklava. Hey, what do you expect from three guys named Kapetanakis, Tsuluhas, and Nikolaou?

If anything, you'll never get bored at the Armview. There's always something new to try, and it's always good!

Haddock Burgers with Tartar Sauce

Makes: 4 servings

Tartar Sauce

2 dill pickles, finely chopped

1/4 cup mayonnaise

1 teaspoon paprika

2 sprigs fresh parsley

2 dashes tabasco sauce

Squeeze of lemon juice

Salt and pepper

Haddock Breading

1 cup all-purpose flour

1/3 cup dry bread crumbs

1/2 cup panko bread crumbs

2 teaspoons dried basil

1 teaspoon chopped fresh dill

1 egg

1 cup milk

Assembly

Oil for deep-frying

4 skinless haddock fillets (3 1/2 ounces each)

4 hamburger buns, toasted

8 slices fresh Roma tomato

4 leaves red leaf or romaine lettuce

Tartar Sauce

In a small bowl, combine the dill pickles, mayo, paprika, parsley, tabasco sauce, lemon juice, and salt and pepper to taste.

Mix well. Chill until needed.

Haddock Breading

In a shallow dish, stir together the flour, bread crumbs, basil, and dill. In another shallow dish, beat together the egg and milk.

Assembly

Pour 2 or 3 inches of oil into a large heavy pot and heat to 340°F (or use a deep-fryer).

Dip a piece of haddock into the milk mixture, letting excess drip off; dredge fish in the crumb mixture, coating all sides.

Fry the breaded haddock for 6 to 7 minutes or until crispy and cooked through. Transfer to paper towels to drain. Repeat with the remaining pieces of fish.

Spread tartar sauce on the bottom of each toasted bun. Place a piece of haddock on top and finish with tomatoes, lettuce, and the top of the bun.

Boneheads BBQ

EST. 2010
1014 BARRINGTON STREET
HALIFAX · NS · B3H 2P9
WWW.LICKTHEBONE.COM

As a guy whose ancestors arrived here in 1963, I have a special place in my heart for Halifax. Yet as much of a homecoming as it may seem every time I return to the city, there's one type of food I never really expected to find in a place where seafood is king: southern barbeque. But that's exactly what you get at Boneheads, thanks to the passion of owner Cindy Wheatley, who travelled all over the US in search of the finest southern-style barbeque cooking this side of the Mississippi.

It didn't matter to Cindy that her friends called her a *bonehead* for trying to introduce an alien cuisine to fish-eating Haligonians. Cindy knew what she wanted. In fact, she believed so strongly in the cuisine that she named her restaurant in honour of her friends' skepticism. Now they apologize with every bite!

No doubt lots of those bites have been of Boneheads' pulled pork, a food that's almost as fun to prepare as it is to eat. Pulled pork here begins as a whole pork shoulder (sometimes called pork butt . . . insert twelve-year-old-boy giggle) that is carefully trimmed, then rubbed with a magical (at least according to chef and Boss Hog Al McPherson) spice mix and popped in the smoker. But the pork gets really fun when it comes out ten hours later. That's when the pulling begins. In fact, whenever a pork shoulder comes out of the smoker, all employees gather round and pull the tender bits of meat off the shoulder with their gloved hands. Once the pork

Owner Cindy Wheatley was so enamoured of the BBQ joints she found in the southern US that she modelled Boneheads after them.

Boneheads' pulled pork is so succulent it takes no effort to pull at all; it literally falls apart in your fingers.

has been sufficiently pulled, Al sautés it up with Boneheads' homemade barbeque sauce. Try it with Boneheads' tangy purple apple slaw, and you're sure to be licking your lips for hours to come.

Yet what stops the show for me at Boneheads is their smoked chicken wings, a southern twist on an old standby that's like none I've ever had before. Most BBQ joints deep-fry their chicken wings. Not so here at Boneheads, where the yawning mouth of the smoker awaits all meat. It's only a bit of vegetable oil, some more secret spices, and into the smoker. When ready to be served, the wings are tossed on the charbroiler for a few seconds to give them a charred flavour, tossed in a pan of browned butter, then popped in the oven. Why the pan of butter, you ask? Simple: butter makes *everything* better.

Boneheads' wings are all I need for the party in my mouth to get hoppin', but any dipping-sauce freaks can choose from one of three homemade sauces, too: Southern Gold, Smokehouse Sweet, and Kickin' Red.

Yet Boneheads also knows how to blend their southern BBQ roots with good ol' Canadiana, which is where their Burnt-End Poutine comes in. Now I know burnt ends are not the kinds of things typically found on a restaurant menu, but at Boneheads, Al takes the crispy ends of cooked beef brisket (called *the bark*) and adds them to his homemade poutine gravy. Top with old Cheddar, chopped tomatoes, and green onions, and it's classic poutine—with a hint of beef jerky.

So if you like it slow and low (and couldn't possibly have another bite of lobster), Boneheads is the place for you.

It didn't matter to Cindy that her friends called her a bonehead for trying to introduce an alien cuisine to fish-eating Haligonians. Cindy knew what she wanted.

Smoked Chicken Wings with Chipotle Ranch Dressing

Makes: 4 to 6 servings

Note: This recipe requires a smoker.

Smoked Wings

4 pounds whole or split chicken wings
1/2 cup vegetable or olive oil
Wood of your choice for smoking

Boneheads Wing Rub

1/2 cup sea salt
1/2 cup lightly packed brown sugar
1/2 cup white sugar
1/4 cup freshly ground black pepper
1/4 cup each chili powder, paprika, and
**   ground cumin**
2 tablespoons each garlic powder and
**   onion powder**
2 tablespoons cayenne pepper

Chipotle Ranch Dressing

1/2 cup mayonnaise
1/2 cup sour cream
1/3 cup buttermilk
1 tablespoon chipotle pepper paste
1/2 teaspoon salt
1/4 teaspoon each garlic powder and
**   onion powder**
1/8 teaspoon freshly ground black pepper

Boneheads Wing Rub

Combine all ingredients.

Chipotle Ranch Dressing

Place all ingredients in a bowl and whisk to combine.

Smoked Wings

Preheat smoker (or grill) to 225°F.

Rinse the chicken wings and pat dry. Place the wings in a foil pan or on a baking sheet and lightly coat with vegetable oil. (This helps the rub stick and keep the wings moist.) Sprinkle wings generously with 1 cup of Boneheads Wing Rub, making sure to turn and coat the entire wing. (You can also use a large resealable plastic bag to toss the wings, first in oil and then in rub.)

Place wings, evenly spaced, directly on the rack in the smoker and smoke for 1 hour or until a meat thermometer registers 165°F. Turn the wings over halfway through, and adjust positions if necessary to account for any hot spots in the smoker. Grill for a few minutes on both sides, and serve with Chipotle Ranch Dressing for dipping.

Note: Smoking times can vary greatly depending on wing size, outdoor weather conditions, smoker temperature, etc., so the above time is just a guideline. A meat thermometer will tell you when your wings have reached a safe temperature and are done.

Charlene's Bayside Restaurant & Cafe

EST. 2008
9657 HIGHWAY 105
WHYCOCOMAGH · NS · B0E 3M0

Charlene's holds a special place in my heart. It's in the small town of Whycocomagh, one of the first places I ever visited on hauntingly beautiful Cape Breton Island. And it was the first place I've ever been served something called a Bucket of Mud, which is the dessert all desserts want to be when they grow up. In fact, the Bucket of Mud is so damn good, you might skip the meal altogether (*not* a wise idea!) and head straight for the dessert menu.

Though Charlene MacNeil started working in the restaurant business when she was sixteen, it wasn't until 2008 that she decided to open her own restaurant. I'm glad she did!

Created by Charlene's sister, Michelle, the Bucket is a multi-layered monster, beginning with a foundation of thick, creamy, homemade chocolate pudding. Sprinkle a pile of homemade chocolate brownie chunks on top, followed by a layer of whipped cream. If you're starting to feel the sugar high already, button up, because you ain't seen nothing yet. The Bucket continues with another layer of each of these delights, ultimately capped off by a final blob of chocolate pudding, a generous sprinkling of caramel chocolates, chopped pecans, chocolate sauce, and butterscotch topping. My teeth hurt just writing this!

Ridiculous, you say? Perhaps. But there just might be times you *want* to see your kids bounce off the walls. If so, Charlene's has got you covered! If the Bucket isn't your proverbial cup o' tea, you can always go for their award-winning carrot cake, a three-tiered affair that boasts homemade cream cheese icing between the layers. The top of each piece is decorated so beautifully that you might think twice about digging in. Don't bother . . . eat, people, eat!

Now, I know I've thrown you off with this dessert-first groove, but let me assure you there's so much more to Charlene's than just the sweet stuff. In fact, if you ask many happy munchers what brings them to Charlene's, you're likely to hear "seafood!" in reply. And there's nothing more regal than what Charlene herself calls the king of the sea: lobster.

Lobster here comes in many forms. The Lobster Roll is a huge local favourite, and little wonder! How many other places do you know that put the meat of an entire lobster on a freshly

It's the people you'll remember here at Charlene's just as much as the food. You'll always feel welcome, and by the time you've finished your meal, chances are you'll have made a few new friends to boot.

Simplicity is the secret to Charlene's famous roll: lobster, mayo, salt, pepper, lettuce, and bread combine for classic Nova Scotian comfort food.

baked bun? As Charlene's son (and chef) Elliot says, the roll is simple by design: if you're ordering lobster, you want to taste it.

Lobster is also a big part of Charlene's famous Seafood Chowder, combining with scallops, haddock, halibut, clams, shrimp, and crabmeat (plus a couple of secret ingredients you're not allowed to know) in a soup so thick you could walk on it (assuming you're into soup walking—I am!). And if it's potatoes or other kinds of filler you crave, don't bother looking in *this* bowl; Charlene's chowder is too pure for any root vegetable. If it ain't from the sea, it ain't going in!

Charlene's makes Fish Cakes the old-fashioned way, using fresh cod and potatoes, and serving them with homemade baked beans, chow-chow relish, and cottage cheese. The Seafood Basket is big enough for two, and features fried haddock, shrimp, scallops, and clams. Heck, Charlene is so caring she'll even serve you something that once lived on land. Her Bay Burger is a 6-ounce homemade patty topped with bacon and cheese and served on a home-baked bun.

In the end, though, it's the people you'll remember at Charlene's just as much as the food. You'll always feel welcome, and by the time you've finished your meal, chances are you'll have made a few new friends to boot . . . maybe with Charlene herself!

Charlene's famous Seafood Chowder made its commercial debut at the international Fancy Food Show in San Francisco. It's been keeping customers smiling ever since.

Bucket of Mud

Makes: 8 servings

Brownies

1/3 cup shortening or butter
1 cup brown sugar
1 egg
3/4 cup all-purpose flour
1/4 cup cocoa powder
1 teaspoon baking powder
1/2 teaspoon salt
1/2 cup chopped nuts

Chocolate Pudding

1 cup sugar
1/2 cup cornstarch
1/3 cup cocoa powder
1/4 teaspoon salt
1/2 cup cold water
2 cups hot water
1 teaspoon vanilla extract

Assembly

2 cups whipping cream, whipped
A handful of pecans
Mini caramel chocolates
Chocolate sauce
Butterscotch topping

Brownies

Preheat oven to 375°F. Grease an 8-inch square cake pan.

In a small saucepan, melt the shortening. Remove from heat and beat in the sugar, then the egg.

Into a large bowl, sift together the flour, cocoa powder, baking powder, and salt. Stir in the nuts. Add the shortening mixture and stir until combined well. Pour into prepared pan.

Bake for 20 minutes or until the cake is pulling away from the sides of the pan. Cool on a rack, then cut into small pieces.

Chocolate Pudding

In a medium bowl, whisk together the sugar, cornstarch, cocoa powder, and salt. Add the cold water and whisk until smooth. The mixture should flow a bit but not be watery.

Add hot water to a medium saucepan set over medium heat. Slowly whisk in the cocoa mixture—it will thicken quite quickly. Cook, stirring constantly, for 3 to 4 minutes.

Remove from heat and stir in the vanilla. Let cool, uncovered.

Assembly

Layer an inch and a half of the cooled chocolate pudding in a serving bowl. Cover with three-quarters of the brownie pieces. Top with three-quarters of the whipped cream. Top with the remaining pudding.

Spoon a dollop of whipped cream in the centre and surround with the remaining brownie pieces. Sprinkle with the pecans and chocolates. Drizzle with chocolate sauce and butterscotch topping.

Ches's Famous Fish & Chips

EST. 1951
9 FRESHWATER ROAD
ST. JOHN'S · NL · AIC 2NI
WWW.CHESSFISHANDCHIPS.CA

When it comes to fish and chips, Ches Barbour ruined the people of St. John's. Back in 1951, Ches fulfilled his life's dream by opening the first Ches's with his wife, Betty, at his side. In those days, Ches would go out every morning in a small boat and catch enough fish for the day. Then he'd come back, fillet it all himself, and start cooking it for his eager customers. And though Ches and Betty have since passed on and four more Ches's have opened around the province, their business has stayed in the family, run by their daughter, Cathy . . . and continues to wow happy diners with what they say are the best damn "fi and chi" in Newfoundland, if not all of Canada.

The secret to Ches's deep-fried delights is the batter, a family recipe so closely guarded that relatives run the risk of being disowned if they flap their lips. I'm not really sure what goes in it (all they showed me was the flour, baking powder, and water), but as chef Scott Lamkin says, it's the tender loving care they infuse that makes the difference. That and a little elbow grease, actually. For while most places use industrial mixers to mix their batter, Scott and the crew are doing it all by hand . . . er, forearm.

Once the batter is mixed to perfection, the carefully selected and trimmed cod pieces are rolled in flour and dipped lovingly in the batter. But rather than toss the fish into the fryer, Scott swims each piece across the top of the oil, then lays it in gently. I don't know if this is the secret, but I can tell you that by the time it arrives at your table, the fish is crispy on the outside, light and flaky on the inside, and not the least bit greasy. It's fried-fish perfection. Pair that with Ches's equally delectable fresh-cut fries (Scott says they burn through 15,000 pounds every week), and you'll think you've died and gone to Davy Jones's Locker.

But Ches's isn't all about the fish, and they make some of the best damn chicken wings you'll ever taste,

Today Ches's looks much like it did when its doors first opened back in 1951, and the food is every bit as good.

Ches would go out every morning in a small boat and catch enough fish for the day. Then he'd come back, fillet it all himself, and start cooking it for his eager customers.

too. I don't know what kind of chickens they grow in Newfoundland, but these things are *huge*! Dipped in a thinner version of the batter that envelops the fish, the chicken wings come out of the fryer super crispy on the outside and steaming on the inside. Don't bother with any dipping sauce; these babies are just perfect flying solo.

As you can imagine, the deep-fryer sees a lot of action at Ches's. But the menu is not restricted to fried foods, not by any stretch. In fact, my favourite meal here was made at the hands of Ches's granddaughter Jennifer, who started working at the restaurant at a young age, went away to culinary school, then came back to be one of the main chefs in the flagship location on Freshwater Road. And one of Jennifer's best-loved creations is her Stuffed Cod.

The Stuffed Cod begins with a couple pieces of fish laid in a baking dish, then topped with a layer of delicious home-made dressing (a

Just what kind of chickens do they have in Newfoundland, anyway? Though I'd rather not run into one of these monsters, I'm quite happy to eat their wings.

combination of bread crumbs, Newfoundland savory, onions, melted butter, and spices). Topped with yet more cod, a sprinkle of diced onions, cooked bacon, and shredded white Cheddar, Jennifer's masterpiece is cooked in a steamer, from which it emerges moist and flaky, a one-of-a-kind taste sensation.

And guess what? The Barbour family will even be happy to serve you something other than fish and chips, if you're *that* kind of person (hell, they'll even serve you a homemade dessert). But when everyone you ask in St. John's about fish and chips points to the iconic blue building on Freshwater Road, why would you want anything else?

Ches's Stuffed Cod

Makes: 4 servings

Stuffing

1 1/2 cups fresh bread crumbs

1 tablespoon finely chopped onion

1 1/2 teaspoons dried savory

2 tablespoons butter, melted

Salt and pepper

Stuffed Cod

2 1/2 pounds cod fillet (preferably fresh)

Salt and pepper

1 tablespoon finely chopped onion

2 slices bacon, cooked and crumbled

1 1/2 cups shredded white Cheddar cheese

Stuffing

In a bowl stir together the bread crumbs, onion, savory, and butter. Season with salt and pepper to taste.

Stuffed Cod

Preheat oven to 325°F.

Layer half of the fish in an 8-inch square baking dish. Season with salt and pepper to taste.

Spread the stuffing over the fish. Top with another layer of fish, and season with salt and
pepper.

Cover fish and bake for 30 minutes. Sprinkle with the onion and bacon. Top with the Cheddar.
Bake, uncovered, for another 15 minutes or until the fish flakes easily.

Coastal Waters Restaurant & Pub

EST. 1986
36404 CABOT TRAIL
INGONISH · NS · BOC IKO

We all have different ways of showing love. Some of us are effusive, others quiet. But for a small part of the population—like Jason LeBlanc and Keith Moore, the co-owners and chefs at the Coastal Waters Restaurant—love is something best shared with a laugh. That's why a trip to the Coastal Waters, on Cape Breton Island's Cabot Trail, is more than just a meal. For while Jason and Keith are serving up delicious home-cooked meals by the hundreds, it's the welcoming atmosphere and constant jokes and jibes that help create an experience people never forget.

Coastal Waters was born when Jason and Keith met in college and became instant friends. After graduation, they considered moving out west, but when opportunity presented itself at home, they leapt. The pair bought Coastal Waters in 2006 and have transformed it into a must-stop destination on the Cabot Trail (even for stinky cyclists who haven't showered in a week). The old place was gutted, and a pub with a renowned menu was born.

Coastal Waters is one of those special places that welcomes everyone with open arms. On some nights, co-owner Jason LeBlanc and his band perform live music.

Standing atop that menu is the Ringer, a burger whose legend has grown to such proportions that people ask for it without even seeing a menu. The Ringer starts with a flame-broiled patty topped with bacon, mozzarella, and buttermilk-battered onion rings. What makes it extra special is the Coastal's signature Ringer BBQ Sauce, a tangy mixture that Jason and Keith concocted in the kitchen one night after a few too many drinks. Yet as Jason tells it, the sauce tasted even better the next morning! Since then it's become a staple at the restaurant.

Ringer Sauce also makes an appearance on the Stuffed Burger Special, a beef patty jammed with bacon, onion, cheese, and mushrooms. The patty is baked, coated with an even bolder barbeque sauce, then served with fresh-cut fries. What, no beef for you? Then wrap your hands around the Chicken Burger Special, in which a grilled chicken breast is smothered in homemade sun-dried tomato pesto mayonnaise.

But you don't set up shop this close to the Atlantic Ocean without making seafood a focal point of your menu, and the Coastal delivers with a variety of classic seafood dishes such as fish cakes, seafood platters, and haddock. The hot Crab Dip is a house specialty, built upon the backs (and legs!) of crabs pulled from local waters, then supplemented with a creamy mix of Parmesan, green onions, green pepper, all-purpose dressing, lemon juice, and Worcestershire sauce. Served with homemade tortilla chips, it's a creamy taste of the sea.

The seafood parade also includes pasta, and one of my favourites is the Shrimp and Scallop Carbonara—a steaming bed of linguine bursting with fresh shrimp and scallops and doused in homemade carbonara sauce. As if that weren't enough, the bowl is rimmed with freshly steamed mussels. The Coastal's Seafood Chowder mixes generous portions of scallops, shrimp, clams, and haddock with cream, thyme, garlic, and homemade fish stock . . . but never potatoes, which Jason calls "filler."

You won't find any filler on the Coastal's dessert menu . . . unless you consider flour, butter, and sugar to be filler. The Cinnamon Skillet showcases a deliciously sweet homemade cinnamon bun warmed in a cast-iron skillet and topped with vanilla ice cream and caramel sauce. Coconut Cream Pie takes a homemade coconut cream filling and lays it to rest—temporarily at least—in a pie crust made from scratch, before topping it with whipped cream and toasted coconut. Those aching for a little fruit in their dessert might turn to the Strawberry Shortcake, where massive homemade tea biscuits are topped with mounds of fresh whipped cream and strawberries.

Customers at the Coastal will tell you that this is the place for real Cape Breton food. If Cape Bretoners are *really* chowing down on Ringer Burgers and Cinnamon Skillets with any kind of regularity—then someone find me a realtor.

Want some? Though my conscience (and waistline) told me otherwise, it wasn't easy for me to put down this delicious crab dip, which was supplemented perfectly with homemade tortilla chips.

Coastal Cinnamon Skillet

Makes: 12 to 14 cinnamon rolls

2 cups all-purpose flour

1 cup white sugar

2 tablespoons baking powder

1 teaspoon salt

3/4 cup shortening

1 cup water

3/4 cup butter, at room temperature

1 cup brown sugar

Cinnamon

Preheat oven to 400°F. Line a baking sheet with parchment paper.

In a medium bowl, whisk together the flour, white sugar, baking powder, and salt. Using a pastry cutter or 2 knives, cut in the shortening until mixture looks like coarse crumbs.

Slowly add the water while stirring with a fork; when a dough starts to form, mix with your hands until the dough can be made into a ball. (If the dough is too sticky, sprinkle it lightly with flour.)

On a floured work surface, roll out the dough into a rectangle 1/4 inch thick. Spread the butter over the dough, all the way to the edges. Sprinkle evenly with brown sugar. Sprinkle with cinnamon to taste.

Starting at a long side, roll the dough into a log. Push down the far edge to seal. With a sharp knife, cut the log into 1-inch pieces. Arrange the rolls, cut side up, 3 inches apart on the baking sheet.

Bake for 18 minutes or until browned.

Serve immediately or reheat cinnamon buns in a skillet. Serve topped with ice cream and caramel sauce.

Déjà BU!

EST. 2010
49A BOULEVARD SAINT-PIERRE OUEST
CARAQUET · NB · E1W 1B6
WWW.DEJABU.CA

T ruth be told, there aren't that many restaurants in the pages of this book that qualify as downright *romantic*, but déjà BU! is as close as you're going to get. Overlooking the waters of Chaleur Bay, déjà BU! offers its customers more than just a meal. That's just fine with chef and owner Robert Noël, a trained sommelier who is as passionate about ambience as he is about the food he serves.

And what food! Déjà BU!'s menu is comfort classics with a gourmet twist, and people from as far away as Moncton (a three-hour drive) and Fredericton (a three-and-a-half-hour drive) come to Caraquet with the sole intention of indulging their taste buds. They know this: Robert makes no bones about using the richest ingredients in his meals, so if you're counting calories or averse to extra butter, cream, or cheese, you might want to find somewhere else to eat!

Given its proximity to the ocean, déjà BU! features lots of fresh seafood, beginning with the dish that rocked my socks and messed my hands, the Lobster Grilled Cheese. Robert (or Bobby Christmas, as he's known around these parts) starts with two giant pieces of sourdough bread, which he sits in a pan of hot butter. Then he spreads homemade truffle mayonnaise on one side and covers it in a heap of lobster, which itself has been tossed in hot butter. If there's any butter left in the pan, it gets drizzled on the sandwich, too!

If you're counting calories or averse to extra butter, cream, or cheese, you might want to find somewhere else to eat!

Then comes a mixture of sliced Gruyère cheese and grated Parmesan, and a slice of prosciutto. After a few minutes in the oven, the sandwich can only be described in two words: *c'est fantastique!* The Lobster Grilled Cheese is served on a bed of french fries, but there's nothing ordinary about these, either. In keeping with Robert's mandate of making the ordinary extraordinary, he fries his Yukon Gold potatoes in duck fat, making them as crispy as they are addictive.

Butterholics will also love the Lobster Mac & Cheese, which combines Gruyère and Parmesan with a rich Mornay sauce, all tossed together with macaroni and endless hunks of lobster. Topped with melted butter and a squirt of white truffle oil, Robert's mother's recipe will bring you to your knees.

Yet the dish that sits atop the uniqueness scale at déjà BU! has to be its Poutine aux Palourdes (bar clam poutine), which combines duck-fat fries with deliciously chewy local Blancs d'Arcadie cheese curds and a traditional beef gravy that is jacked up on clam juice and a hefty portion of bar clams. Devotees of the dish say it's the best poutine they've ever had, one that combines the earthy pull of beef gravy with the taste of the sea. If clams aren't your thing, there's always the Lobster Poutine; Robert adds a veal reduction to the gravy for added complexity. And if you really want to take your poutine tasting to the next level, try the Duck Poutine, which adds duck confit to the classic blend. You can even add Quebec foie gras to it!

This mix of the classic and the unexpected sums up déjà BU! Customers are made to feel like they're old friends visiting Robert's house, and are served meals they won't find anywhere else. Even the interior, which uses recycled materials to create a modern feel, is a blend of old and new. And it should come as no surprise that the wine list, chock full of dozens of Robert's favourites, brings the young and old together in harmony.

It's a perfect combination for watching the sun go down while your belly fills up . . . and up . . . and up.

Cardiologists take note! The Lobster Grilled Cheese (*above*) combines quality with quantity, stuffing an improbable amount of butter-laced lobster onto sourdough bread.

Déjà BU! regulars swear by Poutine aux Palourdes (bar clam poutine), but there are lobster and duck versions, too.

Lobster Mac & Cheese

Makes: 2 to 4 servings

Macaroni

1 pound torchietti or macaroni

4 to 8 ounces lobster claw meat, in large pieces

1 tablespoon unsalted butter

1/2 teaspoon salt

1/8 teaspoon pepper

White truffle oil

Truffle slices or peelings (optional)

Mornay Sauce

1/4 cup unsalted butter

3 tablespoons finely chopped onion

1/4 cup all-purpose flour

4 cups whole milk

1 stalk lemongrass, cut into 2 or 3 pieces

1/2 cup whipping cream

Salt and pepper

1/4 cup shredded Gruyère cheese

2 tablespoons grated Grana Padano or Parmesan cheese

Mornay Sauce

Melt the butter in a medium saucepan over medium heat. Add the onion and cook, stirring frequently, for 3 minutes. Stir in the flour and cook, stirring, until light golden (not too dark), about 2 to 3 minutes. Add the milk, a cup at a time, stirring constantly until smooth.

Add the lemongrass and cook for 15 minutes or until the flour taste is gone. (Meanwhile, bring a large pot of salted water to a boil for the pasta.)

Stir in the cream and reduce sauce until thickened, 4 to 5 minutes.

Strain the sauce and season with salt and pepper to taste.

Add the cheeses and stir until melted. Reduce heat to low and cook for 5 minutes.

Assembly

Cook the pasta in a large pot of boiling salted water for 8 to 10 minutes or until al dente.

Meanwhile, in a small skillet over medium-low heat, warm up the lobster meat in the butter.

Drain pasta well and toss with the Mornay sauce, salt, and pepper. Transfer pasta to a serving dish; add a drizzle of white truffle oil and slices of truffle (if using). Spoon the lobster meat and the lobster-infused butter over the pasta. Serve immediately.

Landmark Cafe

EST. 1989
12 MAIN STREET
VICTORIA BY THE SEA · PEI · C0A 2G0
WWW.LANDMARKCAFE.CA

F or the thousands of people who visit Victoria by the Sea every year to enjoy an authentic PEI seaside village, the Landmark Cafe offers everything its name promises, and more.

Back in 1989, owner Eugene Sauvé bought a local grocery store from one of his neighbours and decided to pursue his culinary dream. More than two decades later, the Landmark stands as a local dining destination, one that serves meals as unique as they are delicious and filling. Maybe that's why customers swarm the place. From local families to retirees to visitors to theatregoers (the Victoria Playhouse is across the street), the Landmark is *the* place to eat on the shores of Northumberland Strait.

Eugene is the heart and soul of the Landmark, and is involved in almost every aspect of this family-run business, especially on the kitchen side of things. Eugene is a veritable nutty professor in the kitchen, dreaming up, testing, and re-testing his unique recipes for years before they reach the perfection he demands from them.

For instance, Italians like me have a very clear idea of what constitutes a lasagna. Not so Eugene. He starts what he calls

Charming environment, good people, delicious eats: it's all here at the Landmark.

his "meat lover's lasagna" with tons of lean ground beef sautéed with vegetables, herbs, and spices, along with chili flakes, Louisiana hot sauce, lots of red wine, balsamic vinegar, and Dijon mustard to boot. Giant dollops of creamy goat cheese go between the layers of pasta and meat mix. Top with shredded mozzarella and Cheddar, some fresh tomato slices, and you've got a truly extraordinary taste experience. Just don't tell my Zia Felicetta, OK?

Eugene serves his one-of-a-kind lasagna with the freshest beet salads your taste buds have ever wrapped themselves around, the product of ingredients picked the same day in the family garden. In fact, Eugene is a bit obsessed with getting all his food fresh from local producers . . .

The Landmark Café's cast and crew perform culinary theatrics every night in Victoria by the Sea.

or his own backyard. But that's one kind of obsession that works for me!

No PEI restaurant located this close to the sea would offer a menu devoid of fish, and Landmark answers the call with one of the most delicious fresh haddock specials around (it's not a regular menu item). Eugene starts with an entire fillet, which is battered and coated in herbs, peppers, and the Landmark's special combination of bread crumbs. Pan-fried in butter for a few minutes, the fish arrives at your table soft, moist, and insanely good.

Other landmark dishes at the Landmark include pork tenderloin (an incredibly rich dish topped with a wine and Roquefort cheese sauce), meat pie (a recipe Eugene inherited from his mother), and a seafood chowder unlike any I've ever tasted. Dessert fans will love the Landmark's chocolate pecan pie, a mouth-watering blend of eggs, chocolate chips, pecans, and either Grand Marnier or chocolate liqueur.

So whether you're in Victoria by the Sea to watch a play, check out the local artists, or enjoy the beautiful waters of the Gulf of St. Lawrence, don't miss the Landmark Cafe with its unique culinary delights.

Eugene is a veritable nutty professor in the kitchen, dreaming up, testing, and re-testing his unique recipes for years before they reach the perfection he demands from them.

Leave it to Eugene to dream up a lasagna that includes goat cheese and Dijon mustard . . . and tastes like a slice of heaven.

Landmark Pan-Fried Haddock

Makes: 4 servings

1 large egg
1/2 cup milk
1/2 cup panko bread crumbs
1/2 cup Italian bread crumbs
1 teaspoon Cajun seasoning
1/4 cup dried or chopped fresh tarragon
Pepper
4 large fresh skinless haddock fillets
2 tablespoons salted butter
4 large garlic cloves, minced

Whisk the egg and milk together in a shallow dish. In another shallow dish, combine the panko and Italian bread crumbs, Cajun seasoning, tarragon, and pepper to taste.

Add the haddock fillets to the egg mixture and turn to coat entirely. Dredge the haddock in the crumb mixture, coating both sides generously.

In a large nonstick skillet over high heat, melt the butter with the garlic until the butter starts to bubble; be careful not to let the garlic burn. Add the fish and turn the heat down to medium-high. Fry the fish for 2 minutes or until golden and crispy on the bottom. Flip, and fry for another 2 minutes or until the fish is golden and crispy on both sides, with a moist interior.

Magnolia's Grill

EST. 1987
128 MONTAGUE STREET
LUNENBURG · NS · B0J 2C0

Yea, baby! Pass me some o' dat Lobster Linguini!

Some people are like magnets, attracting others to them with their warmth, charm, and positive energy. That's exactly what you get with Nancy Lohnes, the owner and chef at Magnolia's Grill. Nancy has one of the warmest hearts you'll ever meet, and it's her energy that fills this small place with love and beauty . . . not to mention delicious, imaginative, and ever-changing comfort food of the highest order.

If you've never been to Magnolia's, then you're not only missing Nancy and her gourmet creations, you're also missing Lunenburg, which was designated a UNESCO World Heritage Site in 1995. Old-town Lunenburg has a seaside charm that is hard to find today, so why not combine some of the best eats on the East Coast with a stroll back through time?

There are so many delicious things to eat at Magnolia's, but for a pasta lover like me (who goes into withdrawal without at least two weekly fixes . . . not a pretty sight!), the dish that stole my heart was Nancy's Lobster Linguini, a customer favourite at Magnolia's. As the name suggests, the "lobling" starts with healthy chunks of lobster sautéed in butter, to which Nancy then adds a splash of hot sauce, sherry, cream, and Parmesan cheese. Toss with perfectly cooked pasta, and the result is a meal so good you'll want to kiss the chef. As a matter of fact, I did!

Magnolia's is Lunenburg at its best, and Lunenburg *is* seafood. And Nancy does seafood up *right*, beginning with her signature Fish Cakes, the restaurant's most popular dish. Nancy uses her grandmother's recipe for Dutch Mess, which begins with haddock and potatoes boiled together in a huge pot, a process that infuses the potatoes with the flavour of the fish. In the meantime, salt pork and onions are fried until brown and crispy, then added to the strained

Just how special is Magnolia's? All I can tell you is this: when the crew and I were in Nova Scotia recently to shoot another episode of You Gotta Eat Here!, we all piled into a car and drove to Lunenburg for a meal with Nancy.

When you're working with Nancy (*centre*), it's smiles all around for the women of Magnolia's Grill.

fish and potato mix. Add *lots* of butter and whipping cream and mash it all together: this is then refrigerated, then mixed with eggs.

Once the mess has cooled, it's formed into patties, rolled in flour, and fried in butter. Served with a homemade rhubarb chutney, the result is a cake with a crisp crust but a soft and tender inside that makes your mouth sing. Just don't make like the many visitors to Magnolia's who order the fish cakes because they're watching their weight: there's nothing low-cal about these! (Have I mentioned the butter?)

The menu at Magnolia's is rich with variety, each dish a reflection of Nancy's twenty-plus years as a chef. The Creole Peanut Soup is a spicy yet decadently rich mixture that brings people back year after year. Scallops come right off the boat that docks across the street. They're so fresh you could eat them raw. But with Nancy cooking, why would you?

For dessert, Magnolia's Key Lime Pie is an old-fashioned undertaking, with Nancy squeezing the limes herself for her filling. And to those salespeople who occasionally try to sell Nancy a filling mix for her pies: don't bother! Like everything else here at Magnolia's, it's all done by hand. The same goes for her Mrs. Zinc's Chocolate Sloppy, a chocolate pudding cake inspired by local recipes and named by an Australian waitress.

Just how special is Magnolia's? All I can tell you is this: when the crew and I were in Nova Scotia recently to shoot another episode of *You Gotta Eat Here!*, we all piled into a car and drove to Lunenburg for a meal with Nancy.

We were not disappointed!

1 pound linguine

2 tablespoons unsalted butter

8 ounces cooked lobster meat, chopped

1/2 teaspoon hot pepper sauce

1/3 cup dry sherry

Salt and pepper

1/2 cup whipping cream

1/3 cup freshly grated Parmesan cheese

Chopped fresh parsley

Cook linguine in a large pot of boiling salted water until al dente. Drain and set aside.

Meanwhile, melt the butter in a large skillet over medium heat. Add the lobster and stir just until the lobster is heated through. Stir in the hot pepper sauce. Add the sherry and salt and pepper to taste. Cook for 3 minutes or until the sherry is reduced. Stir in the cream and let it bubble up and thicken.

Add all but 2 tablespoons of the Parmesan along with the linguine. Stir until the pasta is heated through.

Divide the pasta among plates and top with the remaining Parmesan and the parsley.

New Glasgow Lobster Suppers

EST. 1958
604 ROUTE 258
NEW GLASGOW · PEI · COA INO
WWW.PEILOBSTERSUPPERS.COM

Take one delicious lobster, add all-you-can-eat appetizers and dessert, then toss in fifty-plus years of history. The sum is New Glasgow Lobster Suppers, a true Island institution that's built a legacy out of an alien-looking crustacean with a natural affinity for butter.

Yet as synonymous as the New Glasgow is with lobster, it's equally associated with owner and general manager Carl Nicholson, who has worked at the restaurant for more than thirty years and whose family legacy traces back to the restaurant's inception. Carl's parents were original partners in the restaurant, which was founded in 1958. The building had no kitchen and no washrooms back then, and all the food was prepared elsewhere and brought on site. Carl started at the New Glasgow as a fifteen-year-old dishwasher, and now oversees a restaurant that is open every night from May to October, can seat five hundred people, and will serve eight hundred meals on a busy night.

It doesn't matter what age, size, or shape you are . . . it's a family affair at New Glasgow Lobster Suppers.

Now if you want to know anything about the New Glasgow, you have to know a thing or two about lobsters, because they go through a lot of them! In fact, the restaurant sells so much lobster that they have their own cold-water tanks, which allow them to keep lobsters throughout the season (PEI lobsters can't be caught in July, since that's when they moult). The cold water also keeps the lobsters sleepy and serene, which prevents them from ripping each other apart. As Carl says, these critters can be downright *nasty*.

That doesn't prevent people from eating them by the thousands, though. The New Glasgow offers saltwater-boiled lobsters in 1-pound, 1 1/2-pound, 2-pound, 3-pound, and 4-pound sizes.

And if you want to make the most of your dining experience, do as the locals do and don't just focus on the claws and tails. The best flavours await inside the lobster's many nooks and crannies, so spend some time exploring your meal.

Just leave room for all the accoutrements, because chef Mike Forrest gives you lots to choose from at the New Glasgow. As much as you can eat, in fact—and maybe even more. The all-you-can-eat menu begins with freshly baked rolls and whole wheat bread that arrives at your table still steaming. There's seafood chowder, beef vegetable soup, and freshly steamed cultivated Island blue mussels.

You'll also get a salad plate with your meal, which includes coleslaw and a garden salad with house dressing. My favourite part has to be New Glasgow's potato salad, a traditional mix of potatoes, chopped hard-boiled eggs, onion, celery, celery salt, and homemade mayonnaise.

Now, let's just say that you've come to the New Glasgow *Lobster* Suppers and you're not in the mood for, er, *lobster*. Will Carl unceremoniously toss you out the door? He should . . . but he won't. In fact, Carl and his crew are so accommodating that they'll even offer a few alternatives to the crustacean that's made them famous. There's an Atlantic Scallops entrée, as well as Atlantic Haddock and Atlantic Salmon. Landlubbers have a choice of Island Roast Beef, Tender Sweet Ham, or Chicken Supreme. There's a Vegetarian Stir-Fry for herbivores, or you can eschew the main course altogether and just buy the all-you-can-eat appetizers and desserts.

Now, offering the ordinary human as much dessert as he or she can consume is a dangerous undertaking, especially when the sweets are as good as baker Joan Blanchard's creations. Of Joan's many sweet temptations, the Mile-High Lemon Meringue Pie is a local hit. Tangy and sweet, it's the perfect finish to a giant meal. And if you like it so much you want more, go right ahead!

Take one delicious lobster, add all-you-can-eat appetizers and dessert, then toss in fifty-plus years of history. The sum is New Glasgow Lobster Suppers, a true Island institution that's built a legacy out of an alien-looking crustacean with a natural affinity for butter.

Crustaceans, beware! They're taking you down by the thousands round these parts.

Proper Maritime
Boiled Lobster with
Dinner Rolls

Makes: 4 servings of lobster and 24 rolls

Boiled Lobster

1/2 cup salt for every 12 cups water

4 lobsters

Dinner Rolls

3 cups warm water

1 tablespoon active dry yeast

1 1/2 teaspoons sugar

8 cups all-purpose flour

1 tablespoon salt

1/2 cup shortening

2 eggs

1/2 cup sugar

Dinner Rolls

In a small bowl, combine 1 cup of the warm water, yeast, and sugar; stir to combine and let stand until foamy, 5 to 10 minutes.

In the bowl of a stand mixer (or other large bowl), combine 4 cups flour of the flour and the salt. Using a pastry blender or fork, cut in the shortening until well combined. Make a well in the centre.

In a small bowl, beat together the eggs and sugar. Pour the egg mixture, yeast mixture, and the remaining 2 cups of warm water into the well.

If using a stand mixer, mix on low speed with the dough hook until a shaggy dough forms. Add the remaining 4 cups of flour, 1 cup at a time, mixing on low speed for 5 minutes or until the dough is no longer sticky and pulls away from the side of the bowl cleanly.

If mixing by hand, stir until the dough comes together. Turn the dough out onto a floured surface and knead for 15 minutes, adding enough of the remaining flour to make a smooth, elastic dough.

Place the dough in a large oiled bowl and cover with a cloth. Let dough double in size, about 1 hour.

Preheat oven to 325°F. Spray two 12-cup muffin pans with cooking spray.

Cut dough into 48 balls. Roll balls between your palms and place 2 balls side by side in each muffin cup. Let rolls rise, uncovered, until they double in size again, at least 4 hours.

Bake rolls for 11 minutes or until golden brown. Serve hot with lots of butter.

Boiled Lobster

Fill a large pot with water; add salt. Bring water to a boil. Drop in the lobsters. (Do not crowd the pot.) When the water begins to boil again, start the timer.

Boil 1-pound lobsters for 10 minutes. Boil 1 1/2-pound lobsters for 15 minutes. Boil 2-pound lobsters for 20 minutes. (Add 5 minutes per half pound of additional weight after that.)

To check doneness, remove a lobster with tongs and pull on one of the legs. If it comes off easily, the lobster is done.

Potato Salad

Makes: 12 servings

Timing note: Boil the potatoes a day ahead, because they must chill overnight. The mayonnaise can be made a day or two ahead; keep it covered and refrigerated.

Mayonnaise

1/4 cup + 1 tablespoon all-purpose flour
1/3 cup sugar
2 tablespoons dry mustard
Pinch of salt
1/3 cup + 1 teaspoon white vinegar
2 eggs
1/2 cup whole milk
1/2 cup 10% cream

Potato Salad

2 1/2 pounds russet potatoes
1/2 cup finely chopped celery
1/4 cup finely chopped onion
4 hard-boiled eggs, chopped
Celery salt and pepper
Pinch of paprika for garnish

Mayonnaise

Bring water in the bottom of a double boiler (or a saucepan) to a boil, then reduce to a simmer.

In the top of the double boiler (or in a heatproof bowl), whisk together the flour, sugar, mustard, and salt. Whisk in the vinegar. Add the eggs and whisk together. Add the milk and cream and whisk until blended.

Heat over simmering water, whisking periodically, until the mayonnaise thickens (this may take up to 2 hours). The mayonnaise should be thick enough to hold the whisk upright.

Set aside in the refrigerator.

Potato Salad

Boil the potatoes in a pot of salted water just until tender. Drain, peel, then chill overnight.

Dice the potatoes and transfer to a large bowl. Add the celery, onion, eggs, celery salt and pepper to taste, and reserved mayonnaise. Mix thoroughly.

Serve sprinkled with paprika.

Rick's Fish 'N' Chips & Seafood House

EST. 1992
5544 ROUTE 2
ST. PETER'S BAY · PEI · COA 2AO
WWW.RICKSFISHNCHIPS.COM

I f you're planning on chatting with Rick Renaud when you're at Rick's Fish 'N' Chips & Seafood House in St. Peter's Bay, just make sure you don't show up between 2 and 4 p.m. on weekdays. That's when he's driving the school bus.

It's this kind of down-hominess that makes Rick's a legend. There's nothing pretentious about Rick or the restaurant that bears his name. What you see is what you get, both with the man and with the food.

Rick's came to life when Rick and his wife, Seana, bought a small takeout joint in 1992. Business started booming almost immediately, and by 1998 the old place couldn't take it anymore. So in the spring of that year the red-roofed building was erected, and a landmark was born. Today

Straight-shooting and down to earth, Rick is the heart and soul of what has become a PEI institution.

Rick employs twenty-one people, a far cry from the three who held the reins in the early years. And they all hold true to one common cause: combining fresh, simple, and delicious seafood with good old-fashioned hospitality.

As the name suggests, the cornerstone of Rick's menu is fish and chips, and he doesn't overcomplicate the issue. Haddock or sole fillets are cut fresh every morning, around the same time another daily batch of batter is being prepared. Rick likes to say his batter recipe—water, flour, and baking powder—comes from an old Englishman, but whatever the source, it's working. The fillets are coated in the thin batter, then washed across the top of the hot oil before being set free to the gods of the deep-fryer.

When they come out a few minutes later, they are a crunchy taste of fish heaven, my brothers and sisters! Each piece is golden and crispy (and never greasy) on the outside, warm, moist, and

There's nothing pretentious about Rick or the restaurant that bears his name. What you see is what you get, both with the man and with the food.

flaky on the inside. And let's not forget those delicious PEI "bodadoes," which Rick and his crew lovingly transform into hand-cut fries with every meal.

Though most people end the food conversation at Rick's with fish and chips, there *are* other things to order, and the restaurant has steadily expanded its selection of offerings over the years. One of the most popular is the Cajun Mussels, which takes fresh local mussels, steams them to perfection, then dips them in Rick's "old Englishman" batter before hitting the deep-fryer. Once they're done, Rick tosses the crispy mussels in a paper bag loaded up with his own famous Cajun spice blend—Rick's Mix—which is also available for purchase. And while I'm a huge fan of mussels, I've never had them this way, though I hope to again! Crispy and chewy, and with an unexpected kick of heat, they were absolutely delicious.

Somebody find the old Englishman who gave Rick his batter recipe and thank him for me. This stuff is heavenly!

Other specialties of Rick's house include the Seafood Pizza, which was loaded with enough fresh seafood to make sea critters for miles around swim for cover. Homemade dough is covered in a base of garlic and oil, then piled with a hefty handful of mozzarella. Then comes the seafood—scallops, haddock, mussels, and shrimp—followed by even more mozzarella. Rick will gladly serve you his Maritime Cajun Bake, a southern-spiced white fish casserole baked with plum tomatoes and cornflake crumbs. The crust is hearty enough to stand up to tons of seafood, but not too thick that it overpowered. If it's a liquid lunch you crave, then have one Rick's way and order the curried Seafood Chowder, which adds a South Asian twist to a creamy union of fish and shellfish.

The way I see it, though, Rick's is all about the crunch of crispy pieces of fish enjoyed out on the deck on a warm summer afternoon. If you don't believe me, just ask Rick. He'll be the guy driving the bus.

Rick's Seafood Pizza

Dough (enough for three 12-inch pizzas)

3 1/2 cups all-purpose flour

1 tablespoon whey powder (available from baking supply stores)
   or powdered milk (for flavour)

1 teaspoon salt

1 teaspoon sugar

4 teaspoons shortening

1 1/2 cups cold water

1 tablespoon instant yeast

Toppings (per pizza)

2 garlic cloves, finely chopped

3 to 4 tablespoons high-quality olive oil

1 cup shredded mozzarella cheese

10 to 20 mussels, steamed and shucked

20 cooked scallops, cut into small pieces

Cooked lobster chunks (fresh or canned)

6 to 8 cooked shrimp

4 ounces cooked white fish, cut into small pieces

Any other seafood of your choice

Rick's Mix or other Cajun seasoning

Dough

In a large bowl, combine the flour, whey powder, salt, and sugar. Cut in shortening with a pastry blender until the mixture looks like coarse crumbs. Stir in the water until a dough forms. On a lightly floured surface (or in a stand mixer), knead for 1 minute. Add the yeast and knead for another 5 minutes or until the dough is firm but smooth and elastic.

Cut into 3 equal portions. Let sit for 1 hour, covered with a cloth.

On a lightly floured surface, roll out dough to fit your pizza pan.

Note: Leftover dough may be frozen for later use.

Assembly

Preheat oven to 425°F.

Stir garlic and oil together and let sit for 10 minutes.

Brush garlic oil evenly over pizza dough. Sprinkle mozzarella evenly over the pizza. Arrange seafood toppings on top and sprinkle with Rick's Mix and more mozzarella.

Bake for 12 to 15 minutes, until crust is golden and cheese is bubbling.

Let sit for 5 minutes before cutting.

Saint John Ale House

EST. 2003
I MARKET SQUARE
SAINT JOHN · NB · E2L 4Z6
WWW.SAINTJOHNALEHOUSE.COM

I love Jesse and Peter. That's Jesse Vergen and Peter Stoddart, the executive chef and owner, respectively, at the Saint John Ale House, one of my all-time hands-down rock-solid favourite places of all time. Fun, adventurous, loving, and kind, Jesse and Peter are the heart and soul of the Ale House, where the food is as creative as they are and served in an environment so relaxed you'll feel like you're in your best friend's living room.

The only difference between Jesse and Peter and your best friend, though, is that your best friend *never* made food like this (unless, of course, Jesse and Peter *are* your best friends). Take, for instance, their monstrous Lobster Roll, which uses the meat of an entire lobster and has been known to scare would-be diners with its sheer girth. Not satisfied to plunk his lobster into an ordinary hotdog roll, Jesse starts with a thick hunk of sourdough loaf that he fries in a generous portion of homemade lobster oil until the bread is golden brown and crispy.

But Jesse isn't one to just toss his lobster meat anywhere. He lays fresh lettuce in the V of the bread, piles in the lobster salad, and—for an added of touch of, you guessed it, lobster!—drizzles lobster mayo over the sandwich and sprinkles lobster roe on top. In short, it was freakin' incredible! The bread has a crispy grilled cheese–like texture and was filled with so much delicious lobster I almost wept. Actually, I would have wept, but I was too busy eating.

What now? When he's not hamming it up, Jesse Vergen is the creative genius behind the taste-tempting treats at the Saint John Ale House.

And as serious as Jesse and Peter are about food, that doesn't mean they can't have a good time with it, too. And there's nothing more fun on the Ale House's menu than the Buttermilk Fried Chicken, which starts with tender hunks of boneless, skinless chicken soaked overnight in buttermilk spiked with a shot of hot sauce. Then they're rolled gently through a blend of flour and spices, dipped in another buttermilk and hot sauce wash, and pulled through the flour once again before heading off to chicken heaven: the deep-fryer.

These tenders are served on a plate bulging with Jesse's homemade kettle chips and topped with spicy mayonnaise. But here's where Jesse hits his ha-ha stride: he sprinkles pop-in-your-mouth candy all over the chicken, which adds an extra level of bang to the affair. In the end, the chicken is popping all over your mouth but filling it with warm, tender goodness, too—another incredible food experience from the boys at the Saint John Ale House.

Given the name of the place, it just wouldn't be right for the Ale House to let you walk away from a meal without sampling some kind of alcoholic beverage, regardless of the form. Don't worry if you're about to get behind the wheel, though. They've got you covered with their Chocolate Guinness Cake, which sandwiches sweet Guinness syrup and gooey hazelnut praline spread between layers of chocolate cake. Topped with a rich chocolate ganache (don't worry, Jesse has a PhD in fatology and he says the cream in the ganache is good for you) and served with homemade whisky caramel and Irish whipped cream, it's like a shooter on a plate—a perfect way to end a meal.

Of course nobody would look at you sideways if you did have a pint or two with your food. They do, after all, have the largest beer selection in the area, not to mention their Moosehead Cask Ale, which is made exclusively for the Ale House and draws people from far and wide who just want to get their hands on a glass of the precious brew. Like many things at the Ale House, it was a one-of-a-kind experience. I love that ale.

But not nearly as much as I love Jesse and Peter.

Chocolate Guinness Cake, which sandwiches sweet Guinness syrup and gooey hazelnut praline spread between layers of chocolate cake, is served with home-made whisky caramel and Irish whipped cream.

The Ale House is a magnet for people who share one common trait: the love of good food. The restaurant's homey feel doesn't hurt, either!

Lobster Roll

Makes: Enough for 1 very
hungry person

Lobster

Water from the Bay of Fundy (or heavily salted water)
1 live Atlantic lobster (2 pounds)

Lobster Mayo

Tomalley and roe from 1 lobster
2 egg yolks
1 tablespoon Dijon mustard
1 cup canola oil
Juice of 1 lemon
Salt and pepper

Assembly

3-inch-thick slice sourdough bread
1 tablespoon butter, softened, or lobster oil
Romaine lettuce

Lobster

In a large pot, bring ocean water (or heavily salted water) to a boil. Plunge the lobster in head-
first. Cover and boil for 15 minutes.

Remove the lobster and place on ice for 15 minutes to cool.

Shuck the meat from the lobster, reserving tomalley and roe for the lobster mayo. Save some
roe for serving.

Lobster Mayo

In a medium bowl, whisk together the reserved lobster tomalley and roe, egg yolks, and mustard. While whisking, slowly add the oil until emulsified. Season mayo with lemon juice and
salt and pepper to taste.

Assembly

Heat a skillet over medium heat. Make a cut three-quarters of the way down the middle of the
sourdough slice to resemble a hotdog bun. Butter the outsides liberally and fry until both
sides are crispy.

Open the bun gently and stuff with crispy lettuce. Add all the lobster meat. Top lobster meat
with *lots* of lobster mayo and a sprinkling of roe.

Buttermilk Fried Chicken Strips with Spicy Mayonnaise and Popping Candy

Makes: 4 to 6 servings

Spicy Mayonnaise

1 cup mayonnaise

3 tablespoons Asian hot sauce

2 tablespoons sweetened condensed milk

Buttermilk Fried Chicken Strips

16 ounces boneless, skinless chicken breasts or thighs, cut into strips

2 cups buttermilk

1/2 teaspoon hot pepper sauce

Oil for deep-frying

2 cups quick-mixing all-purpose flour

3 tablespoons paprika

2 tablespoons salt

1 tablespoon each celery salt, onion powder, ground cumin, dried basil, and black pepper

1 teaspoon each garlic powder and curry powder

1 pkg (0.3 ounce) watermelon-flavoured popping candy

Spicy Mayonnaise

In a small bowl, stir together the mayonnaise, hot sauce, and condensed milk. Chill until
needed.

Buttermilk Fried Chicken Strips

In a large bowl, combine the chicken, buttermilk, and hot pepper sauce. Cover and refrigerate
for at least 4 hours.

Preheat oven to 200°F. Pour 2 to 3 inches of oil into a large heavy pot and heat to 350°F (or
use a deep-fryer).

In a medium bowl, stir together the flour, paprika, salt, celery salt, onion powder, cumin, basil,
black pepper, garlic powder, and curry powder.

Remove the chicken strips from the buttermilk. Working in small batches, dredge chicken in
the seasoned flour, dip back in the buttermilk, and dredge in the flour again.

Fry for 4 to 6 minutes, until the chicken is golden and the internal temperature is 160°F.

Drain on paper towels, then transfer to a baking sheet and keep warm in the oven. Repeat with
the remaining chicken.

Season with salt and pepper to taste.

Serve the chicken strips drizzled with spicy mayonnaise and sprinkled with popping candy.

Salvatore's Pizzaiolo Trattoria

EST. 1994
5541 YOUNG STREET
HALIFAX · NS · B3K 1Z7
WWW.SALVATORESPIZZA.CA

I've always believed that if you want to reveal the essence of a good pizza, you have to start with the basics: crust, sauce, and cheese. It's been a long time since I met someone who shared my Pure Pizza Theory. Then I met Chris Cuddihy, the chef and owner of Halifax's Salvatore's Pizzaiolo Trattoria, a man who knows that once you've got these three things mastered, the rest will come easy. And let me tell you, Chris has them down to a T.

Yet as simple as it sounds, mastering the nuance of crust-sauce-cheese is not as easy as you might think. Chris came upon his recipes while working at a New York restaurant called Salvatore's New York Pizza. When the restaurant closed in 1992, Chris got permission from his former bosses to keep the name and their recipes, which he brought back to Halifax, determined to keep the traditions alive. And so he has: Salvatore's is consistently voted Halifax's best pizza in local arts and entertainment magazines.

Given his Pizza Purist tendencies, there was no way Chris was going to let me start with anything but his Original Pizza, a classic combination of crust-sauce-cheese and a sprinkle of Parmesan and dried basil. Chris assembles every pie he makes with care and planning, and the Original is no different. Instead of dredging sauce

When you have the best pizza in Halifax, everyone wants a slice! That's why you'll find an eclectic mix of people inside, from art students to suburbanites.

across the virgin dough, Chris lays the cheese down first, then the sauce. He says it improves the texture of each slice and prevents toppings from sliding off (*when* he lets you put toppings on, that is). The result was Italian food at its best: simple and delicious.

The Bianco in Stephano is another Salvatore's original, a cornmeal-rimmed pizza that starts with a layer of mozzarella punctuated by dollops of ricotta. Add raw sliced onions, parsley,

Parmesan and Romano cheeses, and herbs, and it's into the oven for Stephano. But it's not ready to eat until it comes out piping hot and is sprinkled with chopped tomatoes, more Parmesan, and fresh lemon juice, a light and refreshing groove that's perfect for summer.

A Halifax dining experience would not be complete without a seafood twist, and Salvatore's is no different. Enter the Clam Pie Marinato. That's right, *Clam Pie* . . . as in *clams* on a pizza. Maybe it's the blend of baby clams, garlic, dried Mediterranean peppers, fresh parsley, and extra virgin olive oil that he lets sit for a few hours before putting it on the dough. Maybe it's the fresh lemon juice he squeezes on top after it comes out of the oven. No matter the secret, though, the end result is a thing of beauty. I can tell you one thing. The next time I'm at Salvatore's, *this* is the pizza I'm ordering!

If for some bizarro reason you're not into pizza when you go to Salvatore's, they serve up a bevy (you heard me . . . bevy) of delicious heroes, all on exquisite homemade bread. (They use the same dough for both bread and pizza crust.) Sal's Roasted Ham Hero starts with hand-roasted garlic rosemary ham piled on fresh garlic bread and topped with smoked mozzarella, tomatoes, sautéed mushroom, onions, and Romano cheese. I had a great Meatball Hero at Sal's, too. Overflowing with moist and tasty meatballs and doused with homemade tomato sauce, onions, and black olives, it was the perfect takeout dish after a long day of shooting.

But if you want the full Salvatore's experience, stay for a while. If you're a purist like Chris, you'll know that food tastes better when it's served fresh from the kitchen to your table.

Chris came upon his recipes while working at a New York restaurant called Salvatore's New York Pizza. When the restaurant closed in 1992, Chris brought the name and recipes back to Halifax, determined to keep the traditions alive.

I wasn't a huge fan of seafood-and-cheese combinations until I tasted Salvatore's Clam Pie, which won me over completely.

Salvatore's Meatballs

2 pounds ground grass-fed, pastured beef
1/2 cup dry bread crumbs
1/4 cup minced onion
2 eggs, lightly beaten
1 garlic clove, minced
1 tablespoon dried oregano
1 teaspoon each salt and pepper
1/2 teaspoon dried thyme

The Meatball Hero

2 Italian baguettes
1/4 cup garlic butter
Mayonnaise
Shredded mozzarella cheese
A few large cooked meatballs, sliced
    1/8 to 1/4 inch thick
1 1/2 cups pizza sauce
Kalamata olives, pitted and sliced
1/2 medium Spanish onion, thinly sliced
Freshly grated Grana Padano cheese
Salt and freshly ground pepper
Dill pickle

Meatballs

Preheat oven to 400°F.

In a large bowl, combine the beef, bread crumbs, onion, eggs, garlic, oregano, salt, pepper, and
thyme. Mix well. Shape mixture into 3-inch balls. Arrange balls in a baking pan large enough
to hold them in one layer.

Cover with foil and bake for 40 to 60 minutes or until a meat thermometer reads 160°F.

Set a wire rack over a baking sheet. Transfer meatballs to rack to drain. Let cool so meatballs
are easier to slice.

Hero

Preheat oven to 475°F.

Slice bread in half horizontally and then into 6-inch sections. Spread garlic butter on both cut
sides.

Place the bottoms of the sandwiches buttered side up on a baking sheet. Spread a layer of mayonnaise on each slice. Add a layer of mozzarella. Arrange a row of sliced meatballs on each
bun and spoon pizza sauce along the row.

Top the sandwiches with olives, onions, and a generous sprinkle of Grana Padano.

Bake the loaded sandwich bottoms for 7 to 10 minutes, until the mozzarella melts.

Meanwhile, arrange the sandwich tops buttered side up on a second baking sheet. When the
first tray comes out, put your tops in and toast them, about 4 minutes.

To serve, place a bottom half on each plate, season to taste with salt and pepper, and add the
top of the sandwich. Garnish with a pickle.

Tide & Boar Gastropub

EST. 2011
700 MAIN STREET
MONCTON · NB · EIC IE4
WWW.TIDEANDBOAR.COM

I think almost every pub across Canada serves poutine. But how many serve it with hunks of slow-roasted boar? That's the kind of surprise that awaits you at the Tide & Boar, where the imagination and creativity of owners Matt Pennell and Chad Steves—two young guys hell-bent on making their culinary mark on Moncton—know no bounds.

It's not like these guys stumbled across their profession by accident. Matt—who is the pub's head chef—and Chad met at culinary school in Halifax, then travelled the world on a quest to find great ingredients and unique ways of preparing food. When they returned home to New Brunswick, they decided to open a pub together, but one where the food is as important as the spirits.

And if the Boar Poutine is any indication, then these guys have struck the perfect balance between booze and beast. The poutine starts with a massive boar shoulder (who knew a boar was so damn *big*?) that is soaked in brine, rubbed with sugar, herbs, and spices, then seared in a very hot oven. Afterwards, the shoulder is slow-roasted for as many as eight hours in a pan full of its own stock, a process that makes it so tender it literally falls apart in your hands when it's done.

Matt assembles the poutine by first piling a mound of hand-cut fries on a plate and topping them with mozzarella cheese, caramelized onions, cheese curds, and the boar meat (which by now has been sautéed in a deliciously rich chicken-boar gravy). And if wild pig isn't quite surprising enough an addition to your poutine, Matt adds another layer of sometin-sometin by pouring his homemade ketchup on the pile, which adds an unexpected—and delicious—zing! to the proceedings. Just don't expect Matt to pour gravy on his wonderfully crispy fries, which he says makes them soggy. Instead, he serves gravy on the side, so you can add it right before you go to town.

Though food is the focal point of any visit to the Tide & Boar, the meals are not treated with kid gloves. They're meant to be shared and enjoyed.

And that's just the beginning of the uncommon taste sensations Matt and Chad have in store for you. Their Polenta Fries are a new twist on an old Italian standby, one that starts with classic polenta mush that Matt spreads on a baking tray then puts in the fridge to cool for a few hours. Once the polenta has firmed up, he cuts it into crinkle-cut wedges and deep-fries them. Served with the Tide & Boar's homemade salsa verde, it's a deliciously different perspective on cornmeal that combines a crispy exterior with warm, mushy love on the inside . . . much like me!

Matt also lends his creative talents to dessert, and the Tide & Boar's Beeramisu is one of those dishes that pleases in every way imaginable. Visually, the gently layered Beeramisu is served in little Mason jars that look as cool as they sound. But your mouth isn't left out of the equation, either. The Beeramisu—which combines layers of sweetened mascarpone cheese and cream mixture with layers of chocolate—is drizzled with a reduction of Guinness stout and sugar, which adds a subtle and unique twist. Stick a couple of homemade ladyfingers in the top and you'll have no choice but to agree with the hundreds of customers who swear by the Beeramisu: it's the perfect dessert.

Did you know that the wild boar is the wild ancestor of the domestic pig? Did you know it tastes really, really good on poutine?

Modern and rustic, the Tide & Boar is a great place for a meal and a drink in Moncton. If you're like me and the crew, you'll find yourself going back over and over again to a place where the eats are never . . . boaring.

(Sorry. That was really bad. Seriously, I'm *really* sorry.)

(Not sorry enough to take it out, though.)

If the Boar Poutine is any indication, then these guys have struck the perfect balance between booze and beast.

Beeramisu

Makes: Enough for 10 to 12 servings

Ladyfingers

6 egg whites

2 tablespoons + 5 teaspoons sugar

4 egg yolks

1 1/4 cups all-purpose flour

Mascarpone Mixture

3 cups whipping cream

1 cup sugar

1/2 cup water

2 tablespoons glucose

2 egg yolks

2 cups mascarpone cheese

Beer Syrup

1 bottle or can (600 mL/2 1/2 cups) stout
   beer such as Guinness

2 3/4 cups sugar

Chocolate Ganache

1 pound dark chocolate, chopped
   (3 1/2 cups)

1 1/2 cups whipping cream

Ladyfingers

Preheat oven to 300°F. Line a baking sheet with parchment paper.

With an electric mixer, beat the egg whites with 2 tablespoons of the sugar until stiff peaks form.

In a separate bowl, beat together the egg yolks and the remaining 5 teaspoons of the sugar until thick and pale yellow.

Using a rubber spatula, fold half of the egg whites not quite thoroughly into the yolk mixture. Sift the flour over the yolk mixture and gently fold it in. Fold in the remaining egg whites.

Spoon the batter into a pastry bag fitted with a 1/2-inch plain tip. Pipe 2-inch fingers of the batter about 1 inch apart on the baking sheet.

Bake until golden brown, 8 to 9 minutes. Transfer ladyfingers to a rack to cool.

Mascarpone Mixture

With an electric mixer, whip the cream until stiff peaks form; refrigerate.

In a small saucepan, cook the sugar, water, and glucose until the syrup registers 120°F on a candy thermometer.

Just before the syrup is ready, in the bowl of a stand mixer, begin beating the egg yolks on medium speed. Beating constantly, slowly pour the syrup into the yolks, being careful to avoid the beaters. Once the syrup is incorporated, beat in the mascarpone cheese. Gently but thoroughly fold in the whipped cream.

Spoon the mascarpone mixture into a pastry bag and refrigerate.

Beer Syrup

In a medium saucepan, simmer the stout and sugar over medium heat until reduced by a quarter. Let cool.

Chocolate Ganache

Just before assembling the beeramisu, in the top of a double boiler (or in a heatproof bowl) over simmering water, stir the chocolate and cream until melted and smooth.

Assembly (for each serving)

Fill a half-pint preserving jar (or glass serving bowl) one-quarter full of the mascarpone mixture. Rap the jar on the counter to help the mascarpone even out and settle.

Fill the next quarter of the jar with half of the chocolate ganache. Chill to set the chocolate.

Fill the next quarter of the jar with mascarpone mix and the remaining chocolate ganache. Top with ladyfingers and a tablespoon of beer syrup.

Urban Deli

EST. 2009
68 KING STREET
SAINT JOHN · NB · E2L 1G4
WWW.URBANDELI.CA

Twenty years ago, Elizabeth Rowe walked into Schwartz's Deli in Montreal and her dream was born. Since then, Liz has toured some of the most famous delis across North America, learning secrets from the masters along the way and adding her own distinctive twists to morph classic sandwiches into her own creations. Add a family atmosphere that keeps people coming back over and over again, and it's easy to see that Liz's dream has come true.

The cornerstone of any good deli is the sandwich, and the Urban does them right! One of the highlights of the menu is the Muffuletta (say muff-uh-LET-uh, people!), a New Orleans classic that uses a rough-chopped olive salad as its base. Not surprisingly, the brainiacs at the Urban designed their own olive tapenade, a blend of Manzanilla and Kalamata olives, pepperoncini peppers, capers, pearl onions, garlic, and lemon juice.

This tapenade is spread on a gigantic hollowed-out Italian loaf, followed by heaping layers of corned beef, turkey, ham, and slices of aged white Cheddar. But you can't eat it yet! Chef Andrew Brewer wraps the Muffuletta and lets it sit for a couple of hours to let the flavours mingle before you can indulge. Then the monster loaf is cut into quarters like a cake—and it's time to dive in! And oh! The flavour of the tapenade is so tangy, it just pops in your mouth and makes the taste of the meat jump out even more. A true deli classic!

But that's just the beginning of the sandwich parade at the Urban. For an even more exclusive twist on an old classic, try their Uptown Big Beef Bad Boy sandwich (try saying that on

Some restaurants start almost by chance. Others are dreams, the product of years of research and planning, a place where guests can enjoy great food in a warm, friendly environment. Enter the Urban Deli.

camera!), which sees an eye of round roast injected (yes, *injected!*) with a syringe of brewed coffee and beef stock. I don't know who came up with this idea, but it seems more logical than asking the cows to drink the coffee, eh? Trust me, I've tried!

The roast is then stuck full of garlic cloves and covered with a rub of sugar, smoked paprika, cumin, and cayenne before going in either the smoker for four hours or

Owner Liz Rowe is committed to serving her customers, and will listen intently to feedback about a meal. It's all part of offering the tastiest deli food around.

the oven for eight. Once cooked and sliced, the roast beef is dipped in beef jus to moisten while a blend of red onions, red peppers, and pepperoncini is sautéed on the grill. Then let the mounding begin! A warmed sourdough is coated with deli mustard, then piled high with the beef and pepper blend, topped with provolone cheese, and popped in the oven to melt together. And like customers here swear, this sandwich is pure delight. The ingredients all work together to form a symphony of deli perfection.

At the Urban, there's something for the sandwich lover in all of us, from smoked meat to meatloaf, Reuben to meatball. And if meat and bread ain't your thing, there are salads, soups, pasta, and desserts, too.

Yet it's not just the food that makes the Urban a special place. Sure, you can sit at your own table or booth, but why bother when the centrepiece of the dining room is a fifteen-foot, 150-year-old communal table? I realize that may sound a bit intimidating to the hermits in the crowd, but the Table is a great place to meet new friends, catch up with old ones, and realize that we're all part of something bigger than ourselves.

Just don't expect your new friends to share their food with you, OK? That's pushing things just a bit too far. Especially when it's this good!

It's not just the food that makes the Urban a special place. Sure, you can sit at your own table or booth, but why bother when the centrepiece of the dining room is a fifteen-foot, 150-year-old communal table?

Muffuletta Sandwich

Makes: 4 servings

Muffuletta Sandwich

1 round crusty Italian loaf
11 ounces sliced corned beef
4 ounces sliced smoked turkey
6 ounces sliced ham
4 thin slices aged white Cheddar cheese

Olive Tapenade

1 cup pitted green olives
1/2 cup pitted Kalamata olives
1/4 cup capers, drained
4 pepperoncini, stems removed
5 pearl onions, peeled
1 to 2 garlic cloves
2 teaspoons dried oregano
1 teaspoon pepper
4 teaspoons lemon juice
1/2 cup olive oil

Olive Tapenade

In a food processor, combine the green olives, Kalamata olives, capers, peperoncini, pearl
onions, garlic, oregano, and pepper; pulse 8 to 10 times to roughly chop the ingredients.
Add the lemon juice and olive oil; pulse once or twice to mix. Set aside.

Muffuletta Sandwich

Cut the Italian loaf in half horizontally to produce a rounded lid and a flat bottom. Hollow out
the top and bottom of the bread, leaving a shell about 1 inch thick.

Brush the inside of the bottom half with 2 tablespoons of the oil from the olive tapenade
(the oil will have floated to the surface). Layer the corned beef, smoked turkey, and ham in
the hollow. Cover with cheese slices.

Spread 1/2 cup of the olive tapenade on the inside of the top of the bread. Place the top over the
bottom and gently press down. Wrap the sandwich in plastic wrap and refrigerate for at least
2 hours to allow the flavours to blend.

Unwrap the sandwich and cut into 4 wedges. Warm in the microwave for about 1 minute.
Serve with pickles, coleslaw, or pasta salad.

Note: Leftover olive tapenade will keep in the fridge, covered, for up to 2 weeks.

Water-Prince Corner Shop and Lobster Pound

EST. 1985
141 WATER STREET
CHARLOTTETOWN · PEI · CIA IA8
WWW.WATERPRINCELOBSTER.CA

When PEI native Shane Campbell got tired of the construction game, he took a right-hand turn and found himself at the intersection of Water and Prince. Now the Water-Prince Corner Shop and Lobster Pound bears Shane's stamp and has made its imprint by serving up some of the freshest seafood you can get anywhere . . . not to mention the lobsters he ships all across the country.

You won't find anything fancy at Water-Prince, just good, fresh food cooked well and served with love. Shane's philosophy has always been "keep it simple, keep it fresh, and you'll keep them happy." It's a mantra you can't argue with. During the summer and autumn months, the lines start forming first thing in the morning and seem to linger all day long.

And nothing keeps them coming back like his Homemade Seafood Chowder, a classic PEI brew that chef Doug McAleer takes his time making so he gets it just right every time. In one pot Doug boils up a heap of halibut, in another he boils potatoes; the water from both eventually becomes the broth for the chowder. In a third pot he whips up a roux, which will help thicken the chowder . . . when he gets to that point, that is.

In a fourth pot Doug sautés up buckets of chopped bacon, onions, and celery, followed by salt cod, haddock, halibut, scallops, clams, pollock, and lobster. All of this goodness gets added together, along with fish bouillon, tarragon, clam juice, and finally, the roux. If you're beginning to feel this is, um, an *involved* process, you're beginning to catch on. Call it Chowder: The Mini-Series.

But good things come to those who wait, and I can only agree with the countless happy diners who have eaten Doug's chowder: this is a classic Maritime soup. The love that goes into it is palpable, and there was so much fresh seafood stuffed in my bowl I could almost stand my spoon up. This, my brothers and sisters, is the real deal. Ditto for their fish cakes: crispy, golden blends of salt cod, haddock, and salmon that are sure to set your taste buds atwitter.

Shane's philosophy has always been "keep it simple, keep it fresh, and you'll keep them happy." It's a mantra you can't argue with.

Wait, you mean all Islanders don't dress like this? I prove to everyone within snickering distance that I did, indeed, come from away.

Each bowl of Water-Prince chowder comes with one of chef Alice Sullivan's homemade biscuits. Now I don't know what biscuits represent for you, but for an Italian kid raised on pasta, homemade biscuits were something I never ate but always fantasized about. I envisioned my friends' grandmothers serving them soft, warm biscuits at dinner, a cozy way to mop up the gravy on their plates.

Well, Alice's biscuits are everything I had dreamt about and more. She makes them without measuring anything, and intuitively knows how much of each ingredient to use. Then she rolls the dough, cuts it into shape, gently brushes each biscuit with a milk-and-egg wash, and bakes to golden-brown perfection. Light, fluffy, and delicious, they were the perfect accompaniment to the symphony of seafood in the bowl before me.

But you can't talk about a place that calls itself a *Lobster Pound* without mentioning the little critters. The Water-Prince serves up lobster ranging in size from 1/2-pound to 2-pound monsters, each served with potato salad and Island mussels, which are steamed in garlic and white wine. If it's a bit of everything you crave, there's always the Deluxe Seafood Platter, which features fresh lobster, half a pound of Island mussels, golden pan-fried Northumberland scallops, and a choice of homemade potato salad, hand-cut french fries, or baked PEI potato.

If you really want to throw a wrench in the operation, you can always order a burger at the Water-Prince, or even chicken fingers. Just don't be surprised if one of the locals sidles up to you and says, "You're a CFA, aren't you?" (That's "come from away," don't ya know.)

Shucking oysters is a piece of cake for a guy like me . . . OK, so maybe not *me* exactly. But I'm sure there must be guys *like* me who can do it!

Timing note: The salt cod needs to soak overnight.

1/4 pound salt cod
2 pounds halibut carcass
3 cups peeled and cubed potatoes (about 4 1/2 medium potatoes)
1/2 pound bacon, finely chopped
1 cup each finely chopped onions and celery
1/4 pound haddock fillet, chopped
1/4 pound cooked crabmeat
1/4 pound cooked lobster
1/4 pound cooked scallops, chopped
1/2 pound unsalted butter
3 cups all-purpose flour
3 tablespoons fish bouillon powder
1 teaspoon dried tarragon
1 teaspoon white pepper
2 to 4 tablespoons whipping cream per serving

Soak the salt cod in water in the fridge overnight.

In a saucepan, cover the halibut carcass with about 6 cups of water. Bring to a boil, reduce heat, and simmer for 1 hour. Strain, reserving the stock, and pick off any meat to be included in the chowder. Discard bones.

Meanwhile, boil the potatoes until tender. Drain and set aside.

Drain and rinse the salt cod. Break it into chunks and set aside.

In a large skillet over medium-high heat, sauté the bacon until lightly browned. Add the onions and celery; cook until tender. Add the haddock fillet. Sauté for 7 minutes, until the fish is cooked. Add the crab, lobster, scallops, and salt cod; sauté until the fish is starting to colour. Set aside.

In a large saucepan, melt the butter over medium heat. Add the flour and cook, stirring constantly, for 3 minutes; do not let the flour colour. Remove from heat.

In a second large pot, bring the reserved fish stock to a boil. Whisk in the fish bouillon powder, tarragon, and pepper. While whisking, slowly crumble in the flour and butter mixture. Return to a boil.

Remove from heat and add the fish mixture, halibut pickings, and potatoes. Stir well.

If serving immediately, stir in the cream and heat through. Or let cool, then refrigerate overnight. Stir in the cream and gently reheat chowder.

Water-Prince
Fish Cakes

Makes: 6 servings

Timing note: The salt cod needs to soak overnight.

1/2 cup diced salt cod

3 medium potatoes, peeled

8 ounces haddock

8 ounces salmon

2 tablespoons unsalted butter

1 small onion, finely chopped

1 egg, beaten

1 teaspoon dried dillweed (or 2 teaspoons chopped fresh dill)

1 1/2 cups dry bread crumbs

Pinch each of salt and pepper

Soak the salt cod in water in the fridge overnight.

In a large saucepan, cover the potatoes with cold water. Bring to a boil over medium heat and cook until the potatoes are fork-tender. Drain potatoes, then mash. Set aside.

Drain the salt cod and place in a second saucepan. Cover with cold water and bring to a boil; cook for 10 minutes. Drain and set aside.

Place the haddock and salmon in a saucepan and cover with water. Bring to a boil and cook for 5 minutes or until the fish is cooked. Drain and set aside.

Melt butter in a large skillet over medium heat. Add the onion and cook until soft and translucent. Remove from heat.

In a large bowl, combine the mashed potatoes and onions; mash together. Add the salt cod, haddock, salmon, onion, egg, dillweed, 1 cup of the bread crumbs, and salt and pepper; mash into the mixture. Form mixture into 6 fish cakes, 1 1/2 inches thick. Dredge the fish cakes in the remaining bread crumbs, turning to coat all sides.

In the same skillet over medium heat, and working in batches if necessary, fry the fish cakes until golden on both sides.

Serve with tartar sauce.

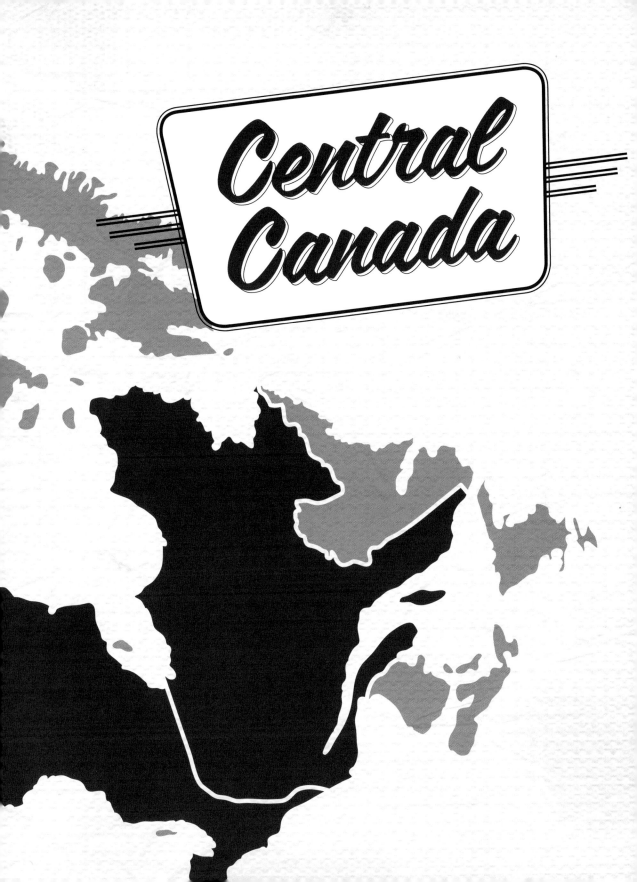

Baffo's Pizza & Pasta

EST. 1971
31 QUEEN STREET EAST
BOLTON · ON · L7E IC2
WWW.BAFFOS.COM

Hey you, big chain-store pizza place . . . Yeah, I'm talkin' to you. If you think you can push the little guy around, think again. Here in Bolton, one of your kind opened up right across the street from Baffo's. Now there's only one still standing. I'll give you a hint: it ain't the chain.

It's not because the people of Bolton and the surrounding area are blindly loyal. They know good food when they eat it, and they know that no chain can match the handmade pizza and pasta Baffo's has been creating since 1971, thanks to the dedication of owner Aldo Buccioni.

As a boy, Aldo worked in bakeries across Toronto, learning everything there is to know about the fine art of dough making. When he moved to Bolton in 1971 to open Baffo's (which was then strictly a pizza joint), Aldo did all the cooking himself. Well, times may change, but the food at Baffo's hasn't. The restaurant has since moved to a bigger building and Aldo doesn't cook anymore, but that hasn't stopped the legions of customers who descend upon Baffo's for an experience they just can't get anywhere else.

A big part of that experience is the pizza, which at Baffo's is the exclusive terrain of chef Elio Romano. Elio makes all of his own dough by hand, and none more lovingly than the one that goes under the pizza you won't find anywhere else: the Baffo's Famous Chocolate Brownie Banana Split Pizza. This is dessert pizza at its finest, beginning with the handmade chocolate dough. From there it's layers of goodness, with a cream cheese and ricotta blend, pineapple, strawberries, brownie chunks, peanuts, and deep-fried bananas. After a short blast in the oven to heat up the bananas, the pizza is topped with whipped cream, drizzled with chocolate syrup, and jammed in the mouth as quickly as humanly possible. Warm, crunchy, gooey, and sweet, it's a pizza any Italian would be proud of.

Clearly, Elio is not scared of stepping out of the pizza box, which he does again and again. Witness the Lobster and Roasted Red Peppers Pizza. Given its shellfish tendencies, this creation doesn't use tomato sauce, but instead lines the dough with olive oil. Then comes the chopped garlic, lots of roasted red peppers, heaps of lobster meat, and hunks of feta cheese. Five minutes in the oven later and you've got one Baffolicious creation! *Salute!*

There are a dozen pizza styles at Baffo's, and you can create hundreds of others from a host of toppings. The Baffo's Special, the most popular on the menu, starts with a layer of tomato sauce, followed by what Elio calls the best mozzarella money can buy. Then comes the spicy pepperoni, mushrooms, green peppers, onions, olives, and bacon, and a second layer of mozzarella. For me, it tasted like childhood all over again. The Bacon Triple Cheese Burger pizza combines ground beef, tomato sauce, bacon, and a blend of mozzarella, Cheddar, and Monterey Jack.

Über-popular though it may be, pizza is but a small part of what Baffo's does. In addition to a full complement of appetizers (try the Baffalo Wings), soups, and salads, the restaurant serves up genuine Italian pasta dishes that customers rave about. The Penne Gorgonzola is one of the most popular, and tosses al dente penne with pancetta, cremini mushrooms, asparagus, and tomatoes in a Gorgonzola cream sauce. Spaghetti and Meatballs is a classic that's been on the menu since the day Aldo opened his doors. Not one to be limited by convention, chef Mark Brasier adds a rich twist to an Italian standby with his Lobster Lasagna.

That place across the street? They served lasagna, too. Not for all that long, though.

Whether you're having a business meeting, eating with your children, or going out on a first date, Baffo's welcomes you with open arms.

The people of Bolton know good food when they eat it, and they know that no chain can match the handmade pizza and pasta Baffo's has been creating since 1971.

Where do I get a hat like that? Chef Elio Romano is all smiles when people enjoy the food he was put on Earth to make—pizza.

Tomato Sauce

1/4 cup olive oil

1 large sweet green pepper, sliced

1 large sweet red pepper, sliced

1 large onion, sliced

1 garlic clove, minced

2 tablespoons each chopped fresh oregano and basil

2 tablespoons black pepper

1 teaspoon salt

1 can (28 ounces/796 mL) stewed tomatoes (or 4 cups homemade)

Meatballs

2 1/2 pounds ground veal

2 1/2 pounds ground beef

1/4 cup grated Parmesan cheese

1/4 cup dry bread crumbs

1 tablespoon finely chopped garlic

1 1/2 teaspoons each chopped fresh basil and oregano

1 1/2 teaspoons salt

3/4 teaspoon pepper

2 eggs, lightly beaten

Assembly

8 ounces spaghetti
1/4 cup olive oil
1/4 cup finely chopped garlic
12 meatballs
Shredded Asiago cheese for garnish
Pea shoots for garnish

Tomato Sauce

Heat the oil in a medium saucepan over medium heat. Add the green and red peppers, onion, and garlic; cook, stirring frequently, until the onion is translucent. Do not let the vegetables brown. Stir in the oregano, basil, black pepper, and salt. Add the stewed tomatoes and simmer until the sauce reaches a nice consistency, 30 to 45 minutes. The sauce will still be chunky.

Meatballs

Preheat oven to 325°F.

In a large bowl, mix together the veal, beef, Parmesan cheese, bread crumbs, garlic, basil, oregano, salt, pepper, and eggs until well combined. Shape into 3-ounce meatballs; place meatballs in a large baking dish and bake for 20 minutes.

Increase temperature to 365°F. Ladle over just enough tomato sauce to cover the meatballs. Bake for another 35 minutes.

Assembly

Cook the spaghetti in a large pot of boiling salted water until al dente; drain.

In a large saucepan, heat the oil over medium-high heat. Add the garlic and cook just until fragrant.

Add the pasta and gently toss. Add 2 to 3 cups of the tomato sauce and the meatballs and toss again. Simmer until hot, then empty into a large serving bowl.

Serve garnished with Asiago cheese and pea shoots.

Note: Leftover meatballs may be frozen.

Penne Gorgonzola

Makes: 4 servings

Gorgonzola Sauce

1/4 cup olive oil

1 small onion, chopped

2 tablespoons minced garlic

3/4 cup white wine

4 cups whipping cream

1/2 cup shredded Asiago cheese

1/2 cup crumbled Gorgonzola cheese

Salt and white pepper

1/4 cup cornstarch

1/4 cup water

Assembly

8 ounces penne

1/4 cup olive oil

1/2 cup sliced mushrooms

1/2 cup diced fresh plum tomatoes

1/4 cup crushed garlic

4 ounces pancetta, thinly sliced

8 spears fresh steamed asparagus

Shredded Asiago cheese for garnish

Pea shoots for garnish

Gorgonzola Sauce

Heat the olive oil in a medium saucepan over medium heat. Add the onions and garlic; cook, stirring, until the onions are translucent. Add the wine and stir to loosen the onions and garlic from the pan. Add the cream, stir, and bring almost to a boil. Reduce heat and simmer for 15 to 20 minutes, until thick enough to coat a spoon.

Strain the sauce into a bowl to remove the onions. Pour the sauce back into the saucepan and return to a simmer. Stir in the Asiago and Gorgonzola cheeses, about 1/4 cup at a time, and simmer, stirring, until the cheese has melted. Season with salt and white pepper to taste.

Stir the cornstarch into the water; add to the sauce, a little at a time, to thicken as desired.

Assembly

Cook the penne in a large pot of boiling salted water until al dente; drain.

Heat the oil in a large saucepan over medium-high heat. Add the mushrooms, tomatoes, and garlic; sauté until mushrooms just start to soften.

Add the pasta and toss. Add the gorgonzola sauce and toss again. Simmer until hot, then empty into a large serving bowl.

Top with the prosciutto and asparagus. Serve garnished with Asiago cheese and pea shoots.

Boomers Gourmet Fries

EST. 1998
26 ERIE STREET
STRATFORD · ON · N5A 2M4
WWW.BOOMERSGOURMETFRIES.COM

Like people, restaurants develop their own personalities, and at Boomers Gourmet Fries, that personality can be summed up in one word: Sue. Sue Pasquale is the cantankerous yet lovable owner and chef at Boomers, a woman whose perspective on deep-fried Yukon Gold potatoes is every bit as individual as her take on life. As devoted customers at this tiny fry-and-burger joint will tell you, Sue is Boomers, and Boomers is Sue!

Opened in 1998 as an extension of a local fry truck, Boomers took on its current personality in 2001, when Sue bought the businesses. She's been expanding the menu ever since. Now, not only can you enjoy twelve of the most unique combination of fries and homemade gravy your taste buds can possibly imagine, there's also a slew of delicious burgers (including the S.O.B., named after Sue herself!) and even fish and chips.

The challenge at Boomers is finding a place to park your behind. The place is a huge local favourite, so consider yourself lucky if you find a seat at the counter inside or at one of the two benches outside. Either way, the decor at Boomers is light, bright, and fun, from the red-and-yellow walls to the handwritten chalkboard menu.

And oh, did I mention the food? Sue may be Stratford's toughest woman, but she's a sweetheart when it comes to dreaming up new taste temptations. For you traditionalists in the house, there's classic poutine, but I'm saving my money for more exotic combinations like the Italian Poutine, which is highlighted by a homemade marinara sauce so good you could put it on a plate of gnocchi. (Hey, gnocchi are potatoes, too!) Sue says the secret to her sauce is her exotic (!) blend of salt, pepper, and chilies, but I say it's *love*. That and maybe a pinch of yelling.

If you think putting marinara sauce on a plate of fries is a bit on the wackier side of the menu ledger, you ain't seen nothin' yet! Sue will serve you a plate of Black Bean Chili Fries that tastes like a burrito, only better. Here the lightly salted potatoes are topped with Monterey Jack and mozzarella, black bean chili, sour cream, and a squirt of hot sauce. Salsa Fries continue the Tex-Mex theme, and are smothered with Monterey Jack and mozzarella, along with homemade salsa and a dollop of sour cream.

Then there's the Cosmopolitan, which puts a twist on classic poutine by using sweet potato fries instead of Yukon Golds. But if you really want to push the limits of french-fry convention at Boomers, go for the Goat Cheese Poutine. Top those golden sticks of potato goodness with a scoop of fresh chèvre, gravy, cracked black pepper, and some basil oil, and you will enter potato nirvana. And calories don't exist in potato nirvana! Om!

Sue knows there's more to life than just fries, though, so she offers some pretty tasty burgers for her customers, too. Boomers boasts more than fifteen burger topping combinations, and every one can be made with a beef, boar, turkey, or veggie patty. Just make sure you eat them the way Sue wants you to! My turkey burger—the Guacamolean—was smothered in homemade guacamole, shredded cheese, and sour cream, and there was *no way* Sue was going to let me put any ketchup on it.

But who am I to argue with Sue, a woman who can toss a 50-pound sack of potatoes over her shoulder like it's a baby? Like most good patrons of Boomers, I do what Sue says. As one happy diner told me, she has a way of abusing customers that keeps them going back for more. I know I will.

At 20 by 13 feet, there's nothing grandiose about Boomers . . . until you taste the food, that is. Regular customers and tourists sit side by side at a communal table to enjoy Sue's delicacies.

As one happy diner told me, Sue has a way of abusing customers that keeps them going back for more. I know I will.

Don't hurt me! The child of a German mother and Italian father, Sue uses her heritage to inspire many of her poutine recipes. Here she gives me a good stern talking to about the way of the fry.

Italian
Poutine

Makes: 4 servings

Basil Oil

Leaves from 1 bunch fresh basil
Leaves from 1/4 bunch fresh parsley
1/2 cup canola oil

Marinara Sauce

1 tablespoon olive oil
2/3 cup finely chopped onion
1/3 cup finely chopped carrot
1/3 cup finely chopped celery
2 large garlic cloves, finely chopped
1 can (5 1/2 ounces/156 mL) tomato paste
1 can (28 ounces/796 mL) whole plum tomatoes, crushed
1 tablespoon salt
1 1/2 teaspoons black pepper
1/4 teaspoon hot pepper flakes

Poutine

French fries
1 cup white Cheddar cheese curds
Cracked black pepper

Basil Oil

Blend the basil, parsley, and oil in a blender or food processor until smooth; set aside. (Can be made ahead and refrigerated for up to 2 weeks.)

Marinara Sauce

Heat the oil in a medium saucepan over medium heat. Add the onion, carrot, and celery; cook, stirring constantly, until softened. Add the garlic and continue to stir for 1 minute. Add the tomato paste and cook, stirring, for 2 minutes. Stir in the crushed tomatoes, salt, black pepper, and hot pepper flakes. Reduce heat, cover, and simmer for 1 hour.

Poutine

Arrange french fries on 4 large plates. Crumble a layer of cheese curds over the fries. Pour marinara sauce on top. Drizzle with the basil oil. Season with cracked black pepper to taste.

Bubi's Awesome Eats

EST. 1977
620 UNIVERSITY AVENUE WEST
WINDSOR · ON · N9A 5R5
WWW.BUBIS.ORG

Vampires, consider yourselves warned. Go to Bubi's and turn to dust. Non-demonic creatures, consider yourselves warned, too. Every Bubi's customer has one thing in common: a love of their deliciously addictive Bubi Sauce (also called Cup o' Bubi's), which is so garlicky that for days to come, you'll smell like you bathed in it.

Here at Bubi's (home of the 8-pound burger), the infamous sauce goes on or with just about everything on the menu. And even though you know you shouldn't eat it, even though you know nobody's going to come near you, even though you know you're going to sweat garlic for the next three days, you don't care. You can't stop eating the stuff!

Bubi Sauce actually owes its origins to a botched recipe for spinach salad dressing that turned out far too garlicky for owner Michael "Buddy" Miloyevich, who tinkered with the recipe to try to offset the garlic. Although the dressing never worked out, the sauce was born!

Chef Kevin Buckridan is my Bubi Sauce dealer, hooking me up with a garlic fix whenever I start to twitch.

Today, sauce-making responsibilities fall on the shoulders of Anna Chiodo, Bubi's prep chef. She mixes eggs, oil, lemon juice, Dijon mustard, white wine vinegar, and seasonings to make a French mayonnaise. Meanwhile, a food processor purées celery, onions, capers, anchovies, and a million cloves of garlic. Mix the two together and voilà! Bubi Sauce!

I was dipping Bubi Sauce like a lunatic when it was served with Best of the Breast, Bubi's take on chicken fingers (but *don't* call them chicken fingers!). These tender strips of chicken breast marinate in an egg-and-milk wash before being breaded in a bread-crumb-and-oregano mixture. Then they're baked for a few minutes to fuse the coating to the chicken before going into the deep-fryer.

These chicken pieces are a mind-blowing combination of crispy and tender, made all the more enticing by the addition of Dillion Fries, another accidental delight at Bubi's. Cook Dillion

When owner Buddy Miloyevich's grandmother died, his family didn't know what to do with her Victorian home. The ambitious Buddy decided to convert it into his own restaurant, and Bubi's—named after his grandmother—was born.

Einhorn thought it would be a good idea to toss some steak-cut fries in a heap of garlic butter and Parmesan cheese. Never one to turn his back on a food experiment, chef Kevin Buckridan tried it and an instant classic was born. Heck, they were so good I even tried to make them at home! (For the record, they were nowhere near as good as Bubi's.)

But most people come to Bubi's for the burgers, the selection of which is mind-numbing. Buddy makes the hamburger meat in 50-pound batches, mixing together fresh beef, eggs, lots of garlic (you should have guessed this one, right?), bread crumbs, Worcestershire sauce, soy sauce, and chicken soup base. And not only do you choose the type of burger you want, you also get to choose the size. Homemade patties can be as demure as 1/3 pound at Bubi's, but those with larger appetites can go for 2/3 pound, 1 pound, 2 pounds, 4 pounds, 6 pounds, or all 8 pounds of the heart-stopping Bunda's Big V8.

I was in a light kinda mood the day I ate at Bubi's, so Kevin hooked me up with a Gonzo Burger, two juicy patties double stacked and served with ham, cheese, and lettuce. Kevin says it's so messy only guys will eat it. I'm not so sure.

If messy is what you crave, look no further than the Bastien's Chili Cheez Train, which is piled so high with famous homemade chili, gravy, and drippy nacho cheese that you'll forget there's a patty and piece of rye bread underneath this open-faced beauty. More sophisticated palates might go for the Black Olive Almond Pesto burger, which adds a spread of the same name to cream cheese, tomato, and onion. Or try Bubi's Black Olive Almond Pesto over a crispy-yet-creamy hunk of deep-fried Brie, served on a wedge of garlic-buttered pita.

There's something for everyone at Bubi's, though, and if you're not in the mood for a burger, Bubi's Chocolate Peanut Butter Cheezcake is a force to be reckoned with. One bite and you'll forgive this cheesy, peanutty mocha dream for not having garlic. I know all the vampires out there will.

Even though you know you're going to sweat garlic for the next three days, you don't care. You can't stop eating the stuff!

Bubi's Chocolate Peanut Butter Cheezcake

Makes: 6 servings

Note: This recipe requires a food processor.

Timing note: Bake the cheezcake a day ahead, because it must be refrigerated overnight.

Crust

1 1/2 cups graham cracker crumbs

1/3 cup unsalted butter, melted

1/3 cup sugar

Icing

1 1/2 cups icing sugar

1/2 cup unsalted butter, softened

1/4 cup coffee, at room temperature

1 1/2 teaspoons vanilla extract

Cheezcake

5 eggs

2 cups sugar

2 tablespoons vanilla extract

3 pkg (8 ounces/250 g each) cream cheese

2 cups peanut butter

1 1/2 cups sour cream

1 cup 18% or whipping cream

1 cup store-bought French cocoa icing (or any other icing that is 20 to 25% chocolate)

Crust

Preheat oven to 350°F.

Mix all ingredients together and press evenly into the bottom of a 10-inch springform pan.

Bake for 8 to 10 minutes or until firm and slightly browned. Let cool.

Cheezcake

Note: If you have a large-capacity food processor, you can make the cheezcake in one batch.

Preheat oven to 350°F.

Combine the eggs, sugar, and vanilla in a large bowl. Divide the mixture in half. Return half of it to the food processor. Process until smooth.

Add half of the cream cheese and process to combine. Add 1 cup of the peanut butter, 3/4 cup of the sour cream, 1/2 cup of the cream and 1/2 cup of the icing; process until very smooth and well whipped. Empty the mixture into a large bowl.

Add remaining egg mixture to the food processor and process until smooth. Add the remaining cream cheese and process to combine. Add the remaining peanut butter, sour cream, cream, and icing; process until very smooth.

Combine the two batches of mixture and pour into the cooled crust.

Bake for 30 minutes or until small dark circles start forming around the edge of the cheezcake. The edge will rise up ever so slightly. Turn oven off and leave the cake in the oven for another 20 minutes. Remove and cool to room temperature, then cover and refrigerate overnight.

Icing

Combine all ingredients in a food processor and blend until smooth. (This icing can get very thick and heavy, so feel free to add more coffee to yield a thinner icing.)

Assembly

Remove sides of pan and transfer the cheezcake to a serving plate. Spread icing over the cake. Slice and serve.

Busters Barbeque

EST. 2007
177 HIGHWAY 17
VERMILION BAY · ON · POV 2VO
WWW.BUSTERSBBQ.COM

When the term "southern barbeque" was coined, someone forgot to tell the wordsmith about Busters Barbeque. Because while you're sure to get some of the best barbeque you've ever tasted here at Busters, you've got to head *north* to get it!

Busters is about as remote as it gets. To get there, you have to either drive twenty-four hours from Toronto, or fly to Winnipeg and drive into Ontario for four hours. Just make sure you've got your eyes peeled for Vermilion Bay, an unincorporated community so unassuming that small towns look at it and say, "Wow . . . you're *small*!" But that doesn't stop Busters—which bills itself as the only award-winning barbeque restaurant on the Trans-Canada Highway—from serving up food with big-city flair.

If you've got twenty-four hours to kill for the most worthwhile road trip of your life, put Busters on your must-see map.

Busters offers up a hefty menu's worth of food, including barbeque sandwiches, burgers (made from a special blend of ground beef brisket and steak), wraps, salads, and steaks, but it's their smoked chicken, ribs, and pork that keep happy diners begging for more. The secret to Busters' success? Their dedication to good food, and their Blueberry Barbeque Sauce, whose reputation has grown to legendary proportions in these parts.

The sauce is the brainchild of Kevin and Karen Welniak, who purchased Busters Family Restaurant in 1994. Busters was reopened as a barbeque joint in 2007 by son Stosh and his wife, Natalie, who have made such a reputation for themselves that people will drive hours to eat here . . . and for good reason! The sauce starts with a base of succulent wild blueberries, simmered slowly. A couple hours later you've got one of the most unique damn barbeque sauces you've ever laid your lips upon. Take it hot (with habanero peppers) or mild, partner.

Given the popularity of the Blueberry Barbeque Sauce (it's won multiple awards throughout North America), it's easy to see why Stosh and Natalie make it a part of so many dishes, including one of my favourites, the St. Louis Style Pork Side Ribs. This off-the-bone beauty starts with a spray of liquid smoke and vinegar, followed by Busters' rub of secret ingredients, a blend designed to highlight the apple, hickory, and cherry woods used in the smoker, which is out behind the restaurant.

Anyone within a nostril's distance of Busters is sure to notice the delectable smell of smoke wafting through the air, a scent most find hard to resist.

Busters touts itself as the only award-winning barbeque restaurant on the Trans-Canada Highway. I'm not sure if it's the only one, but you can't argue with the award-winning part!

After several hours in the smoker, the ribs are laid on the charbroiler, where they're finished off with a hefty portion of blueberry goodness, just one of about a hundred rib racks that Busters serves every day. And the taste? To die for, my brothers and sisters. To die for.

Busters' smoked chicken is prepared in much the same way. Its crispy skin almost seems fried, but the meat is so tender, with just the right hint of smoke, that you know this bird has never seen an oil bath. Each Busters main dish comes with fries and their homemade cornbread, homemade baked beans, or homemade coleslaw.

Their Carolina Pulled Pork Sandwich starts as a pork shoulder, but after about ten hours in the smoker it's ready to be pulled into tender bits that are then sautéed in blueberry sauce, piled high on a panino, and topped with coleslaw. And the Brisket Sandwich? Each piece of gently smoked beef literally melts in your mouth.

We were lucky enough to get our hands on Busters Jalapeño Sausage, a free-form sausage grilled in corn husks and jacked up with Busters Championship Seasoning.

You may not happen to find yourself in Vermilion Bay any time soon. But if you've got twenty-four hours to kill for the most worthwhile road trip of your life, put Busters on your must-see map. With its great casual vibe and incredible barbeque, this place has gotta be tasted to be believed.

Smoked St. Louis Ribs

Makes: 4 to 6 servings

Note: This recipe requires a charcoal grill.

2/3 cup cider vinegar
1/3 cup liquid smoke
4 to 5 pounds St. Louis cut pork ribs, silverskin removed
Busters Championship Seasoning or your favourite dry rub
Hickory wood chips (or wood pellets or sawdust if using an electric smoker)
Busters Blueberry Barbeque Sauce or your favourite barbeque sauce

Combine the cider vinegar and liquid smoke in a spray bottle. Spray both sides of the ribs with
the liquid smoke mixture, then coat both sides of the ribs with the seasoning rub.

Smoker method: Preheat smoker to 250°F. Smoke the ribs for 2 hours. Seal the ribs tightly in
foil, then return to smoker for another 2 hours.

Grill method: Prepare 6 smoke packs, filling foil packets with hickory pellets or sawdust and
sealing tightly. Make a small hole in each packet with a toothpick. Place 1 packet on the coals
and preheat grill to 250°F. Smoke the ribs for 2 hours, replacing smoke packets every 45
to 60 minutes. About 15 minutes before ribs are ready, preheat oven to 250°F. Seal the ribs
tightly in foil or a tightly covered roasting pan and transfer to the oven for another 2 hours.

About 15 minutes before ribs come out of the smoker or oven, preheat grill.

Coat ribs with barbeque sauce and grill for 3 to 5 minutes per side to finish.

Busters Jalapeño Sausage in Corn Husks

Makes: 8 servings

Note: If you're grinding your own meat, use the coarse grinding plate.

16 dried corn husks (available in Latin American grocery stores)
1/4 cup chopped seeded jalapeño peppers (or leave seeds in for spicier sausage)
1 tablespoon chopped garlic
1 tablespoon sugar
2 teaspoons Busters Championship Seasoning (or seasoning of your choice)
1/2 teaspoon each nutmeg and cayenne pepper
1/4 teaspoon ground allspice
1/4 teaspoon kosher salt
1 teaspoon chicken bouillon powder dissolved in 1/4 cup cold water
2 1/2 pounds ground pork butt
Busters Original or Habanero Blueberry Barbeque Sauce (or barbeque sauce of your choice)

Preheat smoker or grill to 250°F.

In a large bowl, soak the corn husks in water for at least 20 minutes.

In another large bowl, combine the jalapeños, garlic, sugar, Busters seasoning, nutmeg, cayenne, allspice, salt, and chicken bouillon mixture; stir well to combine. Add the ground pork; mix with your hands until well combined.

Lay 8 soaked corn husks curving up on a work surface. Spoon 3/4 cup of the sausage mixture into each corn husk. Place a second husk on top of the sausage mixture, curving down. Roll the edges of the husks inwards to wrap the sausage tightly. Tie a piece of string around each end of the husks to seal.

Smoke or grill the sausages for 20 minutes or until a meat thermometer reads 160°F.

Cut the strings, unroll the husks, and serve with barbeque sauce.

Café Polonez

EST. 1978
195 RONCESVALLES AVENUE
TORONTO · ON · M6R 2L5
WWW.CAFEPOLONEZ.CA

I t's a sad fact of the restaurant world that eateries come and go, with far more failing than succeeding. So to find one that's got more than three decades of history under its belt is a feat, particularly when it serves specialty cuisine. Yet that's exactly what Café Polonez has managed to do since 1978, largely by offering their passionate and dedicated clientele some of the most authentic and delicious homemade Polish food money can buy.

Soup's on! Café Polonez is proud of their beet brews, although their Beet Root Soup with Dumplings is unlike anything I've ever had. I've always pictured Polish beet soups as thick with puréed beets, stick-to-your-ribs affairs that warmed you on a blustery winter's day. This was completely different, though: a light purple broth filled with succulent pork or mushroom dumplings that were truly delightful. Chef Irene Zychia's Cold Borscht starts out the same way, but adds kefir—a yogurt-like product—along with chopped fresh cucumber, onions, and dill, served cold over a split hard-boiled egg. You don't have to be Polish to love it! There was something about fresh dill and the kefir that made the borscht rich, yet fresh at the same time.

Disco was king and gold was $200 an ounce when Café Polonez was born. Since then it's built a legacy of delicious, home-cooked Polish delights.

If there's one food that keeps 'em coming back to Café Polonez over and over again, it's the homemade *rozne nadzienia*—perogies—which come in four different varieties: Cheddar and potato, cottage cheese and potato, sauerkraut and mushroom, and minced pork. The fillings are wrapped lovingly by the hands of chef Danusia Olesinska, who has likely made millions of these things in her time. The perfect little dumplings can be boiled or fried, and are served under a blanket of bacon and sautéed onions, with a side of sour cream.

Now I don't know what your experience with perogies has been, but if you're anything like me, you're used to the frozen ones in a bag. Filling? Maybe. Taste sensation? Nah. But when you get them rolled out and hand-stuffed by master hands, they are one of the most perfect foods you can put in your mouth. Little wonder that devoted customers say they're the best perogies they've ever had.

The European hit parade just keeps on rolling at Café Polonez, with a host of Polish classics featured on the menu, not to mention the daily specials. From Herring to Ground Meat Cutlets, Hunter's Stew to Polish Sausage, there's a meal to suit everyone's taste. *Nalesniki z serem lub dzemem* are traditional crêpes made by chef Marcin Molek, who fills them with either sweet cheese or strawberry jam. Light, sweet, and delightfully contrasted by the sour cream they're served with, the crêpes are good for breakfast, lunch, or dinner.

The *golabki* (cabbage rolls) are the perfect Polish comfort food, a home-cooked meal brought to your table. At Café Polonez, the boiled cabbage leaves are stuffed with a seasoned minced pork blend, then lovingly rolled before being smothered in tomato sauce. The Hungarian-Style Potato Pancakes are also a huge hit. This Polonez specialty starts with shredded potatoes fried into a pancake and then stuffed with goulash, a savoury pork stew made with paprika, pepper, onions, and garlic. Hearty and delicious, these intriguing cakes hit the spot after a long winter's day.

Tradition, authenticity, and a dedication to fresh, delicious, homemade food. It's what makes Café Polonez a mainstay in an ever-changing culinary landscape.

Since 1978, Café Polonez has offered its passionate and dedicated clientele some of the most authentic and delicious homemade Polish food money can buy.

Timing note: Make the Beetroot Consommé before making the Cold Borscht Soup.

Beetroot Consommé

4 cups beef or vegetable stock

1 1/2 pounds beets (or 5 medium beets), cooked, peeled, and shredded

2-3 stalks of celery, diced

1/4 cup lemon juice

4 teaspoons sugar

1 1/2 bay leaves

Salt and pepper

Cold Borscht Soup

4 cups kefir (fermented milk)

6 cups chilled beetroot consommé

1/2 cup sour cream

2 cups diced cucumber

1/2 pound beets (or 2 medium beets), cooked, peeled, and shredded

1/2 cup chopped green onions

1/2 cup chopped fresh dill

Assembly

1 hard-boiled egg, cut in half (per serving)

Beetroot Consommé

In a large saucepan, combine the beef stock with 5 cups of water.

Add 5 cups of the shredded beets, celery, lemon juice, sugar, and bay leaves. Season with salt and pepper to taste. Bring to a boil. Reduce heat and simmer for 5 minutes, then remove from heat.

Add the remaining cup of shredded beets to give a rich, deep colour. Let cool.

Strain, discarding the solids, and put the consommé in the fridge until cold. Remove bay leaves before serving.

Note: You can also serve the consommé as a hot soup, with chopped fresh dill for garnish.

Cold Borscht Soup

Pour the kefir into a medium bowl. Slowly whisk in the cold beetroot consommé. Add the remaining ingredients and stir until thoroughly combined. Chill if not serving immediately.

Assembly

Cut a hard-boiled egg in half and place in the bottom of each bowl. Pour chilled soup over top.

Filling

1 tablespoon grated onion

2 tablespoons unsalted butter

2 cups mashed potatoes

1 cup farmer cheese or dry-curd cottage cheese

Salt and pepper

Perogy Dough

2 1/2 cups all-purpose flour

1/2 teaspoon salt

1 egg, lightly beaten

1/2 cup water

1 teaspoon canola oil

Filling

In a small skillet, fry the onion in the butter until brown. Transfer to a medium bowl; add the mashed potatoes, cheese, and salt and pepper to taste. Stir until well mixed.

Perogy Dough and Assembly

In a medium bowl, stir together the flour and salt. Add the egg, water, and oil; stir to combine.

On a lightly floured surface, knead the dough for 8 minutes or until smooth. Roll out the dough to 1/8-inch thickness. Cut out 3-inch rounds using a cookie cutter or drinking glass.

Hold a round in the palm of your hand and place a spoonful of filling in the centre. Fold the dough over into a half-moon shape and press together the edges to seal. Place the perogy on a floured baking sheet. Continue with the remaining rounds and filling.

Bring a large pot of water to a boil. Add the perogies, stirring gently with a spoon. Boil for 3 to 5 minutes or until the perogies float to the surface. Remove the perogies with a slotted spoon and drain thoroughly.

Serve perogies topped with warm melted butter, fried onions, and fried chopped bacon. Serve with sour cream.

Cardinal Rule

EST. 2011
5 RONCESVALLES AVENUE
TORONTO · ON · M6R 2K2
WWW.CARDINALRULERESTAURANT.COM

Excuse my French, but at Cardinal Rule, partners Katie James and Marta Kusel take traditional homestyle diner food and flip it on its ass. Want macaroni and cheese? Here it's Maki N' Cheese, where a classic turns sushi. Meatloaf you crave, my dear? You're going to be a fan of their meat muffins. And if you're in for brunch and want a Caesar to wash down your eggs Benedict, why not combine them with the Hail Caesar Eggs Benedict? Or you could try Cardinal Rule's Coconut Quinoa Pancakes, a sweet twist on a breakfast fave.

Such creations come easy to Marta and Katie, whose frustrations in the service industry persuaded them to pool their talents and open Cardinal Rule. A former interior designer, Katie takes care of the front of house and bakes the desserts. Marta is a food freak, especially when she gets talking about her latest culinary invention. Together, they are one hell of a team, as the constant crowds attest.

And why wouldn't you wait for a dish like Marta's amazing Maki N'

Not one to live inside the box, **Marta Kusel likes to add her own eclectic vision to classic diner fare.**

Cheese? For years she worked as a sushi chef, but was never able to enjoy the fruits of her labour since she didn't eat fish. Searching for something else to roll, she stumbled upon macaroni and cheese, and not the fancy stuff, either. Powdered cheese mix turned out to be the only way to achieve the result she wanted, so now she cooks the "traditional" stuff. But here's the twist. Marta then adds a layer of filling to the maki. I had sausage, but she's been known to use jalapeños, salami, or whatever else she feels like that day. Then she rolls it and freezes it. After the roll comes out of the freezer, Marta breads and deep-fries it. Then the log is cut into discs and, as a final touch, pan-fried so each side is golden and crispy. Served with dollops of smoked ketchup

At Cardinal Rule, partners Katie James and Marta Kusel take traditional homestyle diner food and flip it on its ass.

and mustard sour cream, it's an incredibly tasty variation on classic KD.

Now keep your giggles to yourselves, but there's something about the Meat Muffins at Cardinal Rule that makes them hard to resist. Meat Muffins, you say! Indeed, I do say. Think meatloaf meets meatball meets muffin meets phyllo. Confused? Here's the short and skinny: Meat Muffins are baby meatloaves baked in a muffin tin and served in a crispy phyllo cup with a squirt of sweet and tangy barbeque sauce. They're perfect little balls of meat heaven, tasty and tender, and set off by the crispy texture of the phyllo.

Weekend brunches at Cardinal Rule are full-on affairs, and there's something for every taste under the sun. The Chwaley (shwa-lee) is a family-style breakfast for two or four people. Its scrambled eggs, choice of meat, potato latkes, and toast come with a pitcher of Caesars. The Breakfast Pie layers potato latkes, eggs, and other goodies and bakes them in a bacon crust. The Hawaiian Stuffed French Toast stuffs an old-time favourite with peameal bacon and smoked mozzarella cheese, then tops it off with homemade pineapple chutney.

Me, I'm the kinda guy who likes a Caesar with his breakfast, but I don't want to waste time eating and drinking, eating and drinking. Luckily, Marta has put it all together in one meal, the Hail Caesar Eggs Benedict. The focal point of the dish is the red eggs, which are poached in Clamato juice and are served on an English muffin with Genoa salami and traditional hollandaise sauce. You also get a couple of homemade potato latkes, which round out yet another amazingly inventive food creation at Cardinal Rule.

It's just another way that Katie and Marta are putting smiles on their customers' faces every day of the week. Chilled, groovy, traditional, and modern all in one, Cardinal Rule sits dangerously close to the top of my must-eat list.

Marta's Maki N' Cheese is a crowd pleaser of the highest order, despite the unconventional ingredients.

Meat Muffins

Makes: 12 servings
(4 muffins per person)

Muffin Wrappers

1 pkg (16 ounces/454 g) frozen phyllo pastry, thawed

2 tablespoons butter, melted

Meat Muffins

5 pounds ground chuck

1 1/2 cups dry bread crumbs

1/4 cup chopped fresh parsley

1/4 cup 2% milk

2 teaspoons kosher salt

1 1/2 teaspoons pepper

1 teaspoon each onion powder and garlic powder

6 eggs, lightly beaten

Barbeque sauce for drizzling

Muffin Wrappers

Preheat oven to 375°F.

Place 1 sheet of phyllo on a work surface (keep remainder covered with a damp towel to prevent drying out); brush sheet lightly with some of the butter. Top with a second sheet; brush with butter. Repeat two more times, for 4 layers. Cut into 2 1/2- to 3-inch squares. Mould each square to the bottom of an upside-down 24-cup mini-muffin pan, folding in the sides around each cup. Repeat with a second mini-muffin pan.

Bake for 12 to 15 minutes or until golden brown. Remove from muffin cups and set aside. (Do not turn off oven.)

Meat Muffins

Grease two 24-cup mini-muffin pans.

In a large bowl, combine the ground chuck, bread crumbs, parsley, milk, salt, pepper, onion powder, garlic powder, and eggs; mix together well by hand. Scoop approximately 1/4 cup mixture into each muffin cup.

Bake for 25 to 30 minutes, until brown and firm.

Assembly

Place a meat muffin in each muffin wrapper and serve with a drizzle of barbeque sauce on top.

Chez Claudette

EST. 1983
351 AVENUE LAURIER EST
MONTREAL · QC · H2T 1G7

When the exhaustive history of Montreal cuisine is finally written, there will be one dish that'll stand out as having defined the heart, soul, and taste buds of the city: poutine. Adel Bakry and Jo-Anne McNeil—the owners and chefs at Chez Claudette—know this all too well, which is why they offer up to twenty-five different twists on a fries, cheese, and gravy classic. In other words, if you dream about poutine, this is the dream you dream about.

Perhaps the biggest reason Chez Claudette has built a reputation for serving some of the best poutine in Montreal is that every single order is made from scratch . . . and made with love. How popular is poutine at Chez Claudette? Consider that Adel makes 165 quarts of gravy from scratch every *week*, and you'll start to get the idea.

Of course, the best poutine deserves attention to every detail, and Adel is not one to overlook the foundation of his creations, the fries. No wonder: every week he lovingly hand cuts 1700 pounds of potatoes, so he knows how important they are to his business. Adel will tell you that one of the secrets to his poutine is pure vegetable oil, which he says keeps the fries perfectly crispy.

As you've probably realized, the biggest challenge for visitors to Claudette's house is choosing which poutine they want at any given moment. Most go for the Toute Garnie (All Dressed), the restaurant's most popular dish, which tops its bed of crispy fries with a mélange of sautéed red, green, orange, and yellow peppers, alongside mushrooms, baby peas, and sliced hotdogs.

I'm more of a tomato sauce kinda guy, so the Poutine Italienne caught my eye. The highlight of this dish is Adel's hearty meat sauce, which combines ground beef, tomatoes, chili flakes, oregano, and lots of garlic. Just don't expect Adel to be breaking out the measuring cups any time soon. He can tell when the sauce is right just by looking at it. The Italienne buries its fries under the squeakiest cheese curds you've ever bitten into, followed by heaping mounds of meat sauce.

How popular is poutine at Chez Claudette?
Consider that Adel makes 165 quarts of gravy from scratch
every week, and you'll start to get the idea.

Not sold? Don't worry, there's a poutine for everyone, every whim, and every taste at Chez Claudette. The Trois S offers three types of sausage: spicy Italian, beef hotdog, and German style. The American comes with eight ounces of New York steak and mushrooms, while the Poutine Bourguignon comes loaded with peppers, mushrooms, onions, and ground beef. The Porky adds ham and baby peas to the equation; the Galvaude, a generous helping of chicken and baby peas.

Poutine isn't the only Quebecois classic that Chez Claudette has perfected: their traditional tourtière is a deliciously beefy pie with a flaky golden crust.

Chez Claudette also offers breakfast throughout the day, and will happily transform your breakfast potatoes into a side order of poutine, should you desire. And what better, really, to accompany a plate of eggs, an omelette, or even your eggs Benedict? Looking for a more hand-held meal? Adel and Jo-Anne offer up a variety of classic diner burgers, and their hotdogs are simply delicious.

Me, I believe more in the "When in Rome . . ." philosophy. So when I'm in Montreal, I'm going *all* Montreal. Pass the poutine, *s'il vous plaît.*

He may look sweet and innocent, but Adel Bakry is a *monster* when it comes to fries-gravy-cheese-curd concoctions.

Tourtière
Makes: 1 pie

Pie Shell

4 cups all-purpose flour

1/2 teaspoon salt

1/2 pound shortening

2 eggs, lightly beaten

3 tablespoons 7UP

2 cups cool water

Egg wash (1 egg, lightly beaten)

Meat Filling

1 1/2 pounds ground beef

1 onion, minced

1 cup dry bread crumbs

1/2 teaspoon cinnamon

1 teaspoon salt

1/4 teaspoon pepper

Pie Shell

In a large bowl, stir together the flour and salt. Using a pastry blender or your fingers, cut in the shortening until the mixture resembles tiny split peas. Add the eggs, 7UP, and water. Gently mix with your hands until a dough forms. Do not overwork the dough or the pastry will be tough. Divide the dough in half.

Roll out one half of the dough on a lightly floured surface until 1/8 inch thick. Place pastry in a 6- or 8-inch pie plate and gently press it against bottom and sides. Trim the edge, leaving about 1 inch overhang. Refrigerate while preparing the filling.

Meat Filling and Assembly

In a large skillet over medium heat, cook the ground beef until no longer pink. Be careful not to burn or overcook it.

Remove from heat and add the onion, bread crumbs, cinnamon, salt, and pepper. Fill pie shell.

On a lightly floured surface, roll out the second piece of dough until 1/8 inch thick. Top the pie with the pastry. Gently press the edges together, then trim and flute the edge. Brush the pie with egg wash. Cut a circular or square hole in the middle to release steam.

Bake for 45 minutes or until the crust is golden and the surface is hot.

Serve with mashed potatoes.

Chicago Style Pizza Shack

EST. 1975
534 UPPER SHERMAN AVENUE
HAMILTON · ON · L8V 3MI

Pat Delle Grazie does not screw around when it comes to cheese. The owner and chef at Hamilton's Chicago Style Pizza Shack, Pat loves cheese so much that he always has a giant bucket of it handy, ready to be heaped, piled, and mounded on his next creation. With more than fifty years in the pizza business (Pat and his family first set up shop in Chicago in 1946), Pat knows what makes a tasty pie. And when you make a stuffed pizza that boasts almost two *pounds* of the highest-quality mozzarella, you've gotta have lots on hand!

The Stuffed Pizza is the pie that made the Chicago Style Pizza Shack famous, for good reason. It's made in a deep-dish pan, and starts with a layer of homemade pizza dough laid in the bottom and up the sides of the pan. From then on, baby, Pat is reaching for the bucket over and over again. Almost two pounds of full-fat mozzarella goes in, followed by their fresh homemade tomato sauce and any other kind of topping (or in this case, "middling") your heart desires. Then throw another layer of pizza dough on top, followed by another hearty dose of tomato sauce. Thirty minutes in the oven and the two crusts are baked to a crispy yet soft golden brown, the perfect beginning and perfect end to a trip to

There's a whole lotta deep-dish magic happening behind these doors, as generations of customers have come to know and love.

Cheese Heaven. But beware, pizza lovers: this is one mighty thick pizza, so get both hands ready!

Pat's a passionate guy when it comes to his food, and it shows when it comes out of the oven. And while he'll let you choose your own toppings for one of his masterpieces, you just might consider taking the pressure off and choosing one of his special combinations. One of my favourites is the Roast Beef Pizza, which starts with dough and sauce, followed by a pound and a half of in-house slow-roasted beef. Add some more sauce, banana peppers, raw onions, and mozzarella, and it's a pizza that thinks it's a sandwich. Identity crisis aside, it's damn fine eating. Like all pizzas here, it can be made on crust ranging from crispy thin to indulgently thick.

But just in case you think a place that dubs itself Chicago Style Pizza Shack is all about pizza, think again. Pat's menu is a veritable treasure trove of Italian dishes, including appetizers like bruschetta and fried ravioli, soups like Italian wedding soup, and classic entrées like lasagna and eggplant parmigiana. If that's not enough, there are chicken and veal dishes, and even linguine with red clam sauce.

Pat delighted me with a classic entrée that sent me on a spin of

Steve Howe, number one pizza line cook (*left*), and Pat Delle Grazie (*right*) are the brains behind the many ingenious pizza combinations here, including the No Self Respect Pizza, a hefty combination of pepperoni, meatballs, bacon, and ham.

memory towards my childhood, a dish he calls Chicken Red and White. The red half of the plate is a crispy, juicy chicken parmigiana bathed in Pat's tomato sauce. The white half is a mound of penne topped with homemade Alfredo sauce. Not satisfied, Pat has to sprinkle a handful of cheese over everything, then pop it in the oven to melt. The best part? When you mix the two together, you get a delicious rosé sauce in the middle of your plate. Take a little piece of chicken, add a little pasta, and let the love story unfold right there in your mouth.

Pat even does desserts, just in case, with a couple pounds of cheese swimming in your belly, you've got a little room left for something sweet. Not surprisingly, everything on Pat's dessert menu has cheese in it, from various kinds of cheesecake to a mouth-watering tiramisù. Maybe now you know why Pat doesn't bother counting how much cheese he goes through every week.

Pat loves cheese so much that he always has a giant bucket of it handy, ready to be heaped, piled, and mounded on his next creation.

Roast Beef Pizza

Makes: One 13-inch pizza

Crust

1 pound pizza dough (homemade or store-bought)

Sauce

1 can (28 ounces/796 mL) crushed tomatoes
1/4 cup vegetable oil
2 1/2 tablespoons grated Romano cheese
1 tablespoon sugar
1 tablespoon minced fresh garlic
2 teaspoons dried oregano
1 teaspoon granulated garlic
1 teaspoon salt
1/4 teaspoon crumbled dried rosemary

Assembly

1 pound thinly sliced roast beef
1 cup hot banana pepper rings
1 cup finely chopped Spanish onion
1 pound shredded mozzarella cheese

Crust

Preheat oven to 450°F. Grease a 13-inch pizza pan.

Roll out the dough on a floured surface to fit the greased pan; place dough in the pan. Allow the dough to rest for 30 minutes at room temperature.

Sauce

Whisk together the crushed tomatoes, oil, Romano cheese, sugar, fresh garlic, oregano, granulated garlic, salt, and rosemary.

Assembly

Ladle 1 cup of the sauce onto the dough and spread to within 1 inch of the outer edge. Layer the roast beef over the sauce. Drizzle 3/4 cup of the sauce over the roast beef. Spread the hot pepper rings and onions over the pizza. Finish the pizza with shredded mozzarella, sprinkling it all the way to the edge.

Bake the pizza in the middle of the oven for 20 minutes or until the cheese is golden orange and the edges of the dough are golden brown.

Note: You will not use all the sauce. Leftover sauce may be frozen.

Tiramisù

Makes: 6 to 8 servings

2 cups brewed espresso

2 ounces rum

1 ounce triple sec

34 ladyfingers

5 eggs, separated

6 tablespoons sugar

1 pound (450-g pkg) mascarpone cheese, at room temperature

1 cup crushed chocolate sandwich cookies

Cinnamon

Cocoa powder

4 ounces semisweet chocolate, grated

In a small bowl, combine the espresso, rum, and triple sec.

Lay the ladyfingers in a single layer in a shallow pan and ladle the coffee mixture over the cookies. Cookies should be well soaked but not too soft.

In a large bowl, beat the egg whites until stiff.

In another large bowl, whisk together the egg yolks and sugar. Add the mascarpone and beat just until smooth. (Don't over-mix. The mixture should be fairly thick but still pourable.) Gently but thoroughly fold the egg whites into the mascarpone mixture.

Butter a 10-inch springform pan. Sprinkle the crushed cookies over the bottom and sides.

Arrange half of the soaked ladyfingers, close together in a single layer, in the bottom of the pan (cut to fit as needed). Pour half of the mascarpone mixture over the ladyfingers. Sprinkle with cinnamon, cocoa, and half of the grated chocolate. Make a second layer with the remaining ladyfingers and mascarpone mixture. Sprinkle with cinnamon, cocoa, and the remaining chocolate.

Chill before serving. (The tiramisù can also be frozen. Thaw in the fridge before serving.)

The Dam Pub Gastropub

EST. 2005
53 BRUCE STREET
THORNBURY · ON · NOH 2PO
WWW.THEDAMPUB.CA

I f you're looking for a place to warm your stomach and your heart on a cold winter's day—or even a warm summer's day—the Dam Pub Gastropub is the spot. Everything about it speaks of home, of nights with loved ones, and of good home cooking that tastes just like Mom's.

From the outside, the Dam Pub looks like an old Colonial house, an impression that doesn't end once you cross the threshold. Cozy on the inside, the Dam Pub makes you feel comfortable from the minute you walk through the door. You know you'll be well taken care of here.

A lot of that feeling revolves around chef Suzette Gerrie, whose talents are so extensive she can tackle a menu boasting both a Queen-approved haggis and Cajun crab cakes. Suzette is the primary reason that the food at the Dam Pub is definitely *not* your average pub fare. This is a woman who takes pride in feeding her guests.

Lord knows that's what she did to me! Suzette started by stuffing me full of her classic Shepherd's Pie, which starts with a creamy foundation of buttery Yukon Gold mashed potatoes that's then piled high with a savoury blend of sautéed vegetables and ground lamb, which Suzette tells me is more traditional than ground beef.

You don't have to be a kilt-wearing beaver to indulge in one of the more than 600 whiskies on hand at the Dam Pub . . . but it sure helps stir the conversation!

Suzette finishes off her Shepherd's Pie with more mashed potatoes, but adds a twist by piping the potatoes onto the pie like cake icing, giving the dish a decorative look that made me wanna sing! And OK, so Suzette isn't a huge fan of piping the mashed potatoes directly into one's mouth, but I couldn't help myself! I mean, the piping bag was *right there*!

Part Scottish, part Jamaican, and part Chinese, chef Suzette Gerrie whips up culinary inventions that celebrate comfort food the world over.

You don't have to worry about this sort of thing with the Steak and Kidney Pie, a back-to-basics favourite where the two primary ingredients are baked inside a flaky golden crust.

The Dam Pub will also warm your cockles (that's right, I said cockles) with their Braised Lamb Shank, giant 14- to 16-ounce portions of lamb baked in Suzette's blend of beer, red wine, tomato sauce, demi-glace, and cinnamon. When they come out of the oven more than three hours later, these shanks are fall-off-the-bone, melt-in-your-mouth delicious. Served with mashed potatoes and vegetables, it's the kind of thing you wish you could make every night at home. (In my case, I don't. I'm super lazy.)

For dessert, there's nothing quite like Suzette's Famous Bread Pudding, yet more testimony to how the chef can take a traditional dish and make it exotic. A huge hit with patrons, the bread pudding is made from scratch, beginning with the sweet custard that Suzette mixes with the bread she's cut into neat little cubes. She then adds fruit to the mix, though you never really know what kind of fruit it will be. It all depends on what's fresh and in season, but you can bet your cockles (yup, I said cockles *again*) it's going to be delicious. After the mixture has been baked in a steam bath (to keep it moist) for eighty minutes, it's pulled from the oven and topped with more custard, whipped cream, and more fruit . . . the perfect ending to a perfect meal.

Actually, scratch that. For the *real* perfect ending to a meal at the Dam Pub, why not settle in with one of the more than *six hundred* whiskies they have on hand. Owner Stephanie Price is a bit of a whisky connoisseur, and even travelled to Scotland to learn about "the water of life." If you can't tempt your whisky palate here, you can't tempt it anywhere. It's just one more reason the Dam Pub is a damn classic.

Cozy on the inside, the Dam Pub makes you feel comfortable from the minute you walk through the door. You know you'll be well taken care of here.

Be a nice boy and Suzette just might let you pipe the mashed potatoes on the Shepherd's Pie. It takes years of experience to make it look this good, though. Trust me . . . I tried.

Steak and Kidney Pie

Makes: 8 servings

1 lamb kidney (approximately 2 pounds)

1 1/2 to 2 cups milk

1/2 cup all-purpose flour

Salt and pepper

3 pounds top sirloin beef, cubed

1 tablespoon vegetable oil

2 cups beef gravy

1/2 cup red wine

1 sheet puff pastry, thawed

Egg wash (1 egg, beaten)

Preheat oven to 350°F.

Clean the kidney by cutting out all the white bits, then cut into small pieces.

Blanch the kidney pieces in simmering milk for 10 minutes or until tender. This will remove the smell. Drain and set aside.

In a bowl or resealable plastic bag, combine the flour with salt and pepper to taste. Add the beef and toss to coat well.

Heat the oil in a large pot over medium-high heat. Working in batches, sauté the beef until brown. Transfer beef as cooked to a bowl. When all the beef is cooked, remove the pot from the heat and return all the beef to the pot along with any juices. Stir in the kidney, gravy, and wine. Turn into a baking dish just large enough to hold the filling.

On a lightly floured surface, roll out the puff pastry until 1/4 inch thick. Cut out a piece 1 inch larger than your baking dish. Brush the edges of the dish with egg wash and drape the puff pastry over the dish. Brush with egg wash and cut a few slits in the pastry.

Bake for 20 minutes or until golden.

D&S Southern Comfort B.B.Q.

EST. 2009
6501 RUSSELL ROAD
CARLSBAD SPRINGS · ON · K0A 1K0
WWW.DSBBQ.CA

Has someone hurt you? Are you determined to fill that hole in your soul with food? If so, I've got the burger for you . . . the Determinator. Five and a half pounds of food, the Determinator Hamburger is three 8-ounce homemade all-beef patties layered with three grilled cheese sandwiches. But that's just the beginning. I mean, who's satisfied with just three burgers and three grilled cheese sandwiches? Sheesh.

OK, so it's been a while since your last meal and you just happen to be a gigantosaurus. The Determinator is just the thing for you!

Chef Tom Sedlar dresses up each patty with his smoky barbeque sauce, a tongue-thrilling concoction that is buried under a pile of shredded cheese, followed by a piece of back bacon and a heaping mound of house-smoked beef brisket. Still not enough for you? As a finishing touch, add an onion ring to each patty and jam the entire thing together with foot-long skewers.

Of course, if you're a *really* hungry sort, you can always finish the burger and make your way to the rest of the silver platter before you, like the pound of fresh-cut fries, pound of coleslaw, and six pickle quarters. Manage to finish the entire platter in an hour—by yourself, without throwing up, and without going to the bathroom—and you get your photo on the Wall of Fame and a D&S golf shirt. Fail and your picture is forever emblazoned on the Wall of Shame.

And if I was a betting man, I'd say that's where you were headed. For how many people have defeated the Determinator, you ask? None.

At D&S you're made to feel like a person, not a number.

But don't let me lead you to believe that D&S is defined by only one dish. That would be a gross injustice to a place that emphasizes quality barbeque as much as it emphasizes family. Casual and relaxed, this country kitchen welcomes folks with a homey atmosphere that highlights the simple joy of eating together. At D&S you're made to feel like a person, not a number.

Maybe that's why so many of their dishes are what they call Smoke House Specialties, classics that take a long time to cook and seem to embrace the slowness of life. Here you'll find such neoclassics as Hickory Smoked Brisket, St. Louis Cut Pork Ribs, and the Smoked Roasted Chicken. The BBQ Beef Brisket Wrap takes sliced slow-cooked brisket and adds sautéed mushrooms, onions, diced tomato, shredded lettuce, and a blend of cheese.

If you're looking to stay on the lighter side of the scale, the Armadillo Eggs appetizer combines smoky taste with the pop of a fresh jalapeño. Tom wraps a blend of seasoned beef and pork around a fresh Cheddar-filled jalapeño and shapes it to resemble, well, an armadillo egg. Then it's into the smoker for about an hour, finished on the grill, and doused in the sweet and smoky sauce before being served.

And if you didn't think smoking could go any further at D&S, you haven't checked out the dessert menu, which features, among other things, the Smoky Chocolate Cheesecake and Pecans, a ridiculously rich dessert that never sees the inside of an oven. The cake starts as a creamy chocolate cheesecake hickory-smoked low and slow, then covered with a rich chocolate ganache and dotted with roasted pecans. Rich? Rich!

It's so rich I don't think I'm physically capable of finishing an entire piece (especially after eating the Determinator—which, for the record, I didn't do), but I'll give it the old college try!

I don't know if it gets all that smoky in heaven, but if it does, you can bet your bottom they're serving this Smoky Chocolate Cheesecake at the Pearly Gates Diner!

Armadillo Eggs

Makes: 9 servings (2 eggs per person)

Note: This recipe requires a smoker.

18 jalapeño peppers
1 cup shredded Mexican blend of cheese of your choice (or enough to stuff 18 jalapeño
  peppers)
2 1/2 pounds ground pork
2 1/2 pounds ground beef
1 tablespoon + 1 teaspoon your favourite rub
Barbeque sauce for serving

Wearing rubber gloves, cut off the stem end of the jalapeño peppers. Using the handle of a
  spoon, scrape the seeds out of the peppers. Steam the jalapeños for 3 minutes. (Keep your
  face away from the steam—it may hurt your eyes.) Let the peppers cool.
Preheat smoker to 220°F.
Stuff the jalapeños with the shredded cheese.
In a large bowl, combine the pork, beef, and spice rub. Mix well. Divide into 5-ounce portions.
Wrap a portion of meat around each stuffed pepper, ensuring a tight seal with no cracks.
Smoke the armadillo eggs for about 75 minutes, until the meat is no longer pink inside.
Brush your favourite barbeque sauce over the eggs and serve hot.

Note: We brush our eggs and put them on the grill for 3 or 4 minutes to soak up that BBQ flavour.

Dangerous Dan's Diner

EST. 1999
714 QUEEN STREET EAST
TORONTO · ON · M4M 1H2
WWW.DANGEROUSDANSDINER.COM

'm not sure who likes food more, James McKinnon—the owner and chef at Dangerous Dan's—or his grandfather Dan Wooley, for whom the diner is named. Either way, one thing is for certain: after you've sat down to a meal at Dan's, you're leaving a little bit heavier and whole lot happier than when you first walked through the door. And that, friends, is just fine with both of them. With a menu that boasts dishes such as the Coronary Burger and the Big Pig, what were you expecting—salad?

If my waistline is bigger than it used to be, it's in no small part because the burgers really are bigger at the Double D.

Burgers are the mainstay of Dangerous Dan's menu, and each one starts with a juicy 8-ounce patty. James uses a blend of lean and medium ground beef, which offers enough fat content to make his burgers juicy without being greasy. The meat is mixed by hand with eggs, garlic, oregano, and bread crumbs.

The Coronary Burger Special was named in honour of James's father after he suffered a heart attack. It's an appropriate moniker! The Coronary features two patties fried on the grill and finished on the charbroiler for smoky flavour. Each patty is topped with two pieces of bacon and a slice of cheese. Follow this with one fried egg and serve on a soft bun with lettuce, tomatoes, and pickles, and you've got a mouthful of what customers call one heart-attackalicious burger!

If you didn't think it was legal to throw that much beef on a bun, the Big Pig balances out the cow factor with good ol' Canadian pork, courtesy of four slices of strip bacon sandwiched between two slabs of peameal bacon and balanced atop a sizzling patty. James isn't satisfied with cooking his strip bacon the traditional way, so he instead opts for the deep-fryer. Deep-fried bacon, people! Can you dig it? James says it adds that extra touch of special diner taste: grease! No wonder he considers it fatty art, and his customers keep extra napkins on hand.

Admit it. Your mouth is watering right now, isn't it? Isn't it? This Coronary Burger is what keeps people coming back for more.

The Big Pig is served with a slice of Cheddar, lettuce, and tomatoes, so you don't have to feel like you're not getting your veggies. Other burger options include the Elvis (bacon, peanut butter, and fried banana), the Big Kahuna (pineapple, peameal bacon, and mozzarella), and the Big Shroom (shiitake, button, and oyster mushrooms in teriyaki sauce with deep-fried kale). If eating meat is not up your alley, James will even sell you a Tree Hugger (Veggie) Burger.

But none of those shakes a cow's rump at the Colossal Colon Clogger Combo, which weighs in with 24 ounces of burger, a quarter-pound of bacon, and two fried eggs. Since James knows you're into eating balanced meals, he'll throw in a large milkshake and small poutine to round things out for you.

If you're not feeling like a burger, Dan's has mountains of sandwich options, including my personal favourite, the Cereal Killer, a grilled chicken breast stuffed with peameal bacon and Cheddar, rolled in cornflakes, and then . . . you guessed it, deep-fried! The De Niro sandwich buries a piece of breaded chicken under marinated peppers, onions, balsamic vinegar, mozzarella, and tomatoes. Traditionalists in the audience will be happy with two grilled cheese options, the Uber Amy (Cheddar, mozzarella, feta, and cheese curds) and the Uber Kenny, which adds—you guessed it—bacon to the mix.

Dan's desserts are named as politically incorrectly as his mains, so you've got the opportunity to chew on a Tasty Wang (deep-fried beer-battered banana with ice cream, honey, and whipped cream) or the Chef's Salty Chocolate Balls (two battered, deep-fried chocolates covered in caramel sauce and rock salt). I thought I'd take it easy after my Coronary Burger, so I kept it light with the Deep-Fried Mars Bar.

Oh, and just for the record, Dan's actually does serve salads. And nothing in them—nothing—is deep-fried.

With a menu that boasts dishes such as the Coronary Burger and the Big Pig, what were you expecting—salad?

Deep-Fried Chocolate Bar

Makes: 1 serving

Chocolate bar of choice
Vegetable oil for deep-frying
All-purpose flour
Beer batter (homemade or store-bought)
Ice cream of choice, whipped cream, and chocolate sauce for serving

Remove the chocolate bar from its wrapper. Place the bar in the freezer until frozen, approximately 2 hours.

Pour about 2 inches of oil into a large heavy pot and heat to 300°F. Using tongs, dip chocolate bar in hot oil so that the flour will stick.

Roll the chocolate bar in the flour and then dip in the beer batter to coat evenly. Carefully add to the hot oil and fry for 1 minute or until golden brown and floating. Using tongs, transfer chocolate bar to a plate. Serve with ice cream, whipped cream, and chocolate sauce.

Dangerous Dan's Cereal Killer

Makes: 4 servings

4 boneless, skinless chicken breasts
  (6 ounces each)
4 slices peameal bacon
4 slices Cheddar cheese
2 cups whole cornflakes
Oil for deep-frying
4 kaiser rolls
1/4 cup mayonnaise
4 to 8 leaves lettuce
1 tomato, sliced

Using a mallet, pound the chicken breasts until an even 1/2 inch thick. Place 1 piece of peameal bacon and 1 slice of Cheddar cheese on top of each piece of chicken. Roll the chicken around the bacon and cheese into a tube and pinch the ends.

Pour the cornflakes into a small bowl. Press each piece of chicken into the cornflakes to coat completely. Discard unused cornflakes.

Pour about 2 inches of oil into a large heavy pot and heat to 325°F or hotter (or use a deep-fryer). Working in batches if necessary, fry the chicken for 10 minutes. Remove one from the oil and cut a notch in the middle of it to check for doneness; you shouldn't see any pink. If necessary, continue to fry the chicken until cooked, checking every 2 minutes. Drain on paper towels.

Toast the rolls. Spread rolls with mayonnaise, then layer lettuce on the bottom half of each roll. Top with the chicken. Top with tomato slices and the top half of the bun.

Elgin Street Diner

EST. 1993
374 ELGIN STREET
OTTAWA · ON · K2P INI
WWW.ELGINSTREETDINER.COM

The word *institution* may not have the greatest connotation, but when it comes to the Elgin Street Diner, the word fits to a T, and it's all good! How else can you describe a place that's open every minute of every hour of every day of every year, doesn't have a lock on the door, and boasts down-the-street lineups at three o'clock in the morning? You want breakfast in the middle of the night? They've got it for you! You want dinner before you go to a show? They've got it for you! Any time, any day . . . they've got it for you at the Elgin Street Diner, an Ottawa (dare I say?) *institution*.

Elgin is diner food at its best, and customers here consistently rave about one dish over and over again: the poutine. Poutine is so popular at the Elgin that they sell about seven thousand pounds of hand-cut fries every *week*, most of which comes in the simple yet miraculous form of french fries, cheese curds, and gravy. (Cue the heavenly choir.)

Petty thieves and felons, beware: the doors may never lock, but there's *always* someone inside the Elgin, and usually that someone is a horde of people chowing down on poutine.

Although there are a variety of tantalizing poutine combinations to choose from (enough to merit a separate poutine menu; try the onion ring version . . . it is tas-tee!), the secret to Elgin's many concoctions is their firm, squeaky cheese curds and their intensely rich gravy. In fact, poutine is such a big deal at the Elgin that they even put it on one of their most famous *breakfast* dishes, the Blue Plate Breakfast.

Any time, any day . . .
they've got it for you at the Elgin Street Diner.

Elgin's Blue Plate Breakfast is a gargantuan combination of three eggs, sausage, bacon, ham, baked beans, toast, and, oh yeah—poutine! And what patriotic Canadian would avoid poutine for breakfast, anyway? If you would, then you hate freedom!

If the sheer amount of the Blue Plate Breakfast leaves you gasping for air, you can blame owner and chef Ron Shrybman, who says he opened the restaurant because it's the only thing he knows. Little doubt: Ron has been working in the business since he was thirteen, and he opened the Elgin in 1993, at the ripe old age of twenty-three . . . two blocks from his childhood home.

Yet Ron is about so much more than poutine and breakfast. He does sandwiches, burgers and dogs, a variety of classic platters, soups and salads, lots of main courses, and one of the staples of Elgin-goers for many years: Ron's belly-hugging chili. Ron makes as much as 20 quarts of his homemade chili every day, a hearty mix of onions, herbs and spices, chili sauce, homemade tomato sauce, buckets of sautéed ground beef, and kidney beans. Served with garlic bread, it's a little bit of heaven that goes with just about everything else Ron's got on the menu.

If it's comfort food you're after, nothing satisfies quite like Elgin Street Diner's amazing meatloaf. A simple recipe served up with fluffy mashed potatoes and plenty of that famous gravy, Ron's meatloaf is a taste of home.

Afterwards, why not make like the six-thousand-odd customers who eat at the Elgin every week and indulge in one of their ridiculously thick and creamy handmade milkshakes? Ron and his family (his brother, wife, and mother all work here) feature classics like vanilla, chocolate, and strawberry, plus more exotic options such as chocolate-banana, mochaccino, espresso, and creamsicle.

It's just another reason to put the Elgin Street Diner on your Taste Bud Map, regardless of the time, day, or year.

More than one groggy guest has been known to use the Blue Plate Breakfast to beat the hangover blues.

Elgin Street Diner
Meatloaf

Makes: 2 meatloaves

2 pounds ground beef
2 onions, finely chopped
1 cup dry bread crumbs
1 cup chili sauce
4 teaspoons prepared horseradish (optional)
4 teaspoons onion powder
4 teaspoons each salt and pepper

Preheat oven at 350°F.

In a large bowl, mix all ingredients together with your hands. Pack tightly into 2 regular-sized loaf pans.

Place loaf pans on a baking sheet and bake for 1 hour and 15 minutes or until a meat thermometer registers 160°F, the meatloaf is firm, and juices run clear.

Serve with mashed potatoes and gravy.

Note: Leftovers can be wrapped in plastic wrap and refrigerated for up to 3 days.

The Grilled Cheese

EST. 2009
66 1/2 NASSAU STREET
TORONTO · ON · M5T IM5

I f there's one sandwich that evokes memories of the innocent and lazy days of youth, it's the grilled cheese. These memories come alive at Toronto's Grilled Cheese restaurant, where the atmosphere is as warm and comforting as the food. From the wood floors to the working fireplace, from the country cottage decor to the open kitchen, life at the Grilled Cheese is easy and down-to-earth.

But that doesn't mean the food here is overly simple. On the contrary, the Grilled Cheese serves up its signature sandwich ten delicious and different ways. No, friends, this is not your momma's grilled cheese!

That's just fine with owner and chef Rob Yuill, who ran a grilled cheese shop in New York City until his rent went through the roof and he decided to move his operation north of the border. It didn't take long for the eatery to become a local landmark, loved by people of all stripes who are ecstatic to have a comfort-food option for lunch.

And it doesn't get any more classic than, well, the Classic. Rob starts this one the same way he starts all his sandwiches, by spreading a blend of olive oil, margarine, and butter on two thick slices of fresh bread (choose from white, whole wheat, or rye), between which he puts nothing but slices of Cheddar cheese. The sandwich then makes its way to the press, where it gently rests until it reaches that nirvana state of ooey, gooey goodness. Served with homemade tomato soup, it's a perfect heart-warmer on a cold Toronto day.

From there, the menu gets slightly more complex. The Dill-licious uses a special dill Havarti cheese, which is layered around sautéed onions, sun-dried tomatoes, and home-

When you're voted one of the fifty best reasons to visit Toronto, you're doing something right! The Grilled Cheese's signature sandwiches have been a focal point in Kensington Market since the restaurant opened in 2009.

The Grilled Cheese serves up its signature sandwich ten delicious and different ways. No, friends, this is not your momma's grilled cheese!

There's a reason they call this bad boy the Classic. Bread, blobs of gooey Cheddar cheese, and a bowl of tomato soup are all that any good Canadian needs on a cold winter's day.

made basil pesto. The Blackjack is a fan favourite at the restaurant, in no small part due to Rob's homemade black olive pesto/tapenade, a blend of black olives, garlic, capers, hot sauce, and olive oil. The tapenade is topped with mega-slices of spicy jalapeño Havarti cheese and a mound of wilted spinach before it hits the sandwich press. Once the inside has reached the appropriate state of goo-eyness, the sandwich is opened and slices of fresh tomato added, a trick that keeps them from becoming mushy.

Looking for a little more heft in your hands? Then try the Beast, an enormous compilation of sautéed bacon, turkey, onion, and spinach stuffed between slices of jalapeño Havarti and Cheddar cheeses. One of Rob's own favourites, the Grilled Motzy uses fior di latte mozzarella cheese and tops it with basil pesto and sun-dried tomatoes before grilling. Already a truly sophisticated taste sensation (hey, can *you* say "grilled cheese" and "truly sophisticated taste sensation" in the same breath?), the sandwich then adds arugula and balsamic vinegar to the inside of the warm, gooey mess.

Other sandwich options include the Pizza Grill (basil pesto, pizza sauce, provolone cheese, pepperoni, bacon, and spinach), the Grill Worx (sautéed roasted red peppers, mushrooms, and onions between provolone and Swiss cheese), and the Turk 2000 (sautéed turkey and onions, Cheddar cheese, and last-minute-added tomato slices).

Dessert, drinks? Nah, that's not Rob's way. He's a simple man, and this is a simple place. So there's pop, juice, and water, and not much else. I mean, if you're looking to get adventurous, you could always add bacon, ham, eggs, portobello mushrooms, or turkey to any of his grilled selections. But when you're reliving your youth, even that seems a little too involved.

Grilled Motzy Sandwich

Makes: 4 sandwiches

Note: You will not use all the vinaigrette, but it's excellent on salads.

Balsamic Vinaigrette

1/2 cup balsamic vinegar
1 tablespoon dried oregano
1 tablespoon Dijon mustard
1 1/2 teaspoons sugar
1/2 teaspoon each salt and pepper
1/2 garlic clove
1 to 2 drops hot sauce
3/4 to 1 cup olive oil

Motzy Sandwich

Butter, softened
8 slices bread
1/2 cup basil pesto
3 ounces fior di latte mozzarella, thinly sliced
Chopped sun-dried tomatoes
1 cup fresh arugula

Balsamic Vinaigrette

In a blender, combine the balsamic vinegar, oregano, mustard, sugar, salt, pepper, garlic, and hot sauce. Blend on low speed. With the motor running, add the olive oil in a thin, steady stream until the vinaigrette is emulsified.

Motzy Sandwich

Spread butter on one side of each slice of bread. Turn the bread over and spread pesto on each slice. Layer fior di latte evenly over the pesto. Sprinkle with sun-dried tomatoes.

Heat a large skillet over medium heat (or heat a sandwich press to medium or 220°F). Cook bread slices buttered side down until the cheese melts and the bread is golden.

Open the sandwich, add arugula, and drizzle with balsamic vinaigrette. Close the sandwiches. Cut in half and serve.

Hadley's

EST. 2010
940 COLLEGE STREET
TORONTO · ON · M6H 1A5
WWW.HADLEYS.CA

S o you're walking along College Street in Toronto, eyes glazed over with the blur of a hang-over, and you're wishing to the heavens someone could find a cure for what ails you. That's when the smell of smoke first hits your nostrils. Fear not, devoted party hound, you haven't stumbled upon a fire, you've come to Hadley's! And if it's medicine you seek for that banging in your head, Hadley's has the Remedy.

The Remedy is the brainchild of chef and owner Eric Hadley, who—along with wife Lex Taman—bought an old Portuguese sports bar in 2010 and converted it into what has quickly become a neighbourhood destination for great brunches, classic comfort food, and some of the best smoked meat, cheese, and fish you'll find anywhere. But ask people what dish really stands out for them here, and they'll pick the one Eric concocted when he was suffering the ill effects of one too many adult beverages.

> *Hadley's has quickly become a neighbourhood destination for great brunches, classic comfort food, and some of the best smoked meat, cheese, and fish you'll find anywhere.*

The Remedy is a massive brunch dish that piles as much ingenious homemade food as possible onto a platter. The foundation is a hash of onions, shredded Yukon Gold pota-toes, and secret spices that give it all a dis-tinctively smoky flavour. This is surrounded by home-baked beans and house-smoked pulled pork, all of which is topped with a blend of hand-smoked Emmental, aged white Cheddar, and mozzarella cheeses.

But what makes the Remedy a true standout is Hadley's signature deep-fried poached eggs. Eric poaches a couple of eggs, lays them gently in an ice-water bath for a few seconds, then dredges them through a cornmeal-flour blend before dropping them in the deep-fryer. As a finish-ing touch, the eggs are doused in homemade hollandaise sauce. Incredible! This was one of the most delicious breakfasts I've *ever* had. The eggs are crispy on the outside but still soft, warm, and messy in the middle. And the combination of all the other food on the plate works really well together.

The lunch and dinner menus at Hadley's are extensive and varied. One of my favourite appetizers was the Smoked Whitefish with Pea Pancakes, little gems that combine a base of sweet peas with freshly smoked Ontario whitefish, topped with a dill crème fraîche. The fish was so delicate and the pancakes so tasty, I had to stop myself from begging for more.

Entrées run the gamut from sandwiches (the Pulled Pork must be sampled to appreciate Eric's smoking genius) to exotic dishes like Smoked Duck Risotto. Simple guy that I am, I was more drawn to the Smoked Ribs, served with a side of mac 'n' cheese. The ribs were done to perfection in Eric's custom smoker, and the homemade barbeque sauce added just enough zest to keep my tongue guessing. Meanwhile, the mac 'n' cheese was deliciously creamy, with just a hint of smoky flavour, courtesy of Eric's smoked cheese blend.

Lex is in charge of desserts at Hadley's, and that means she's breaking out her granny's recipes. You're in for a treat if you sample Dottie's Delicious Lemon Tart, which Lex starts with a shortbread and brown butter crust that tastes just like a shortbread cookie. The lemon curd filling is a multi-stage effort that surprised me with the addition of basil, which Lex swears enhances the lemon taste without being bitter. All I do know is this: it was perfectly tart, with just the right hint of sweetness . . . the ideal way to end a meal.

Actually, ending a meal at Hadley's is never quite perfect, because it means it's over. But you know you'll be here again, drawn in by the smell of smoke. That or the banging in your head, that is.

Not just for those suffering the ill effects of one too many the night before, the Remedy is a brilliant combination of tastes, one of the finest breakfast dishes you'll find anywhere . . . period.

Note: This recipe requires a smoker.

Smoked Whitefish

1/4 cup salt

1/4 cup sugar

Zest of 1 lime

Zest of 1 lemon

Zest of 1 orange

1 whitefish fillet (8 ounces)

Apple and hickory wood chips

Pea Pancakes

1 1/4 cups fresh or frozen peas

3 tablespoons 10% cream

1 egg, beaten

3 tablespoons all-purpose flour

1 teaspoon baking powder

Unsalted butter

Assembly

Crème fraîche or full-fat sour cream

Balsamic glaze or segmented lemon slices

Smoked Whitefish

Stir together the salt, sugar, and citrus zests. Rub all over the whitefish. Allow to cure, covered and refrigerated, for 1 hour.

Rinse off the cure and smoke at 185°F for 2 hours.

Pea Pancakes

Blanch the peas, then refresh under cold water. Drain well.

In a small bowl, mash the peas with a fork. Stir in the cream and egg. Mix in the flour and baking powder.

Melt the butter in a large nonstick skillet over medium-high heat. Pour in 1-tablespoon circles of pea mixture. Cook the pancakes until they start to bubble on the top, 2 to 3 minutes. Flip and cook for another minute. Transfer to a plate. Repeat with the remaining batter. Let pancakes cool to room temperature.

Assembly

Place some smoked whitefish on each pea pancake. Top with crème fraîche (or sour cream) and drizzle with balsamic glaze (or segmented lemon).

Serve on a platter with salad greens dressed with olive oil and salt and pepper.

May also be served with caviar (as pictured, with rainbow trout caviar) or a slice of Meyer lemon.

Dottie's Delicious Lemon Tart

Makes: 6 servings

Note: This recipe requires a 9-inch fluted tart pan with a removable bottom.

Crust

1 cup all-purpose flour
1/4 cup sugar
6 tablespoons unsalted butter
1 teaspoon vanilla extract

Filling

4 eggs
4 egg yolks
Zest of 1/2 lemon
2/3 cup lemon juice
2/3 cup sugar
6 tablespoon unsalted butter, cubed
3 whole fresh basil leaves with stems

Crust

Preheat oven to 375°F.

In a medium bowl, mix together the flour and sugar.

Melt the butter in a skillet over medium heat until it starts to turn brown and smells fragrant. Remove from heat and stir in the vanilla.

Add the butter mixture to the flour mixture and stir well. Press the dough into the tart pan.

Bake for 10 to 15 minutes, or until the crust begins to turn golden. Cool on a rack.

Filling

Bring water in the bottom of a double boiler (or a saucepan) to a boil.

Meanwhile, in a small bowl, whisk together the eggs and egg yolks. Set aside.

In the top of the double boiler (or in a heatproof bowl), stir together the lemon zest, lemon juice, sugar, butter, and basil. Heat over boiling water, stirring gently, until simmering. The sugar should be dissolved and the butter should be melted.

To temper the eggs, ladle half of the warm lemon syrup into the eggs while whisking vigorously. Then pour the egg mixture back into the lemon syrup. Heat, stirring constantly, until the mixture reaches 158°F.

Pour the filling through a strainer into the tart shell and refrigerate for at least 2 hours or overnight.

The Harbour Diner

EST. 2008
486 JAMES STREET NORTH
HAMILTON · ON · L8L IJI
WWW.HARBOURDINER.COM

Most chefs have the luxury of working in a large, spacious kitchen, with all the tools of the trade literally at their fingertips, waiting to be spun into delicious culinary creations. Some guys—like Chris Preston, who owns and operates Hamilton's Harbour Diner—aren't quite so lucky. Chefs like Chris are the true magicians, casting their culinary spells in kitchens where elbow room is at a premium. Just how small is the kitchen at the Harbour Diner? Ask our sound guy, Scott. He had to stand in the back alley while we shot.

Demure though the environment may be, that sure as hell doesn't stop Chris from whipping up big meals with big taste at the Harbour Diner. Are those the seeds of doubt I hear sprouting in your brain, Grasshopper? How about Chris's Crab and Lobster Macaroni, a dish that boasts enough cheese to send a lactose-intolerant lumberjack to the emergency room?

The foundation of the dish is Chris's creamy cheese sauce, which starts with garlic sautéed in butter, then adds whipping cream and a four-cheese combination of Parmesan, Monterey Jack, Cheddar, and mozzarella. Now add some spices, lots of rich, tender hunks of fresh lobster and crab,

The old storefront has housed a number of businesses over the past hundred years, including a tearoom and laundromat. But never has it been as successful as it is now that it's home to the Harbour Diner.

and some al dente macaroni, and toss together. Once everything is coated in the delicious sauce, the creamy concoction is ready for the baking pan, but not before it's loaded with more cheese. Topped with grated cheese, more fresh crabmeat, and crostini, this was truly one of the most decadent things I've ever put in my mouth. Like dedicated customers of the Harbour like to say, it's buttery.

If lobster and crab seem just a bit too exotic for the comfort-food lover in you, fear not! The Harbour has you covered. Chris also does old-school classics, including the Harbour Diner Meatloaf, a thick and tasty blend of meat and spices that he finishes off with a quick blast in the grill for a crispy exterior. But what makes this meatloaf so spectacular is the gravy it bathes in, a red wine demi-glace that is cooked for hours in a pot swimming with giant hunks of prime rib. It was one of the richest gravies I've ever eaten.

Like so many classic eateries, the Harbour Diner's primary ingredient is love, thanks to chef Chris Preston and his fiancée, Erin Milward, who manages the books and even serves on busy nights.

But Chris isn't done with you yet. He leans two slabs of meatloaf together like a lean-to on a plate, perched over a heaping mound of Yukon Gold garlic mashed potatoes, buried in sautéed portobello mushrooms, and drowned in the demi-glace. I'm sorry if I'm about to offend every mother out there, but I have to agree with Chris: this is Mom's home cooking ratcheted up three or four notches.

Shepherd's Pie at the Harbour also gets the benefit of Chris's prime rib demi-glace, but it's the fresh peas inside that I loved. The meat blend is rich and savoury, but the popping of the peas in your mouth keeps you wondering. To further add to the texture, Chris puts the pie into the broiler right before serving, to crisp up the mashed potato topping. Yuh-mee!

Not what you're hankering for? Don't worry. The Harbour offers an ever-changing array of massive breakfasts, salads and sandwiches, burgers, steaks, and even a messy pulled pork poutine. Desserts come in the shape of a pie . . . because they *are* pies! Chris's neighbour Linda whips up different homemade ones every day, so ask what they're featuring that day.

In the end, you may have to join the many Hamiltonians who wait outside to get into the Harbour, but look on the bright side: you could be waiting out in the back alley. Sorry, Scott.

Chefs like Chris are the true magicians, casting their culinary spells in kitchens where elbow room is at a premium.

Butter, whipping cream, and four types of cheese not rich enough for you? Toss in some lobster and crab for pure Decadence. With a capital D!

Meatloaf with Peppercorn Demi-Glace and Garlic Mashed Potatoes

Makes: 1 meatloaf serving 7 or 8

Note: This recipe requires a 12- × 5-inch loaf pan and a panini press.

Timing note: Prepare the meatloaf first, then cook the demi-glace and mashed potatoes while the meatloaf is in the oven.

Meatloaf

4 1/2 pounds ground top sirloin

1 onion, minced

2 eggs, lightly beaten

1 1/2 cups dry bread crumbs

1 1/4 cups ketchup

1/4 teaspoon each salt and pepper

Peppercorn Demi-Glace

1/4 cup unsalted butter

1/4 cup all-purpose flour

4 cups beef demi-glace

1 tablespoon mixed peppercorns

Garlic Mashed Potatoes

8 pounds Yukon Gold potatoes (unpeeled)

1 cup milk

1/2 cup margarine

1/2 cup garlic butter

1/2 teaspoon each salt and pepper

Assembly

Sliced onions and mushrooms, sautéed
  until soft

Meatloaf

Preheat oven to 350°F.

Place all ingredients in a large bowl and mix very well. Press mixture into a 12- × 5-inch loaf pan, packing it well and smoothing the top. Place loaf pan in a deep baking pan and add enough hot water to reach halfway up the sides of the loaf pan. (This will help ensure an even cooking temperature during baking.)

Bake until the loaf reaches an internal temperature of 160°F, approximately 1 hour and 20 minutes.

Remove the loaf pan from the water bath and let cool in the refrigerator. (Meanwhile, make the peppercorn demi-glace and mashed potatoes.)

Preheat a panini press.

Loosen the edges of the meatloaf with a knife. *Very* carefully turn pan over onto a cutting board. Remove pan. *Very* carefully slice meatloaf into 3/4-inch slices.

Grill the meatloaf in the panini press for 5 to 7 minutes, or until hot and marked with grill marks.

Peppercorn Demi-Glace

In a large saucepan over medium heat, melt the butter. Add the flour and cook, whisking, for 2 minutes, making sure the flour does not colour. Add the demi-glace and whisk vigorously to remove any lumps. Add the peppercorns and simmer, stirring constantly, until the gravy has a nice consistency and the flour flavour has been cooked out. (Add additional demi-glace if needed.) Remove from heat and keep warm.

Garlic Mashed Potatoes

Chop the potatoes into large chunks and put them in a large pot. Cover with hot water and season with salt. Boil potatoes until tender.

Drain potatoes and return to the pot. Add the milk, margarine, garlic butter, and salt and pepper. Mash well.

Assembly

Lean slices of the meatloaf against mashed potatoes and top with sautéed onions and mushrooms. Scoop mashed potatoes over the middle, and pour the peppercorn demi-glace over everything.

Haugen's Chicken & Ribs Barbeque

EST. 1953
13801 HIGHWAY 12
PORT PERRY · ON · L9L 1A2
WWW.HAUGENS.COM

When a restaurant has been around since Elvis was king, and continues to pack in almost as many people every week as the entire population of the town it calls home, you know there's something special going on. This is Haugen's, a legendary institution where generations of locals and loyal cottagers stop in every week for simple yet delicious barbequed chicken and ribs, and some of the best homemade pies you've ever eaten.

Back in 1953, Ivan Haugen opened a takeout joint that served truckers and pioneering cottagers. Thirteen years later, it was bought by the Tzountzouris family, who expanded the restaurant and embraced the dish that would make Haugen's famous: barbeque. Today, owners Steve and Johnny Tzountzouris keep the family legacy alive, and have watched the popularity of their once modest joint grow to epic proportions: Haugen's is now 8000 square feet, seats three hundred hungry devotees, and serves about six thousand customers every week.

One of the staples of meals at Haugen's is their pork back ribs, which are slow-cooked before being finished on the charbroiler and slathered with Haugen's signature barbeque sauce. Meaty, tender, and delicious, they're the meat that all other meats dream of growing up to be. Then there's the other half of the Haugen's dynamic duo: their barbequed chickens, which are slow-cooked for two hours in one of the restaurant's four massive rotisserie ovens. These are popular birds, people. The kitchen does seven chickens per spit, and six spits per oven. In the end, Haugen's goes through about a thousand birds every week. For those customers who can't decide which Haugen's delicacy to indulge in, there's the ever-popular chicken-and-rib special.

One of the secrets to Haugen's success, like that of any good barbeque joint, is their sauce, a signature topping that customers love or hate, with little middle ground. Either way, the Tzountzouris boys are proud of their sauce, which starts with tomato purée, fresh tomato juice, fresh lemon juice, oregano, and a secret blend of spices. Apparently *lots* of people are fans: the family has couriered bottles of it to as far away as California, and some customers have even been known to drink it straight! Personally, I'll make my tomato-based beverage a Caesar, but hey, that's just me.

If you have any room left for dessert—and lord knows that's not a foregone conclusion!—then you cannot walk out of Haugen's without tasting a piece of Angela's famous pies. Angela is the family matriarch who, along with husband, Chris, bought the restaurant in 1969 before passing the reins to sons Steve and Johnny. Angela figures she's handmade more than a million pies in her day, and she's never used a measuring cup for a single one of them.

I can't decide if I like the coconut cream or the strawberry pie better, but they're both Angie's recipes—and therefore equally delicious. I can't imagine how many strawberries these guys go through in a season, but it must be a lot given how high the pies are piled with them!

One more tip: if you plan on coming to Haugen's, you might also want to start looking at real estate in the area. If you're like most people who stop in here for a quick meal, you might just be coming back for decades to come.

When you've been around as long as Haugen's has, the fashion trends might come and go. But the food stays the same: Good! Damn good!

One of the secrets to Haugen's success, like that of any good barbeque joint, is their sauce, a signature topping that customers love or hate, with little middle ground.

Coconut Cream Pie

Makes: 6 to 8 servings

1 1/2 cups sugar

3/4 cup cornstarch

1/2 teaspoon salt

4 cups hot milk

3 eggs, beaten

2 teaspoons vanilla extract

2 tablespoons margarine

1 teaspoon coconut extract

1 cup shredded coconut

10-inch baked pie shell (homemade
  or store-bought)

Whipped cream for garnish

In a medium saucepan, whisk together the sugar, cornstarch, and salt. Whisk in the hot milk,
  1/2 cup at a time, until smooth. Bring to a boil; boil for 2 minutes, stirring constantly. Add the
  eggs and cook, stirring constantly, until thickened.

Remove from heat and add vanilla and margarine; stir until smooth. Cover the surface with
  wax paper and let cool.

Stir the coconut extract and coconut into the cooled filling. Pour the filling into the pie shell.
  Refrigerate until cold.

Serve with a dollop of whipped cream.

You think you're old? Haugen's was about twenty years old when this photo was snapped! But the passage of time means nothing when the food is simply . . . delicious.

Hoito Restaurant

EST. 1918
314 BAY STREET
THUNDER BAY · ON · P7B 1S1
WWW.FINLANDIACLUB.CA

You've never heard of the Hoito? What kind of good Canadian are you? OK, so the Hoito is in the basement of the Finlandia Club, a patriotic Finnish organization that owes its roots to a country thousands of miles away. But at nearly a hundred years old, the Hoito is one of the most storied restaurants our youthful country has ever known. So read and learn, my child!

The Hoito opened in 1918 in the basement of the Finnish Labour Temple. Back then the restaurant was run as a co-operative, largely for the benefit of local Finnish-Canadian bushwork-ers who finished their long, hard days with monstrous appetites. The idea behind the Hoito was to provide large portions at low prices while still maintaining communal ownership for everyone who ate there. Lit-tle wonder they chose the name "Hoito": the word means "care" in Finnish.

Until the 1970s, the Hoito's loyal cus-tomers spent $6 for a weekly all-you-can-eat food ticket and shared their meals at large group dining tables. When owner-ship was transferred to the Finlandia Club, the restaurant was changed to a more traditional format. And while the Hoito's meals are now priced by the dish, the communal tables are still used and the restaurant has never wavered from its goal of providing hearty, generously portioned meals at fair prices.

The building that houses the Hoito was designed by C.W. Wheeler and built in 1910 by the Finnish Building Company. Today it houses a museum and an annual film festival . . . in addition to the Hoito.

Although head chef Darlene Granholm serves up a wide selection of heart-warming meals at the Hoito, no trip to this place would be complete without a sampling of their legendary Finnish pancakes. For those of us who grew up on thick,

What, you've never worn a hairnet? That's because you've never made Karjalan Piirakka, a pasty stuffed with rice pudding.

cakey pancakes, the cakes at the Hoito are a completely different groove. Thin, but as big as a dinner plate, they sit somewhere on the cake-o-meter between a crêpe and a cake, crispy on the outside but warm and moist in the middle. No matter how you define them, when they arrive piled high on your plate on a frigid Thunder Bay morning, there's nothing like 'em!

Like almost everything here at the Hoito, the pancakes are built on decades of tradition. The recipe and cooking technique are the same as they were nearly a century ago, and people flock here for pancakes at all hours of the day and night. No wonder they go through about thirty-five gallons of pancake batter before *noon* and a thousand eggs a *day* at the Hoito! The pancakes can be served with sticky homemade blueberry, strawberry, or rhubarb sauce (depending on what's in season), or just plain maple syrup. If you've really built up a lumberjack's appetite, you can order them with bacon, ham, or sausage. Just deforested half of Northern Ontario? Throw a few eggs in, too!

But in keeping with its mandate of feeding hungry diners day and night, meals at the Hoito are about more than pancakes. The restaurant also offers a variety of sandwiches, burgers, and dinner plates, including a few Finnish specialties. Karjalan Piirakkas are baked oval pastries filled with rice pudding and sprinkled with cinnamon and sugar. I was lucky enough to dive into a Hot Turkey Sandwich, perhaps the most comforting of all comfort foods. Just don't expect sliced deli meat on your Hoito turkey sandwich. Here they roast giant, fresh turkeys every day, then deconstruct them piece by piece for your sandwich, which ends up bursting with the succulent meat. Feast on this, smothered in homemade beef gravy and served on bread supplied by the bakery next door, and nothing—not even the bone-chilling temperatures of a Thunder Bay winter—can stop you!

The idea behind the Hoito was to provide large portions at low prices while still maintaining communal ownership for everyone who ate there. Little wonder they chose the name "Hoito": the word means "care" in Finnish.

Karjalan Piirakka

Makes: 6 to 8 piirakkas

Rice Pudding

1 cup medium-grain rice

2 cups water

1 teaspoon salt

1 cup milk

1 cup whipping cream

3 tablespoons unsalted butter

Crust

1 1/2 cups all-purpose flour

1 1/2 cups rye flour

1 cup water

2 teaspoons salt

2 tablespoons unsalted butter, melted

Glaze

1/2 cup unsalted butter, melted

1/2 cup milk

Rice Pudding

In a medium saucepan, combine the rice, water, and salt; cook over medium heat until the rice is soft, about 20 minutes.

Reduce heat to medium-low and stir in the milk, cream, and butter; cook for 10 to 15 minutes or until thick and bubbly. Let cool. The mixture may thicken as it cools; stir in more milk if necessary.

Crust

Preheat oven to 450°F. Grease a baking sheet or line with parchment paper.

In a medium bowl, combine the all-purpose flour, rye flour, water, salt, and butter. Stir until the dough comes together.

Turn the dough out onto a floured surface and knead for 3 minutes or until the dough is smooth but still sticky.

Shape the dough into a roll 2 inches thick and slice into 16 pieces with a sharp knife.

Roll each piece into a small circle; spread cooled rice pudding over each circle almost to the edge.

Fold up 1/2 to 1 inch of the edge, pinching the dough so that it stands up by itself, leaving 1 inch uncovered in the centre. Crimp the edges on each side to make oval-shaped pies.

Transfer the piirakkas to the baking sheet and bake for 15 to 20 minutes or until light brown.

Glaze

Stir together the melted butter and milk; dip hot piirakkas in the mixture or brush it on.

Cover the glazed hot piirakkas with a towel until serving.

Serve topped with butter, egg salad, or cold cuts. Store in a covered container in the refrigerator.

Note: Leftover rice pudding may be served as a dessert. Stir in raisins and pour into a buttered casserole dish. Sprinkle cinnamon and sugar on top. Bake at 350°F until warm. Serve with strawberry or blueberry sauce on top if desired.

Finnish Pancakes

Makes: 4 to 6 servings

5 eggs

1/4 cup sugar

2 teaspoons salt

6 cups milk

3 cups all-purpose flour

1/2 teaspoon unsalted butter or margarine

Preheat a griddle to 350 to 400°F (or heat a large skillet over medium-high heat).

In a medium bowl, lightly whisk the eggs with the sugar, salt, then milk. Whisk in the flour 1/2 cup at a time.

Melt the butter on the griddle. Pour batter into skillet, making a plate-sized pancake. Cook until golden brown on both sides, flipping once.

Pancakes can be enjoyed plain, with sauce, with strawberries and whipped cream, or with fried eggs and bacon.

"HOITO"
RESTAURANT

Owned and Operated By
The Boarders Themselves!

PLENTY TO EAT — EVERYTHING THE BEST
CLEAN AND WHOLESOME

Please leave used Serviettes on the table.

314 Bay Street,   Port Arthur, Ont.

Joe Feta's Greek Village

EST. 1995
290 LAKE STREET
ST. CATHARINES · ON · L2N 4H2
WWW.JOEFETAS.CA

When a Greek family opens a restaurant, the unstated philosophy is "the more, the merrier," especially when it comes to relatives. Well, when it comes to Joe Feta's in St. Catharines, that's exactly what you get. And with every extra parent, sibling, uncle, or cousin who joins the party, there's that much more love and laughs, reason enough to visit this classic Greek eatery.

Joe Feta's was opened in 1995 by Gus and Jenny Kountouris, who passed the reins to Ted and Toula Kountourogiannis eight years later. Now George Kountourogiannis (Ted and Toula's son) runs the show, while Jenny, Ted, and George's sister Hellen all pitch in one way or another. Warm, loud, and passionate, they make Joe Feta's the landmark it has become. Then, of course, there's the food.

Souvlaki is a mainstay of both the lunch and dinner menus at Joe's, and

In the oven, the béchamel sauce in George's pastitsio puffs up and becomes golden brown, a delicate topping for a warm, soothing meal.

everyone in St. Catharines seems to know it. Just ask Uncle Angelo; he prepares two to three hundred every day. But souvlaki here is more than just meat on a skewer. The day before the souvlakis are cooked, Uncle Ang expertly cuts and cleans the fresh meat before bathing it overnight in a homemade pepper-garlic marinade. Homemade tzatziki is prepared with yogurt, cucumber, garlic, and savoury herbs to accompany the moist meat, which is charcoal-grilled to perfection, served on a pita, and topped with onions and tomatoes.

There's a host of other traditional Greek specialties on the menu. The moussaka is a hearty dish of sliced potatoes layered with baked eggplant, ground beef, and a super-creamy béchamel sauce, then baked to perfection. Dolmades are grape leaves stuffed with seasoned meat and rice, then covered in Joe Feta's special sauce. Served with rice, roasted potatoes, Greek salad, garlic bread, and tzatziki, they are a trip across the Atlantic with every bite. But no Greek menu would be complete without roast lamb, and Joe Feta's is exceptional. It's not always available, though, so in-the-know customers jump at the chance for this succulent meat slow-cooked on a rotisserie and continuously bathed in Joe's special basting sauce.

One meal at Joe Feta's and you'll understand why the place is regularly named the best Greek restaurant in the area by a local magazine.

George even sold me on his pastitsio, a layered pasta-and-meat dish that tasted surprisingly exotic. This has everything to do with the ground beef, which is sautéed with garlic, onions, dill, parsley, mint, tomato sauce, and the secret ingredient—a cinnamon stick. Once fully infused with the spices, the beef is sandwiched between layers of pasta, the top of which gets blanketed in a thick, rich béchamel sauce and grated Parmesan cheese.

Of course, there's much more on the menu at Joe Feta's, and their variety of seafood and grilled meats will suit any taste. Or maybe you're travelling light, in which case there's a seemingly endless array of appetizers on offer. Of these, the most flamboyant is the saganaki, a fried piece of kefalotiri cheese (a Greek goat cheese), which is set aflame at your table. Messy and hot, the saganaki will grab not only your taste buds but the attention of everyone else in the dining room. *Opa!*

Dessert is a traditional experience at Joe Feta's, with good reason: the Greeks do sweets right! Of course there's Mama Feta's Famous Baklava (topped with her secret syrup), but for an added twist try the Baklava Sundae: a piece of baklava topped with vanilla ice cream and whipped cream, followed by cinnamon, crushed walnuts, and secret syrup. I'm particularly fond of galaktoboureko (try saying *that* three times fast!), which is a rich, cinnamon-infused vanilla custard layered with phyllo pastry and topped with—you guessed it—secret syrup.

And don't be surprised if you're offered a second piece. After all, everyone's family at Joe Feta's.

Souvlaki is a mainstay of both the lunch and dinner menus. Just ask Uncle Angelo; he prepares two to three hundred every day.

Moussaka

Makes: 4 to 6 servings

Meat Sauce

1 tablespoon olive oil
2 cups finely chopped onions
1 1/4 pounds lean ground beef
2 cups chopped plum tomatoes
2 teaspoons minced garlic
2 whole cloves
1 small cinnamon stick
  (or 1/4 teaspoon ground cinnamon)
1 bay leaf
1/2 cup water
Salt and pepper
2 tablespoons tomato paste
1/4 cup dry red wine

Béchamel Sauce

1/2 cup unsalted butter
1/3 cup all-purpose flour
2 cups whole milk, heated
Salt
5 egg yolks, lightly beaten

Potato and Eggplant Filling

2 large russet potatoes
3 pounds eggplant (2 large or 3 medium)
Salt
1/3 cup olive oil (or as needed)

Assembly

2 cups crumbled feta cheese

Meat Sauce

Heat the olive oil in a skillet over medium-high heat; add the onions and cook, stirring, for 10 to 12 minutes or until soft and translucent.

Add the ground beef and cook, stirring, over medium heat for 5 minutes or until the meat loses its raw pink appearance.

Stir in the tomatoes, garlic, cloves, cinnamon, bay leaf, water, and salt and pepper to taste; simmer, uncovered, for about 30 minutes, until thick and flavourful.

Stir in the tomato paste and wine; simmer for 10 minutes or until the wine has developed a sweet aroma. Remove the cinnamon stick and bay leaf. Set aside.

Béchamel Sauce

Melt the butter in a medium saucepan over low heat; add the flour and stir with a wooden spoon until smooth. Increase heat to medium-low. Slowly add the milk, whisking constantly until the sauce begins to thicken; the sauce should be creamy without being too thick. Remove from heat and stir in salt to taste.

Stir in the egg yolks and return to the heat, whisking briskly until well blended; remove from heat and set aside.

Potato and Eggplant Filling

Place the potatoes in a large saucepan and cover with cold water. Bring to a boil over medium-high heat; boil gently for 5 minutes. Drain, cool, and cut potatoes into 1/8-inch slices. Set aside.

Cut eggplants into 1/8-inch crosswise slices; sprinkle with salt.

Heat 1 tablespoon of the olive oil in a large skillet over medium-high heat until shimmering. Working in batches, add eggplant slices and cook for 2 to 3 minutes per side or until tender and lightly coloured. Drain on a rack, and continue with remaining eggplant. Add more oil to the skillet as needed.

Assembly

Preheat oven to 350°F.

Arrange a layer of half the potato slices in the bottom of a baking dish. Pour the meat sauce over the potatoes, spreading the sauce into an even layer. Arrange the remaining potatoes over the sauce. Layer the eggplant over the potatoes. Top with the béchamel sauce.

Bake, uncovered, for 30 to 45 minutes or until the cheese sauce is thick and golden brown.

Remove from oven and sprinkle with the feta. Let moussaka rest for about 20 minutes before cutting and serving.

Opa! If you're looking to add a little flare to your meal, order the Saganaki, too, which is doused in ouzo or vodka before ignition.

The Main Deli Steak House

EST. 1974
3864 BOULEVARD SAINT-LAURENT
MONTREAL · QC · H2W 1Y2
WWW.MAINDELISTEAKHOUSE.COM

A Montreal fixture, the Main was the subject of an award-winning short film called *The Birth of Smoked Meat*.

I f there was a winner-take-all battle royal in Montreal for bragging rights over who's got the best smoked meat, you can bet your brisket the Main Deli Steak House would be among the combatants. For as a ridiculously devoted clientele will tell you, the Main has the best *viande fumée* you can find anywhere, and their poutine and potato verenekes are *très délicieux*. (Adding a little French to your everyday conversations will make you sound super smart!) Throw in homemade desserts, and you'll fight for the right to eat here.

You can't go wrong with the Main's classic Smoked Meat Sandwich. Owner Peter Varvaro starts with a beef brisket that's injected with salt, a process that Peter says protects the meat during its twelve-day brining. Then the beef is massaged with a rub of garlic, mustard seeds, coriander, and a few other magical spices Peter conveniently forgot just as the cameras started rolling. The meat is then smoked for three to four hours, steamed until it's dripping with succulence, then sliced to order and piled on fresh, soft rye bread and doused in mustard. And mama, what a sandwich! The beef was so flavourful my tongue was doing cartwheels.

You can also get your smoked meat fix in combination with another Main classic: the Smoked Meat Poutine, which puts patrons completely over the edge with its combination of textures and flavours. The dish is built around a foundation of squeaky-fresh cheese curds, which are then buried under a mound of hand-cut fries. Then comes homemade gravy, more fries, more cheese curds, more gravy, slices of smoked meat, *more* curds, and (yes!) *more* gravy. If it's Montreal you desire, my friends, there is nothing more authentic than this! Of course, you could always try the Main Burger, which piles smoked meat, mozzarella, and a blend of sautéed onions and mushrooms on a sizzling beef patty.

Cook Barbara Szczygiel is in charge of Potato Verenekes around here, and from the piles of potatoes they're shredding every day, I'd say they're pretty darn popular! Barbara uses her

As a ridiculously devoted clientele will tell you, the Main has the best viande fumée you can find anywhere.

hands to mix the grated potatoes with minced onions, eggs, and flour, then drops them by the giant spoonful into a hot-oil bath. Shake the oil off when they're golden brown and crispy, serve with applesauce and sour cream, and you've got to believe when Barbara says they're the best in the city.

But you don't call yourself a Maison du Bifthèque without serving up delicious steaks, and as the weekly five-hundred-plus orders attest, the Main does its 14-ounce and 20-ounce rib-eyes just right. The steak is prepared with a special spice mix, then grilled to perfection over charcoal. Not enough meat for you? Fear not, the steak comes with liver and a frankfurter to start.

Craving pig? The Baby Back Ribs are another fave among diners here, and with good reason. First the ribs are parboiled with tons of garlic, then boiled again in a sweet in-house barbeque sauce. Each time an order comes in, the ribs are tossed on the charcoal grill and served smothered in more barbeque sauce.

Dessert is another house specialty at the Main, all courtesy of pastry chef Diane Bass, who says it's worth a million dollars to see someone enjoy one of her sweet creations. Diane might go through a lot of butter, sugar, and flour, but the ingredient that makes her treats so special is nothing other than love. The Hummingbird Cake is a layered creation made with pineapple and overly ripe bananas, then dressed with homemade cream cheese icing and hand-coated in chopped roasted pecans. Diane's German Chocolate Cake is to die for, and her cheesecakes come in a variety of flavours, including peanut butter and New York strawberry.

And if you've only been eating store-bought desserts, be forewarned: there's no going back after you've tasted one from the Main. In fact, you'd probably fight someone at the mere suggestion.

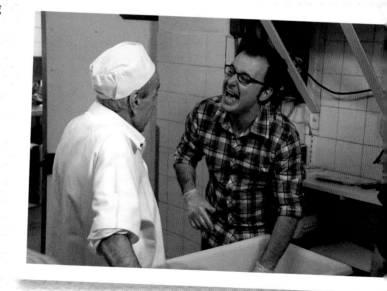

Owner Peter Varvaro not only makes world-class smoked meat, he cracks the occasional joke, too. OK, so here I'm laughing at my own joke, but Peter's are pretty good, too.

Diane's German Chocolate Cake

Makes: 1 cake

Chocolate Cake

4 ounces sweet chocolate, chopped

1/2 cup boiling water

2 1/4 cups cake-and-pastry flour
(not sifted)

1 teaspoon baking soda

1/4 teaspoon salt

1 cup unsalted butter (2 sticks),
slightly softened

2 cups sugar

4 eggs, separated

1 teaspoon vanilla extract

1 cup buttermilk

Coconut Pecan Frosting

1 1/2 cups sugar

1 1/2 cups evaporated milk

4 egg yolks, lightly beaten

3/4 cup butter (1 1/2 sticks)

1 1/2 teaspoons vanilla extract

2 2/3 cups shredded sweetened coconut

1 1/2 cups chopped pecans

Garnish

Chocolate curls

Chocolate Cake

Preheat oven to 350°F. Grease the sides of two 9-inch springform pans and line the bottoms
with wax paper or parchment paper.

Combine the chocolate and boiling water in a large microwavable bowl; microwave on High for
1 1/2 to 2 minutes, until almost melted. Remove from microwave and stir until completely
melted. Set aside.

In a bowl, whisk together the flour, baking soda, and salt.

In a stand mixer fitted with the paddle attachment, cream the butter with the sugar until light
and fluffy. Add the egg yolks 1 at a time, beating well after each addition. Stir in the melted
chocolate and vanilla.

Add the flour mixture, alternating with the buttermilk, making 2 additions of flour mixture
and 1 of buttermilk, beating until smooth after each addition.

In a separate bowl, beat the egg whites until they form stiff peaks. Gently but thoroughly fold
into the batter. Pour the batter into the pans, smoothing the tops.

Bake for 30 minutes or until the cake springs back when lightly touched. Cool in the pans on
racks.

Frosting

In a medium saucepan, combine the sugar, evaporated milk, egg yolks, butter, and vanilla; cook
over medium heat, stirring constantly, until the mixture thickens and is golden brown.

Remove from heat and stir in the coconut and pecans; beat in the saucepan with a wooden
spoon or whisk until frosting is cool and thickened to spreading consistency.

Assembly

Remove the cakes from pans. Set 1 cake on a cake plate. Spread about one-third of the frosting
over the top. Place the second cake on top; frost the top and sides of the cake. Decorate with
chocolate curls.

The Musket Restaurant

EST. 1979
40 ADVANCE ROAD
TORONTO · ON · M8Z 2T4
WWW.MUSKETRESTAURANT.COM

L et's say you love Thai food but can't find a Thai restaurant in your neighbourhood that meets your standards. What do you do? If you're like me, you keep looking until you find one. Not so with Helmut Enser. When Munich-born Helmut couldn't find a restaurant that offered true German-style home cooking, he took matters into his own hands and opened his own. The Musket was born.

Since then, the Musket has become a community fixture, a destination for locals and tourists alike, all of whom know there are few places that offer German cooking as authentic or lovingly made. And while it's Helmut's son Richard who now runs the kitchen, the restaurant still sticks to its roots, offering heart-warming dishes that Helmut himself learned from his mother.

Schnitzel was a big part of that education (surprise, surprise), and both Helmut and Richard know it well. Each schnitzel begins the same way at the Musket: a massive spiced pork cutlet is beaten with a tenderizing hammer, then dredged in flour before being fried in a pan of oil. The Jaeger Schnitzel covers the cutlet with a rich, dark gravy of onions, bacon (pork on top of your pork? I love it!), garlic, mushrooms, red wine, demi-glace, cream, and butter. Like all schnitzel dishes at the Musket, the Jaeger is served alongside a heap of tangy red cabbage and spaetzle, a classic German pasta/dumpling hybrid that's delicious no matter what you call it.

Another classic German can't-miss entrée is the Musket's famous Pork Hock. And while the dish may have taken years for Helmut to perfect, Richard picked up the tradition without skipping a beat. He starts with a bowling-ball-sized pork leg, rubs it with an array of spices, then

The Enser family is the beating heart of the Musket Restaurant, where the laughs flow as freely as the beer, and the real taste of Germany is never far away.

boils it until soft. Then the hock is deep-fried until perfectly golden and crunchy. But there's one more step. When the meat is ready to serve, it's barbequed with mustard seeds, adding yet another dimension of crispiness and locking in the meat's natural flavours. The Pork Hock is served alongside fresh home fries and hand-crafted sauerkraut, and if you're not ordering your lederhosen after this one, something's wrong!

A meal at the Musket is about more than just the food, extraordinary though it may be. The place has a warm, inviting feel, the customers all seem like old friends, and the laughs flow as freely as the beer. Helmut's wife, Joanne—who still acts as the Musket's hostess and server—plays a big part in keeping the dining room hopping, and isn't ashamed to share how proud she is of her husband and son.

And why shouldn't she be? With Richard whipping up recipes like Helmut's Rouladen, there's no reason to feel anything but. The Rouladen starts with finely sliced Angus beef that's blanketed in a layer of Dijon mustard. Then Richard lays in a thick strip of bacon, a quarter onion, and a pickle! The beef is rolled, baked until juicy, and served under a warm smothering of rich beef gravy.

There are a few different desserts on the Musket's menu, but you'd be missing the party if you ordered anything but the homemade Apple Strudel, a Musket specialty. How fresh is the strudel? All you need to know is that Helmut goes to the market to buy apples by the bushel, which will eventually become the dessert's deliciously sweet and tart filling, baked inside homemade dough. There is no better way to finish a classic German meal than with this classic German dessert.

Sing the sweet song of schnitzel and you'll become an honorary member of the German National Accordion Team.

So if you're on the hunt for that quintessential taste of Deutschland and are considering opening your own restaurant, take my advice: don't bother. The Musket beat you to it.

Rouladen

2 slices sirloin beef (each 7 ounces and 1/4 inch thick)

Salt and pepper

2 tablespoons Dijon mustard

2 slices double-smoked bacon

1/2 large onion, cut in half lengthwise

1 large dill pickle, cut in half lengthwise

Rouladen Sauce

2 tablespoons unsalted butter

3/4 large onion, finely chopped

1 teaspoon minced garlic

1 tablespoon tomato paste

2 tablespoons all-purpose flour

1 cup beef stock

1 tablespoon mustard seeds

Pinch each of dried thyme and paprika

1 bay leaf

1/4 cup whipping cream

Rouladen

Preheat oven to 350°F.

Sprinkle beef with salt and pepper. Spread Dijon mustard over top. Place 1 slice of bacon on each piece of beef. Place a quarter of an onion on top of the bacon. Place half a dill pickle beside each onion. Roll up the beef and skewer with a toothpick down the middle of each roll. Place rolls in a small roasting pan.

Roast for 40 minutes or until rouladen are browned and juices run clear. Transfer rouladen to plates and cover loosely with foil to keep warm. Reserve pan drippings.

Rouladen Sauce

When the rouladen are cooked, melt the butter in a small skillet over medium heat. Add the onion, garlic, and tomato paste and cook, stirring, until onion is softened. Stir in the flour and cook, stirring, for 2 minutes.

Whisk in the beef stock. Add the mustard seeds, thyme, paprika, bay leaf, and any juices from the roasting pan. Bring to a boil, stirring, until slightly thickened. Stir in the cream. Remove bay leaf before serving.

Assembly

Place a roulade on each plate and pour the sauce over top until completely covered.

Philadelphia Kitchen

EST. 2011
281 BROADWAY AVENUE
ORANGEVILLE · ON · L9W IL2

As a boy growing up in Philadelphia, Joe Lattari worked in his family's small grocery store, which sold fresh sandwiches by the dozen. So it was at a young age that he learned the secrets behind some of the city's classic food, food like cheesesteaks and meatball hoagies. The only problem for Joe was that his wife, Michelle, lured him to Canada, and there wasn't an authentic Philly cheesesteak to be found for miles. Undaunted, Joe started making Philly classics for family and friends, who raved about his cooking long and hard enough that Joe followed in his family's footsteps and opened up his own sandwich shop. The Philadelphia Kitchen was born.

At its core, the Philadelphia cheesesteak seems like a pretty simple arrangement: bread, steak, onions, and cheese. But to the uninitiated, screwing up a Philly cheesesteak is easier than mastering one. Cook the thinly sliced beef too long and you've got a shoe-leather sandwich on your hands. Burn the onions and the taste changes forever. Too much oil in the mix and your bread becomes a soggy mess. But not to Joe Lattari. He does every sandwich right, every time.

A straight-up sandwich shop that makes no bones about its simple menu, the Philadelphia Kitchen serves it up good, hot, and fresh.

At the Philadelphia Kitchen (PK for those in the know), the cornerstone of the menu is the Philly Cheesesteak, which starts with the cornerstone ingredient: Canadian beef. Joe receives the meat whole and then plays butcher, slicing it thinly and portioning it out for each sandwich. As Joe says, the quality of the meat directly affects the quality of the sandwich, so it better be fresh and it better be done quickly on the grill (and topped with a bit of secret seasoning). Joe then adds sautéed onions to the mix while it's still on the flattop, mounds it all together under a couple slices of mozzarella, then covers the works with a crispy-soft Italian sub roll to fuse it all into the most unbelievable cheesesteak this mouth has ever entertained. Hot *damn!* You're good, Lattari!

For you non-traditionalists in the house, there are loads of other cheesesteak options at the PK. These include the Mushroom Steak, Pepper Steak, Steak Italiano (sautéed spinach and homemade marinara sauce), Italian Stallion (mushrooms, onions, and roasted green and red peppers), and the Pizza Steak.

An eastern American classic migrates north. The Philly cheesesteak takes four simple ingredients and turns them into a mouthful of heaven.

But do not (and that's an order, soldier!) leave this place without trying the Meatball Sandwich. I was shown the meatball ropes by Michelle, who uses the holy trinity of meat for her creations: beef, pork, and veal. She then hand-mixes in chunks of Italian bread that have been soaked overnight in milk, along with Parmesan, eggs, herbs, spices, and bread crumbs. Once those balls have been baked to perfection, they're stuffed into the sub roll, layered with Joe's homemade sauce, and topped with mozzarella. Then it's back in the oven for a quick melt, and you've got a sandwich that you should either kiss or eat. Or maybe both.

If you're a one-meat kind of person, then you might want to try the Veal on a Bun, a simple sandwich that delights the mouth nonetheless. Joe starts by breading a massive piece of tender veal, then deep-frying it just long enough to cook it while still keeping it soft and hot. The meat is tossed in tomato sauce, then placed gently in the signature bread that makes PK sandwiches so distinctive. Topped with more sauce and mozzarella and melted together, it's a crispy, tasty mouthful of love in every bite.

Call them simple if you dare, but to the thousands of devoted customers who make the PK a regular part of their day, these sandwiches are exquisite. For just like Joe himself, the Philadelphia Kitchen is straight up. What you see is what you get.

And we're all *so* OK with that.

To the uninitiated, screwing up a Philly cheesesteak is easier than mastering one. But not to Joe Lattari. He does every sandwich right, every time.

Meatballs

2 pounds medium ground beef
1 pound ground pork
1 pound ground veal
1 cup cubed or torn crustless bread, soaked in milk
2 eggs
1 cup grated Parmesan or Romano cheese
1 tablespoon each dried oregano and basil
1 tablespoon garlic powder
Dry bread crumbs

Preheat oven to 400°F.

Mix all ingredients (except the bread crumbs) in a large bowl. Shape the mixture into meatballs slightly larger than golf balls. If they do not hold their shape, work some bread crumbs into the mixture until meatballs stay together without sticking to your hands. Place on a parchment-lined baking sheet.

Bake for 45 to 50 minutes or until cooked through and browned. Cut a meatball open to make sure that there is no pink inside.

Meatball Sub (per sandwich)

Philadelphia Kitchen's house marinara sauce (or marinara sauce of your choice)
Demi-baguette, cut in half
3 meatballs
Mozzarella

Preheat oven to 350°F.

Spoon some marinara sauce on the bottom of the baguette. Top with three meatballs, more marinara sauce, and mozzarella. Put it in the oven until the cheese melts—about 3–4 minutes.

Phil's Original BBQ

EST. 1998
838 COLLEGE STREET
TORONTO · ON · M6H 1A2
WWW.PHILSORIGINALBBQ.COM

When Phil Nyman had his first taste of authentic southern barbeque, it was love at first bite. In fact, Phil was so enthralled with the cuisine that he started experimenting with his own creations in his backyard and testing them out on his friends. When those same friends started asking when he was barbequing next, Phil knew he was on to something. Phil's Original BBQ was born.

That was 1998. Phil's became a landmark almost immediately, and to this day boasts a faithful following of customers who say if you want the best BBQ in Toronto, there's only one name to know.

The secret to Phil's success lies in the fact that he knows what he does, and he does it well. His menu is a testimony to simplicity, and everything on it is a slow-cooked classic. And if smoke is the number one secret for good barbeque, then good sauce is close behind. And Phil's doesn't disappoint. Both of his sauces—sweet and hot—feature a complex blend of ingredients such as curry powder, chili powder, allspice, cinnamon, and coffee. Throw in a splash (or two!) of cayenne sauce to sass things up a bit in the hot version.

One of the mainstays of the menu at Phil's is the ribs. The boss chooses pork side ribs, which he says are the most tender of all. After careful trimming, the ribs are rubbed with a blend of spices, then placed into the smoker for the slow and low. When an order comes in, the ribs are tossed onto the charbroiler for a little sizzle, then served piping hot with your barbeque sauce of choice.

Phil's ribs are smoked to perfection, tender but still boasting a bit of body and substance. The bones are always clean after you've finished a rack of ribs at Phil's . . . but that doesn't mean the meat fell off on its own. Like each entrée, the ribs come with a choice of two of coleslaw, potato salad, fries, or BBQ beans.

If only we were all as lucky as Phil Nyman, a man who truly loves his work. But when you're playing with smoked pork all day, why wouldn't you be in love?

Pulled pork is done much the same way. After the juicy pork shoulder emerges from a twelve-hour session in the smoker, it's pulled apart with tongs into bite-size chunks before being piled mountain high on a bun and washed in BBQ sauce. If none of those options tickle your fancy, there's always Phil's Cachapas, Venezuelan corn pancakes wrapped around a cheesy layer of mozzarella. And if that's not doing it for you, well, you can always order a beer.

BBQ Beef Brisket is also a classic Phil's dish, served either on a sandwich (which comes with one side dish) or on its own as an entrée. Either way, you're in for a juicy, tender treat when the Black Angus beef hits your gullet. The smokiness is evident but not overpowering, the signature rub adds a hint of mystery, and the meat is never mushy. Phil keeps his sandwiches simple, and instead of loading them up with things that take away from his smoky goodness, he's content to pile tons of meat on a freshly baked bun, douse in sauce, and serve.

For when you're as serious about the smoke as Phil is, there's no reason to get fancy.

The secret to Phil's success lies in the fact that he knows what he does, and he does it well.

Four hours in the smoker is just the beginning for these pork side ribs, which will leave you licking your fingers for hours to come.

3 1/2 cups thawed frozen corn kernels

3 eggs

1/2 cup all-purpose flour

1 tablespoon sugar

1/2 teaspoon salt

4 teaspoons butter or vegetable oil

1 cup shredded mozzarella cheese

Preheat oven to 150°F.

Combine the corn, eggs, flour, sugar, and salt in a food processor; process until the batter is pourable but still has corn chunks.

Heat a large skillet over medium heat and coat the pan with 1 teaspoon of the butter. Pour 3/4 cup of the batter into the pan. Gently shake the pan to spread batter into a 7-inch circle. Cook 3 minutes. Carefully flip, then cook another 1 minute.

Spread a quarter of the cheese over half of the cachapa. Once the cheese is melted, fold over to form a half moon and remove from the pan. Place cachapas on a baking sheet and keep warm in the oven until ready to serve. Repeat with the remaining ingredients.

Pizzeria Napoletana

EST. 1948
189 RUE DANTE
MONTREAL · QC · H2S IKI
WWW.NAPOLETANA.COM

If the essence of good Italian food is deliciousness, then the Girolamo family—the owners and chefs at Pizzeria Napoletana—have the winning recipe.

For more than sixty years, Pizzeria Napoletana has been packing in the customers with classic pasta and thin-crust pizza that has earned the place a legendary reputation in Montreal. And with forty-one pizza and thirty-four pasta options, there's something for everyone.

The key to great taste at Pizzeria Napoletana is their tomato sauce, which goes on just about everything the Girolamos serve. And it doesn't get any fresher than this, starting with hand-crushed tomatoes. Sure, the crushing process can take hours, but the Girolamos know it's the only way to get the authentic Italian taste they desire.

From there, the tomatoes are mixed with olive oil, onions, basil, and garlic . . . and then it's ready for the dough! The sauce isn't cooked before it goes on the dough; it cooks for the first time in the oven. This gives the ingredients a chance to fuse together by the time the pizza's ready.

There is nothing that Linda Girolamo loves better than making the best damn pizza this side of Naples . . . and then watching you enjoy it.

The Girolamos are so dedicated to pizza that they'll even serve you some without sauce. I was lucky enough to have the Toscana, a white pizza that starts with slices of mozzarella cheese (they never use shredded cheese at Pizzeria Napoletana; it changes the taste) topped with chopped tomatoes, black pepper, and olive oil. After it's baked to perfection, a layer of prosciutto and baby arugula are added. When you fold it in your hands, the heat from the pizza wilts the arugula and mmmmmm! It's like Italy, right in your mouth.

There's also the namesake Napoletana pizza, which combines a layer of mushrooms topped with mozzarella, anchovies, and finally, the sauce (the sauce never goes on the dough first; it might make the crust soggy). Sprinkle on a bit of Parmesan after it comes out of the oven, add a splash of olive oil and . . . Madonna! What a taste!

For more than sixty years, Pizzeria Napoletana has been packing in the customers with classic pasta and thin-crust pizza, and with forty-one pizza and thirty-four pasta options, there's something for everyone.

If delicious thin-crust goodness is not your thing, then Pizzeria Napoletana has so many pasta options your head will spin like linguine on a fork. The Girolamos use the same sauce for pasta as they do for pizza, though it has to be simmered for hours before it's pasta-ready. Once it is, though, watch out! It's a focal point of almost every pasta dish they serve.

The Rotolo alla Milanese might be the cheesiest option on the menu. It's a rolled pasta jam-packed with ricotta, Parmesan, and spinach, then smothered in tomato sauce and covered in tons of mozzarella cheese. The Mafaldine Casarecce was deliciously simple. A blend of mafaldine—a fairly wide, ribbon-shaped pasta—tomatoes, pancetta, and arugula, it was a perfect blend of salty and peppery.

Simple yet delicious, every pizza at Pizzeria Napoletana is packed with the flavour that only sixty years in business can provide.

And oh, have I mentioned the Polpette? Because these meatballs are so moist and tender that you have to try them. Linda knows the secret lies in using veal, pork, and beef. After adding parsley, lots of garlic, eggs, Parmesan cheese, and olive oil, Linda adds small bits of panini that she's soaked in milk. This is the secret to moist polpette! The meatballs are then baked under a blanket of tomato sauce. Linda say it's a recipe she learned from her mother and grandmother, and still follows today.

It's that kind of tradition that makes Pizzeria Napoletana a special place. So when customers here tell you it's just like Mama used to make, they're not kidding!

Linda's nonna is the source of her meatball recipe. Personally, I don't care who came up with it, just as long as there's some left for me!

1 pound mafaldine pasta
6 tablespoons extra virgin olive oil
2 garlic cloves
4 ounces thinly sliced pancetta
2 cups diced, seeded tomatoes
Salt and pepper
3 cups baby arugula
1/4 cup grated Parmesan cheese
1/4 cup grated Romano cheese

Cook the pasta in a large pot of boiling salted water until al dente.

Meanwhile, heat the olive oil in a large skillet over high heat. Add the garlic and sauté for 2 min-utes. Remove garlic. Add the pancetta and fry until golden brown. Add the tomatoes and cook for about 8 minutes. Season with salt and pepper to taste. Mix in the baby arugula and cook for 4 minutes.

Drain the pasta and add it to the skillet, mixing it well with the sauce. Cover with Parmesan and Romano cheese. Mix and serve.

Prince Albert's Diner

EST. 1985
565 RICHMOND STREET
LONDON · ON · N6A 3G2

Cozy up at the counter or try your luck grabbing a table. Either way, the food at Prince Albert's is well worth the wait.

Who doesn't like peanut butter, right? Come to mention it, who doesn't like burgers? Wait a second, I think we're on to something here. What if we combined . . . Nah, that's crazy, right? Turns out it isn't so nuts after all. Just ask Bill Spigos and his sister Betsy Kouklakis, who run the restaurant their father, George, bought back in 1996. For them, the combination of peanut butter and beef patty is a winning one: the Wally Burger.

Like all burgers at Prince Albert's, the Wally Burger begins with a fresh beef patty made by Bill and Betsy's mother, Pat, using a recipe she's been perfecting for nearly fifty years. But rather than throw their blend of medium ground (Bill says lean meat is too dry) on the charbroiler, Bill and Betsy fry theirs right on the flattop, keeping it plump and juicy. Slather on a pile of creamy peanut butter and some crispy bacon (the bacon has to go on after the peanut butter so it can melt down into the goo), and you've got a sweet and salty winner that tickles the taste buds!

Now, I realize the idea of a peanut butter burger might be downright scary to some people, and I imagine it's a love-hate thing. But for a guy who never *ever* imagined the marriage of those two ingredients, I have to say I *loved* it. Hey, I've always loved peanut butter and I've always loved burgers. Now I love peanut butter burgers!

Yeah, I was skeptical, too: peanut butter on a burger? Then I tasted it. Betsy will tell you the bacon has to go on after the peanut butter, so it all melts together.

If burgers are your thing, then you can't walk out of Prince Albert's without feasting upon the aptly named You Gotta Eat This Burger, an open-faced monster that features a fried patty buried under a mound of cheese, gravy, and a pile of . . . poutine! It's a tasty treat, but I'm pretty sure Bill is trying to kill someone with it.

As you may have guessed, Prince Albert's is classic diner food at its classic-est, so there's more than just patties and buns here. The Garlic Chicken Burrito takes a char-grilled chicken breast and stuffs it inside a flour tortilla under a thick layer of creamy, homemade garlic sauce, crunchy romaine lettuce, sour cream, and tons of shredded Cheddar. Sure, you *could* try to eat it with your hands, but you will no doubt submit to the messiness of the burrito and eventually go for a fork and knife. They all do.

Speaking of messy, there's something delightfully sloppy about Prince Albert's Coney Fries. Here fresh-cut fries are loaded up with homemade chili and tons of melted mozzarella and Cheddar cheeses. Wash it all down with another diner classic, a thick hand-crafted milkshake. You probably won't be surprised to learn that the most popular flavour is Chocolate *Peanut Butter*. No wonder they go through ten pounds of the stuff every week!

You'll get no apologies from Bill and Betsy, though. They know

Feed me Prince Albert's Diner food and you've got a friend for life! Unlike my pal Bill Spigos, though, I like to stick the T-shirt to my chest rather than actually wear it.

what Prince Albert's Diner is all about, and they make no bones about their old-school approach to classic fare. I, for one, am sold. My motto: it ain't a burger if it ain't got the butter!

Hey, I've always loved peanut butter and I've always loved burgers. Now I love peanut butter burgers!

You Gotta Eat This Burger

Makes: 4 servings

Burger

1 pound medium ground beef

1 egg, lightly beaten

2 tablespoons dry bread crumbs

2 teaspoons chopped fresh parsley

1 teaspoon each salt and pepper

Gravy

1/4 cup meat fat (any kind will do)

1/4 cup all-purpose flour

2 cups water

2 teaspoons each salt and pepper

Assembly

4 slices white or whole wheat bread

Cooked french fries

4 handfuls shredded Cheddar cheese

Burger

Mix all ingredients together in a bowl. Shape into 4 thick patties.

Heat a large skillet or grill pan over high heat. Cook the burgers, turning once, for 4 to 5 minutes on each side or until nicely browned and cooked through.

Gravy

Melt the fat in a medium saucepan over medium heat. Add the flour and cook, whisking, for 2 minutes, making sure the flour does not colour. While whisking, add the water. Continue to stirring frequently, until the gravy reaches your preferred thickness. Remove from heat and stir in salt and pepper.

Assembly

Toast the bread. Pour a bit of the gravy over the bread. Place a burger on top. Top the burger with french fries. Top each serving with a handful of Cheddar cheese. Pour more gravy over top and serve.

Reggie's Hot Grill

EST. 2007
89 HUNTER STREET EAST
PETERBOROUGH · ON · K9H 1G4
WWW.REGGIESHOTGRILL.CA

Take two twenty-five-year-old buddies, a beat-up chip truck, and a well-placed dart and you've got Reggie's Hot Grill, a restaurant where good karma is almost as powerful as the smell of burgers and fries.

Reggie's started in 2007, when best buds Reggie Maranda and Cam Green bought a chip truck, fixed it up with what little cash they had, and let their imaginations run wild with the menu. It wasn't long before most of their customers were regulars, leading them to open a second truck, which in 2009 morphed into Reggie's, a year-round burger joint that has quickly become one of Ontario's must-eat destinations. As for the name, well, the two chose a friendly game of darts to determine whose name would go on the sign. Reggie won.

Reg and Cam will tell you that their secret is their locally sourced ingredients, homemade sauces, made-to-order burgers, and constantly changing menu with bold feature items.

Wondering why Reg (*left*) looks so darn happy? He won the dart game for naming rights of the Hot Grill. Cam's a nice guy, just not so good at darts.

Customers will tell you the secret is Reg and Cam themselves, two of the kindest, happiest, and funniest people you'll ever meet.

But karma only gets you so far, mate. If the food's terrible, nobody's coming back. That's not an issue at Reggie's, for they serve up an array of burgers that keeps customers begging for more. For instance, you won't find the Big Poppa Burger on the regular menu, but it surfaces as a special from time to time. And special it is! The boys first hand-craft a cream cheese and spin-

I loved everything Cam and Reg threw in front of me, but nothing topped the Hawaiian Burger with a side of sweet potato fries and a dollop of butt-whoppin' Lip-Smackin' Mustard!

ach sauce, sandwich a thick layer of it between two patties, and serve it up hot and juicy. It's like a cream-filled doughnut . . . of meat.

Other great burger varieties at Reggie's include the Blue Bayou Burger (topped with homemade blue cheese chipotle and diced bacon), Mozza Burger (served with mozzarella cheese and sautéed mushrooms), and Pepper Jack Burger (the key is the homemade creamy jalapeño sauce and Monterey Jack cheese). But my favourite had to be the featured Hawaiian Burger, which topped a 6-ounce patty with a grilled pineapple ring, back bacon, mozzarella cheese, and Cam's Signature Lip-Smackin' Mustard, which starts out sweet and then kicks your ass when you're not expecting it. It made for one sweet, hot, and *tasty* burger!

Reggie's is also a destination for sandwiches, and there's nothing like the Cranberry Chicken Sandwich, Jerk Chicken Sandwich, or Canadian Sandwich (which features grilled peameal bacon topped with Swiss cheese). Of course, no restaurant that started as a chip truck would keep fries off the menu, and at Reggie's you can get either poutine or Fries Deluxe, which is an intense mess of Cheddar cheese, sour cream, green onions, and tomatoes over fresh-cut sticks of root vegetable heaven.

But dart skills or not, both Cam and Reg are chilled dudes, and this place is as cool as they come. I'm sure you'll have as much fun as I did.

Reggie's started in 2007, when best buds Reggie Maranda and Cam Green bought a chip truck, fixed it up with what little cash they had, and let their imaginations run wild with the menu.

Spinach Cream Cheese Stuffing

2 tablespoons vegetable oil

1 cup chopped Spanish onion

4 or 5 garlic cloves, chopped

4 handfuls fresh spinach

1/4 cup water

Salt and pepper

1 pkg (8 ounces/250 g) cream cheese

Burgers

2 pounds ground beef

1/4 cup Worcestershire sauce

1 1/2 teaspoons onion powder

1 1/2 teaspoons salt

1 teaspoon pepper

Spinach Cream Cheese Stuffing

In a medium saucepan, heat the oil over medium heat. Add the onions and garlic; cook, stirring, for 7 to 10 minutes or until the onions are soft and translucent.

Add the spinach, water, and salt and pepper to taste. Cover and cook until the spinach has wilted. Remove from heat and let cool.

While the spinach is cooling, melt the cream cheese in the top of a double boiler (or in a heat-proof bowl set atop a pot of simmering water).

Purée the spinach in a food processor, then stir it into the melted cream cheese until well combined. Cover and refrigerate to set.

Burgers

Preheat grill to high.

In a large bowl, mix together the ground beef, Worcestershire sauce, onion powder, salt, and pepper. Divide the mixture into 8 patties.

Spread the spinach cream cheese on 4 of the patties; sandwich the cream cheese with the remaining patties, squeezing together the edges to prevent the burgers from opening while cooking.

Place the burgers on the grill and sear on both sides for 2 to 3 minutes. Finish cooking the burgers over low heat.

Serve burgers on hamburger buns with your favourite toppings.

Relish the Best in Burgers

EST. 2010
135 WORTLEY ROAD
LONDON · ON · N6C 3P4

A burger's a burger's a burger, right? Wrong. Wrong, wrong, wrong! So wrong, in fact, that you may be wronger than anyone has ever been. Is *wronger* even a word? No? Well it is now. The point here is that if you think all burgers are created equal, you haven't been to Relish the Best in Burgers, a creation of Adam Green and Kendra Gordon-Green. Eighteen-year veterans of the restaurant industry and owners of a chain of cafés, they noticed a gourmet burger trend during a trip to New York. The pair borrowed a delicious recipe from Adam's mom, and in 2010 Relish was born.

Though Relish is a relative baby by restaurant terms, they have already attained legendary status in the foodie world around London, thanks to the almost unbelievable size, taste, and cre-

When someone writes the epic history of the beloved hamburger, there better be a chapter on Relish the Best in Burgers, where burgers become edible art.

ativity of their burgers. It doesn't matter if you're a local politician, a celebrity, a couple of kids out on a first date, or a family: Relish is on everyone's radar.

And for good reason! Burgers here are many and varied, though they all start with the same foundation: a massive patty. But at Relish you get to choose from ground sirloin, chicken, lamb, bison, portobello mushroom, or a veggie patty. All the meat at Relish is mixed by hand (the meat gets too tough if a mixer is used) and cooked in clarified butter, to give it that drip-down-your-chin appeal.

Picking the patty is the easy part. Once you've made up your mind on that front, you then have to choose from over three *dozen* burger options, and the scale of variety at Relish is mind-boggling. (Number of different patties: 6. Number of different taste combinations: 38. Total number of burgers: 228. Current pant size: I hover between 32 and 34, depending on the brand.) Like it hot? Why not wrap your mouth around the Firecracker, with Havarti cheese, banana peppers, and Holy Mutha Hot Sauce. The Le-Ooh-La-La burger is a continental mélange of bacon, bé-

So, uh, let me get this straight. **You want *me* to put *this* into my mouth?**

arnaise sauce, mozzarella, and caramelized onions, while the Hungry Frat Boy adds Kraft Dinner for that special dormitory taste.

Every burger here is a mountain of taste and substance, but a couple stand out as truly monumental. The Straight to LHSC burger, named after the London Health Sciences Centre (the local hospital), is rumoured to have sent more than one diner there for an angioplasty. The LHSC starts with an 8-ounce patty that is par-cooked, then dipped in tempura batter and deep-fried for good measure. Then comes roasted garlic aïoli, smoked Gouda, peameal bacon, strip bacon, and a sunny-side-up fried egg. OK, so the lettuce, tomatoes, and homemade pickles seem a bit too, um, *healthy* for the LHSC (I mean, they're vegetables, after all!), but they taste great together.

If you really want to stretch the limits of your gastrointestinal capacity, then look no further than the Fat Bastard. This monstrosity features three sirloin patties, Swiss cheese, bourbon BBQ sauce, Thousand Island dressing, bacon, Cheddar, lettuce, tomato, portobello mushrooms, and an onion haystack. (OK, so maybe after this one I went up to a size 36 . . . don't judge!) Finish it and dessert's on the house—as if you've got room. And maybe you do. As some of the patrons here like to say, if you're gonna go all out, go all out!

The Fat Bastard is one of Relish's more notorious offerings, but legions of fans ask for it by name. With a free dessert on the line, I can see why!

Just know one thing about Relish: as delicious as their burgers are, don't think it's easy to get one named after you. I know, because I tried. I begged. I cajoled. I cracked some *really* funny jokes. In the end, I got the world's first-ever Catucci Burger: pesto mayonnaise, bacon, mozzarella, and mushrooms on a sausage patty. It was probably the most delicious burger humankind has ever known. Ask for it when you visit. Tell them John sent you.

As delicious as their burgers are, don't think it's easy to get one named after you. I know, because I tried. I begged. I cajoled. I cracked some really funny jokes.

Straight to LHSC Burger

Makes: 4 burgers

Burger Patties

2 pounds lean ground chuck

2 eggs

1 cup barbeque sauce (homemade or store-bought)

1/2 cup Dijon mustard

6 tablespoons chopped garlic

1 teaspoon roasted garlic

1/4 cup fresh bread crumbs

1/2 cup potato flakes

2 tablespoons ground coffee

Your favourite spice mix (such as Cajun seasoning)

Salt and pepper

Vegetable oil or clarified butter for deep frying

Tempura batter (mix can be purchased at any grocery store)

Assembly

Roasted garlic aïoli

Smoked Gouda

6 slices fried bacon

1 slice fried peameal bacon

1 egg, fried sunny side up

Lettuce

Tomato slices

Pickles

Burger Patties

Combine the ground chuck, eggs, barbeque sauce, Dijon, garlic, bread crumbs, potato flakes, coffee, spice mix to taste, and salt and pepper to taste; mix well. Shape into 4 patties, each about 1 1/2 inches thick.

Heat a griddle or cast-iron pan over high heat. Sear burgers on both sides, then reduce heat and slow-cook until burgers are cooked through, approximately 8 minutes. Let burgers cool.

Pour 2 to 3 inches of oil into a large heavy pot and heat to 350°F (or use a deep-fryer).

Coat cooled burgers in tempura batter and deep-fry until golden, 4 to 5 minutes.

Assembly (for each burger)

Stack all the toppings on a burger inside your favourite bun.

Schwartz's Deli

EST. 1928
3895 BOULEVARD SAINT-LAURENT
MONTREAL · QC · H2W IX9
WWW.SCHWARTZSDELI.COM

When Leonardo da Vinci said "Simplicity is the ultimate sophistication," little did he know that he would be describing the granddaddy of all smoked meat joints in a city that prides itself on being the smoked meat capital of the world: Schwartz's. And OK, so da Vinci lived, like, five hundred years before Schwartz's even existed, but let's not get bogged down in details, shall we?

Simply put, Schwartz's is smoked meat and smoked meat is Schwartz's, as the ridiculously long lines outside the door attest to day and night. The restaurant was founded in 1928 by Jewish Romanian immigrant Reuben Schwartz, and hasn't budged an inch since. Oh sure, the restaurant's decor may have been changed a few times in the ensuing decades, but it still wows its customers with good food rather than fancy knick-knacks: one long, white-tiled room is what you get at Schwartz's. If you're lucky enough to find a free seat inside, you grab it without worrying about who the strangers

If you're looking for fancy, you've come to the wrong place. Ultimately, Schwartz's is about rye bread, mustard, and smoked meat. Window dressing? Not an option.

are around you. Sit, smile, talk, and chow down on the best damn combination of meat, bread, and mustard you've ever imagined. Just don't take *too* long . . . there are other people waiting for your spot!

Tradition is everything at Schwartz's, and they are not ones to mess with success. Chef Frank Silva uses the same process to smoke the hundreds of pounds of beef brisket they serve *every day*, a process that begins with a secret blend of spices born from the mind of old Reuben himself. Then the meat is marinated for as long as ten days, followed by an eight- or nine-hour

Simply put, Schwartz's is smoked meat and smoked meat is Schwartz's, as the ridiculously long lines outside the door attest to day and night.

trip to the smoker. The final step in the brisket's evolution is the steaming, which makes the smoked meat incredibly moist and tender. From there the meat goes to one of Schwartz's master cutters, who take to their jobs with surgical precision.

Now, if you're thinking all smoked meat is made equally, think again. Once you've decided to dig into one of Schwartz's smoked meat classics, you next have to decide what cut of brisket you want. Although the health conscious among us might go for the lean cut, the powers that be here at Schwartz's will tell you to go for the medium fat, which comes from the juiciest part of the brisket.

OK, so you're not a smoked meat fan, you say? Go somewhere else! Well, not really. Schwartz's offers classic deli sandwiches like turkey, salami, and chicken, as well as steaks, ribs, and even liver. Their takeout menu reads more like a grocery store inventory, and you can stock up on things like karnatzel (spicy beef sausages), smoked spiced whole turkey, pickles, coleslaw, and bread.

Order any of these things and you certainly won't be disappointed: Schwartz's quality runs through-out their entire menu. Don't be surprised if you get some strange looks, though. For while the whole world might be changing, you can always count on Schwartz's to stay the same.

If you don't know the person sitting beside you, you soon will. At Schwartz's, everyone shares a common interest: food!

Note: This recipe requires a smoker.

Beef brisket
10 spices of your choice, ground or crushed

Cover the meat in your blend of spices. (You'll have to create your own seasoning, as
Schwartz's blend of smoking spices is top secret.) Cover and refrigerate for 10 days.
Smoke brisket (do not rinse off the spice rub) for 8 hours.
Place the meat on a rack in a steamer. Steam for 3 hours to restore its moisture.
Thinly slice the smoked meat and pile high on your favourite rye bread. Top with your choice of
mustard.

Shish-Kabob Hut Greek Restaurant

EST. 1976
220 KING STREET
PETERBOROUGH · ON · K9J 2SI
WWW.SKHPETERBOROUGH.COM

What is it about Greek people and their giant hearts? Go to any Greek restaurant across this vast country of ours, and you're bound to come across three common themes: love of food, love of family, and love of community. At Peterborough's Shish-Kabob Hut, all three of those traits are alive and well.

The Hut was started back in 1976 by Charalambos (Bob) Vassiliadis, who was born on the Greek island of Chios. As a cook on the *Christina O*—the luxury yacht owned by Aristotle Onassis—Bob met Peterborough native Linda Bilmer during a stopover in Vancouver and fell in love. The couple married in 1967 and soon moved to Peterborough. Not long after, the Shish-Kabob Hut was born.

Bob passed away in 2008, and it's son Don who now runs the operation and continues his father's legacy of delicious eats, a history that has garnered the restaurant a local paper's Reader's Choice Award for best Greek restaurant for thirteen straight years. But Don's not just a fantastic chef and friendly restaurateur; he's also a philanthropist, serving on the boards of several social organizations, hosting fundraisers, and sponsoring local sports teams.

We Italians like to think that moussaka is nothing more than Greek lasagna, but one bite tells a different tale.

Don's streak of kindness permeates his food as well, beginning with one of the Hut's signature dishes, the Hot Peppers and Feta spread, a simple dish that sells like hotcakes (do Greeks even eat hotcakes?). People are addicted to the stuff! Don starts by deep-frying hot Hungarian yellow peppers and sweet red peppers, after which he peels the skins off. After the peppers are ground in a food processor, they're hand-mixed with olive oil and grated cow-and-goat-milk feta. As Don tells it, this kind of feta is harder than the traditional sheep kind, and it absorbs the oil better than softer varieties. The dip is served with grilled pita wedges, and is a tangy-hot way to start a great meal. Other great Greek appetizers at the Hut include dolmades (stuffed grape leaves), spanakopita (phyllo pastry stuffed with a feta cheese and spinach), garides feta (shrimp in garlic tomato sauce topped with feta), and saganaki (kefalotiri cheese flamed with Metaxa brandy).

It should come as little surprise that Greek specialties continue on to the lunch and dinner menus here, including the dish that gave the Hut its name: shish-kabobs—or souvlakis, as they are also called. These tender pieces of fresh beef tenderloin, chicken breast, pork tenderloin, and lamb are marinated in a mixture of oil, oregano, and garlic before being grilled. Here at the Hut, shish-kabobs are served with pita bread, Greek salad, tzatziki, and a choice of Greek potatoes, rice, or french fries.

The Hut also serves up classic Greek comfort food in the form of moussaka, a layered dish that we Italians like to say is, uh, *inspired* by lasagna (though it's really not). Don will tell you it's like lasagna, only better. National pride aside, I love the moussaka for the melt-in-your-mouth grilled eggplant, which is layered in a baking dish under slices of deep-fried potatoes, a sautéed ground beef blend (ground beef, basil, rosemary, thyme, chives, nutmeg, and tomato sauce), crumbled feta, and a thick and creamy béchamel sauce.

Moussaka might be a staple at most Greek restaurants, but one dish you'll likely see only at the Hut is Tigania (tee-gun-YA), a tasty and filling stir-fry coloured brightly by red paprika. The Tigania begins with a sauté of vegetables, to which Don adds Greek sausage, marinated chicken breast, paprika, and lemon juice. Served atop a bed of rice, the dish is unlike anything I've ever had, a true Greek delicacy. Say it with me, people: Tigan-Yeah!

You can taste the love in every bite.

Moussaka might be a staple at most Greek restaurants, but one dish you'll likely see only at the Hut is Tigania. Served atop a bed of rice, the dish is unlike anything I've ever had, a true Greek delicacy. Say it with me, people: Tigan-Yeah!

Chicken Tigania

Makes: 2 servings

Marinated Chicken

1 large boneless, skinless chicken breast (5 ounces), cut into 1-inch cubes
1/2 cup olive oil
1/4 cup lemon juice
1 teaspoon black pepper
1 teaspoon salt
1 teaspoon oregano

Tigania

1 cup water
Marinated chicken
1/2 large Spanish onion, chopped
1/2 sweet green pepper, chopped
1/2 sweet red pepper, chopped
1 soutzoukaki sausage (spicy beef sausage), sliced
4 button mushrooms, chopped
1 tablespoon Spanish paprika
1/2 lemon

Marinated Chicken

Combine chicken with other ingredients and marinate in the fridge, overnight if possible.

Tigania

In a medium saucepan, warm the water over medium heat. Stir in the chicken, onion, green pepper, red pepper, sausage, mushrooms, and paprika. Simmer for 10 minutes, until the chicken is no longer pink inside and the sauce thickens.

Spoon over a bed of rice. Squeeze half a lemon and cracked pepper over the tigania.

Stoneface Dolly's

EST. 1995
416 PRESTON STREET
OTTAWA · ON · KIS 4M9
WWW.STONEFACEDOLLYS.COM

What kind of maniac would line up for forty-five minutes for brunch on a Sunday morning? Hello? Who in their right mind would stand outside in the freezing cold of a January morning and wait . . . Hold on a second, that's me! And the place I've waited outside is none other than Stoneface Dolly's, where a reputation for amazing food has spawned a following so devout, fans will stare in the teeth of a Canadian winter just to get inside. And let me tell you from experience, it's well worth the wait.

Brunch at Dolly's takes many forms, and there's more selection than you could shake a frostbitten finger at. Whether it's eggs Benedict, ribs, steaks, omelettes, soup, sandwiches, or pasta, Dolly's got a brunch dish for everyone. But as far as I'm concerned, nothing touches the French toast, a breakfast dish made über-extra-special by Dolly's homemade molasses bread.

Thick, dark, moist, and unlike any bread you've ever had, molasses bread at Dolly's makes French toast (served with icing sugar, maple syrup, and fresh fruit) an otherworldly experience. No wonder they have to make about a hundred loaves a week! Dolly's Ricotta Blueberry Pancakes are a dreamy interpretation of an old standby, and are served with lemon curd and fresh whipped cream.

Thanks to owner Bob Russell's roots, Stoneface Dolly's also serves a number of South African dishes, giving the dinner menu a decidedly international flair. One of the most popular is the Chicken (or Tofu) Bobotie, a traditional South African dish that wows customers with both its aroma and taste. Bob starts the Bobotie (buh-BOO-tee; try *not* to giggle) by sautéing onion, garlic, ginger, and curry powder before adding raisins and slivered almonds, followed by a blend of apricot jelly, red wine vinegar, and brown sugar. After the chicken (or tofu) has been cooked into the blend, in goes a mix of softened bread and thick coconut cream.

Stoneface Dolly's reputation for amazing food has spawned a following so devout, fans will stare in the teeth of a Canadian winter just to get inside. And let me tell you from experience, it's well worth the wait.

Bob's son Jeff has run Dolly's kitchen for more than ten years. And judging by the taste of the food he produces—like the molasses bread we're making here—he's doing a heck of a job.

Bob's son Jeff has run Dolly's kitchen for more than ten years. And judging by the taste of the food he produces—like the molasses bread we're making here—he's doing a heck of a job.

The Bobotie is served in a toasted bowl of phyllo pastry and topped with a drizzle of cooling yogurt raita. Add a side of coconut basmati rice and Bob's home-made chutney—itself an exotic blend of fruit, spices, and herbs—and you've got an incredible taste sensation, one that hugs your buh-booty! For me, the dish was warm and cozy, like a shepherd's pie with a mysterious twist.

The Red Thai Soup is another faraway taste blast, a spicy party of onions, garlic, ginger, red peppers, Chinese eggplant, bok choy, and fresh cilantro in a coconut cream red curry base that warms your mouth without setting it ablaze. I also loved the tons of vegetables, which were fresh enough to have a firm snap to them. No mushy veggies allowed at Dolly's!

That big menu parade just keeps on rolling at Dolly's, and you'll never find yourself wanting for variety. The Cape Malay–style Fish is a South African specialty of marinated white fish in a mild curry sauce garnished with pickled beets. The Jerk Chicken Club sandwich takes thick slices of homemade whole wheat molasses bread and fills them with spicy jerk chicken breast, romaine lettuce, tomato, bacon, and mayonnaise. The Black Bean Pasta tosses penne in a black bean cream sauce and serves it up with portobello mushrooms and roasted red peppers, along with optional tofu, chicken, or shrimp.

As for the name, well, the story goes that the place was dubbed for the original owner's mother, who was reputed to be an exceptional poker player. When Bob bought the restaurant in 1999 after a career in the technology industry, he changed the place from a small diner to the destination it is today, but the moniker remained.

Just bring your parka if it's cold; you might be waiting for a while.

Breakfast perfected: Dolly's molasses-bread French toast is an exotic twist on an old standby.

Note: This recipe requires 4 tin pie plates.

1/2 cup raisins
1 small Spanish onion
3 tablespoons canola or vegetable oil
1 tablespoon finely chopped fresh ginger
1 tablespoon finely chopped garlic
2 tablespoons + 3/4 teaspoon curry powder
1/4 cup cider vinegar
3 tablespoons brown sugar
2 tablespoons apricot jam
1/4 cup toasted slivered almonds
2 pounds ground chicken
1/4 loaf sourdough bread, cut or torn into small pieces
7 ounces coconut cream
16 sheets phyllo
Butter, melted
Salt and pepper
Raita and sliced banana for serving

Preheat oven to 350°F.

Soak raisins in warm water until plump, then drain and set aside.

Meanwhile, purée the onion in a food processor. Heat the oil in a large saucepan over medium-high heat. Add the puréed onion and cook, stirring frequently, for a few minutes, until the colour starts to change. Add the ginger, garlic, and curry powder; cook, stirring, for 2 more minutes.

Add the vinegar, brown sugar, and jam. Cook until the jam and sugar are completely dissolved. Stir in the almonds and raisins.

Crumble the chicken into the saucepan and cook thoroughly.

While the chicken is cooking, soak the bread in the coconut cream.

Meanwhile, brush a sheet of phyllo with some melted butter. Lay a second sheet diagonally on top of the first; brush with butter. Lay a third sheet diagonally on top; brush with butter. Repeat with a fourth sheet. (When finished, all points should be facing in different directions.) Press into a pie plate. Repeat to fill the remaining pie plates.

Bake for 5 minutes. Let cool.

When the chicken is cooked through, stir in the soaked bread. Season with salt and pepper to taste.

Spoon the chicken bobotie into the phyllo bowls, top with raita and sliced bananas, and serve.

Stoney's Bread Company

EST. 2004
325 KERR STREET
OAKVILLE · ON · L6K 3B6
WWW.STONEYSBREADCOMPANY.COM

Like it loud, boisterous, and always humming with activity? Want a sandwich big enough to choke a horse with enough zip to send your nonno dancing in the streets? Then Stoney's is your place, my friend.

You don't need a PhD in sociology to recognize there's something special about this place . . . and I'm not just talking about the food. Bright and airy, Stoney's is one of those eateries that warms your heart as much as your taste buds. As its devoted patrons tell me over and over again, Stoney's feels like home as soon as you walk in the door. Maybe that's why they all seem so connected to the place. As for the food . . . is it just like home?

Nah, they say. Way better than home cooking. *Way, way* better.

Co-owned by Blake Stoneburgh and Steve Chabot, Stoney's gets its name from Blake's dad, former CFL All-Star Norm "Stoney" Stoneburgh, who spent thirteen years manning the front lines for the Toronto Argonauts. (See what a good son Blake is? Kids, respect your fathers!) Now Blake mans the front of the restaurant while Steve works his magic in the kitchen.

And what magic it is! Steve takes me through his paces, first giving me a behind-the-scenes look (and taste!) of a staple of the Stoney's menu: their famous homemade pizzas. Steve creates as many

Located in Kerr Village just outside downtown Oakville, Stoney's boasts a customer base devoted to the restaurant's extensive menu and consistently delicious offerings. Better yet, it seems like there's always something new to try!

as a thousand of these babies every week, and each one is a masterpiece. The handmade crust is light and crispy, and the toppings are as bountiful as they are delectable. I'm sorry if you caught me drooling over the Catalunya, but the combination of grilled chicken, slow-roasted peppers, caramelized onions, artichokes, Kalamata olives, mozzarella, and feta cheese was just too much

Grab, squeeze, chomp, and . . . Yeah, baby! Stoney's Slow-Roasted Lamb Sandwich is a thing of beauty to behold—but it's even better to eat.

to bear. The Bilbao is piled high with chorizo sausage, mushrooms, roasted garlic, bacon, and Cambozola cheese. As someone told me: "It's just like New York . . . only better!"

Give the credit to the man in the kitchen, because as far as I'm concerned, Steve is a genius. He not only nails the taste every time, he feeds his guests portions that are big enough to satisfy a linebacker. One of my personal favourites is Stoney's Slow-Roasted Lamb Sandwich, a mind-bending combination of buttery smooth lamb, sweet onion marmalade, fresh tomatoes, arugula, three-mustard aïoli (regular Dijon, grainy Dijon, and spicy Dijon . . . the holy trinity of Dijon!) on a soft ciabatta bun. Now I know why old Stoney himself says this is the best sandwich he's ever had!

Norm's word might be law around here, but for my money the Blackened Atlantic Salmon Sandwich gives its lamb counterpart some stiff competition. Blackening at Steve's hands means taking a secret blend of twelve spices that combine for the afterburners he calls a "sweet heat." ("Blackened" means something else when I'm wearing the chef's hat—burnt!) Add some guacamole and mango salsa (both homemade, of course . . . nothing comes from a jar at Stoney's), serve it open-faced on a piece of (you guessed it—homemade!) focaccia, and the result is a sandwich I would date . . . if we Canadians weren't so damn judgmental about man-sandwich relationships. It's the twenty-first century, people. Deal with it!

So go to Stoney's, culinary pilgrim. You may have to wait in line to pay your tab, and you may have to arm-wrestle your neighbour for the last seat in the place. But as far as I'm concerned, it's time and energy well spent.

Stoney's does its Blackened Atlantic Salmon Sandwich the right way: *without* burning it! OK, so my way might be a little more, er, exciting, but their approach definitely tastes better.

The result is a sandwich I would date . . . if we Canadians weren't so damn judgmental about man-sandwich relationships.

Stoney's Pizza Sauce

4 teaspoons extra virgin olive oil

2 tablespoons thinly sliced garlic

3 shallots, thinly sliced

4 teaspoons red wine (any kind)

4 teaspoons balsamic vinegar

1 1/2 cans (28 ounces/796 mL each)
good-quality whole plum tomatoes

4 teaspoons brown sugar (optional)

Kosher salt and freshly ground pepper

Leaves from 1/2 bunch fresh basil,
torn

Leaves from 1/2 bunch fresh oregano,
torn if large

Leaves from 1/4 bunch fresh thyme

Stoney's Pizza Dough

1 pkg active dry yeast (about 2 1/4
teaspoons)

2 teaspoons sugar

1 cup warm water (110°F)

3 cups all-purpose flour

1/2 cup olive oil

1 tablespoon kosher salt

Assembly (for each pizza)

Shredded mozzarella cheese

Sliced chorizo sausage

Sautéed sliced cremini, shiitake, and/
or portobello mushrooms

Roasted garlic

Bacon slices

3 ounces Cambozola cheese, sliced

Pizza Dough

In a measuring cup, dissolve the yeast and sugar in the warm water. Let stand for 10 minutes, until foamy.

In a large bowl, combine the flour, olive oil, salt, and yeast mixture. Stir until a stiff dough forms. On a lightly floured surface, knead for 2 minutes.

Place the dough in a lightly oiled bowl, cover, and let rise until doubled in volume, about 30 minutes.

Pizza Sauce

Meanwhile, in a large saucepan, heat the oil over medium heat. Add the garlic and shallots; cook, stirring frequently, until translucent. Deglaze the pan with the red wine and balsamic vinegar.

Add the plum tomatoes, brown sugar (if using), and salt and pepper to taste. Bring to a boil, reduce heat, and simmer for 25 minutes.

Add the herbs and simmer for another 5 minutes.

Assembly

Set oven rack on the lowest level and preheat oven to 450°F. Lightly grease a pizza pan.

Divide the dough into 4 equal pieces; cover loosely with plastic wrap. On a lightly floured surface, roll out 1 piece of dough into an 11-inch round about 1/4 inch thick. Transfer dough to the pizza pan, and gently push it into place. (If not using remaining dough immediately, chill or freeze.)

Spread a thin layer of the pizza sauce over the dough, leaving a 1-inch border. Sprinkle with the mozzarella. Top with the chorizo, sautéed mushrooms, roasted garlic, bacon, and Cambozola cheese.

Bake for 20 minutes or until the crust and cheese are browned.

Note: Leftover pizza dough may be frozen. Leftover pizza sauce may be refrigerated for up to 5 days.

That Little Place by the Lights

EST. 2007
76 MAIN STREET EAST
HUNTSVILLE · ON · P1H 2C7
WWW.THATLITTLEPLACEBYTHELIGHTS.CA

Huntsville is cottage country, a destination for a bit of R&R away from the city. Just what I hanker for. So when my family was vacationing in the area a few years ago and I couldn't face the prospect of yet another home-barbequed burger, I turned to That Little Place by the Lights, which was said to serve the pasta I was craving.

I won't lie: I was skeptical. For a hard-core noodle man like me, too many places claim to serve authentic Italian food, only to disappoint. But I knew as soon as I walked into That Little Place—where the rich, sweet smell of

When Loris and Annie say That Little Place by the Lights offers a taste of Italy, they aren't kidding.

tomato sauce conjured memories of my youth—that I was in for something special. And once I got to meet Annie and Loris Buttus and taste their impeccable creations, I knew I was home.

Both Italian immigrants, Loris and Annie moved to Canada to follow their dream of opening a homestyle restaurant. It didn't take long. In just a couple short years they have built an institution with their homemade and authentic pastas, pizzas, and gelato. And please forgive me for saying this, Zia Felicetta, but Annie makes the best damn lasagna I've ever eaten, even if she doesn't fancy herself a chef. For when you put as much love into your food as Annie does, the result is pure perfection.

Much of Annie's secret lies in her Bolognese sauce, which starts with sautéed onions, ground beef, and classic Italian herbs and spices. Then it's tomato sauce, crushed tomatoes, tomato paste, and hours of simmering. Annie says the longer her sauce cooks, the better it tastes.

I knew as soon as I walked into That Little Place that I was in for something special.

Bolognese sauce is a key part of Annie's lasagna, though the addition of béchamel sauce instead of ricotta cheese makes it distinctively creamy. Add to this Annie's homemade lasagna noodles—which are so light and tender you'll swear they're a gift from the heavens—and you've got layer upon layer of pure Italian delight, a lasagna so light you can eat a massive piece and still not feel full. *Mamma mia!*

Annie's lighter-than-air magic is also evident in her homemade gnocchi (say nyoh-kee!), a simple recipe of flour, potatoes, and eggs that takes love, patience, and just the right proportions to hit the bull's eye. And does Annie ever hit it! She boils them for just a few minutes be-

When you have as much fun cooking as Annie does, the result is pure perfection, whether it's fresh pasta, gnocchi, pizza, or dessert.

fore tossing them with her Bolognese sauce. You'd never think that a simple recipe like this could result in such a wonderful feeling, but when you do it all by hand like Annie does, there's nothing better.

That Little Place also serves up a wicked thin-crust pizza, courtesy of their very own stone oven. If you're like me you'll go for a classic cheese number (tomato sauce and mozzarella), but the more risqué among us might try things like the Quattro Formaggi (mozzarella, blue cheese, provolone, Parmesan), Capricciosa (mozzarella, ham, black olives, artichokes, mushrooms), or Mama Anna's (mozzarella, Italian sausage, salami, ham, and bacon).

Since Annie's delectable creations are so damn light, you've got no excuse for avoiding dessert, which might be her hugely popular tiramisù or apple pie. But you're in for a real treat if you try Loris's homemade gelato. Back in the day, Loris ran a gelateria just outside Venice; now he's churning out delicious frozen treats for the people of Huntsville using only the freshest ingredients possible. Blueberries were in season when I was there, and I could taste bits of blueberry skin in the cup Loris fed me. It was the perfect way to end an Italian meal.

Of course, a couple kisses on the cheek couldn't hurt, either, and I'm sure Annie and Loris would be happy to serve those up, too, since everyone who comes through their door is considered family.

I swear Annie does something magical with her lasagna. How else could you eat a piece this massive and not feel full afterwards?

Annie's Gnocchi

Makes: 8 to 10 servings

Annie's Meat Sauce

2 tablespoons vegetable oil

1 tablespoon butter

1 onion, chopped

1 pound ground beef

1 teaspoon each crumbled dried rosemary,
dried oregano, dried parsley, dried basil,
dried thyme, and chili flakes

4 cups canned plum tomatoes

4 cups tomato purée

1 can (13 ounces/369 mL) tomato paste

Salt and pepper

Annie's Gnocchi

4 medium baking potatoes (unpeeled)

2 large eggs, lightly beaten

1/4 teaspoon salt

2 cups all-purpose flour

Meat Sauce

Heat the oil and butter in a large pot over medium heat. Add the onions and cook, stirring
frequently, until they are golden brown. Add the ground beef and cook until brown.

Stir in the rosemary, oregano, parsley, thyme, basil, and chili flakes, then add the plum tomatoes, tomato purée, and tomato paste. Fill each empty can halfway with water and add to
the sauce. Cook, uncovered and stirring occasionally, for 1 1/2 hours or until your preferred
thickness. Season with salt and pepper to taste.

Gnocchi

Boil the potatoes until they are easily pierced with a fork. Drain and let cool. Once cool, peel
them and mash them.

Turn the mashed potatoes out onto a lightly floured work surface. Make a well in the centre
and fill with the eggs and salt. Using a wooden spoon or your hand, start mixing in the
potato from the sides of the well. When all the potato is incorporated, knead the dough,
adding as much flour as needed to make a firm dough.

Divide dough into 4 equal pieces. Dust work surface lightly with flour. With your hands, roll
each piece into a rope about 1/2 inch think. Cut dough into 1/2-inch-long pieces. Place on a
baking sheet dusted with flour while you proceed to shape and cut the rest of the dough.

Bring a large pot of salted water to a boil. Use a bench scraper to scoop up gnocchi and drop
into the boiling water. When the gnocchi rise to the surface, they are ready. Using a slotted
spoon or wire strainer, transfer to a bowl.

Toss gnocchi with Annie's Meat Sauce and serve.

Tre Sorelle

EST. 2004
133 MISSISSAGA STREET EAST
ORILLIA · ON · L3V 5A9
WWW.TRESORELLEORILLIA.COM

Take three hot-blooded Italian women, recipes that go back seven decades, and a dedication to delicious, homestyle meals and you've got Tre Sorelle ("three sisters"), where hand-crafted pasta is the order of the day, and everyone is part of *la famiglia*.

Tre Sorelle started out small, with the sisters selling homemade pasta, meatballs, and sauce at a local farmers' market. Customer response was so intense that they had no choice: a sit-down restaurant was in the stars, and Tre Sorelle was born. Now not only does each sister have a job to do, but other family members have been drawn into the vortex as well.

She's not just a master lasagna maker. She's also a ton of fun to be around. Lisa Partichelli and I ham it up over one of her multi-layered miracles.

Gina White is the pasta queen, specializing in ravioli. Lisa Partichelli also makes pasta, though she is the master sauce maker at Tre Sorelle. Third sister Carla Paluzzi still resides in Toronto, so her involvement in running the restaurant is not as hands-on as that of her sisters, though she is in charge of the website and publicity. Not enough family for you? Throw in matriarch Diane Paluzzi (baker); her husband, Domenic (pasta maker—these guys make a *lot* of pasta!); Lisa's husband, David (helped design the restaurant's interior); and Gina's daughter Miah (rolls the meatballs), and you can see why Tre Sorelle is truly a family affair.

And who else but family would serve you homemade butternut squash ravioli as good as Gina's? She starts by making a sweet and creamy filling of roasted butternut squash, ricotta, Parmesan, and nutmeg. Then there's the dough, another simple recipe Gina could make in her sleep: water, vegetable oil, flour, and semolina flour. After the dough's been kneaded to perfect consistency, it's rolled through a hand roller. From there, each ravioli is lovingly made in Gina's ravioli cutter. Five minutes in a pot of boiling water and you've got little pillows of joy.

What makes these ravioli extra special is the sauce: a sweet and salty mix of sautéed pancetta, caramelized onions, and olive oil. It's a treat you'll come back for again and again.

Pasta is not just Gina's territory, though, as Lisa whips up one of the best lasagnas this side of the Roman Colosseum. Of course the noodles are homemade, which is always the best way to distinguish a good lasagna from a truly great one. Once the layering begins, the fresh pasta is woven with tomato sauce and ricotta cheese. Lisa uses a trick her nonna taught her: she doesn't include ground beef directly in her sauce, but dedicates an entire layer to it. The lasagna is topped with a final

Not only a place to tickle your taste buds, Tre Sorelle is also warm and inviting, happily embracing old-world Italian charm without feeling too much like Nonna's kitchen.

layer of mozzarella and Parmesan, then baked to creamy, meaty perfection. As satisfied customers here will tell you, you can't make food this good unless you really love what you're doing.

Of course there are loads of other pasta options at Tre Sorelle, from homemade manicotti (choose from a variety of fillings, including ricotta, butternut squash, chicken and cheese, or spinach and cheese) to spaghetti and meatballs. And if you're one of those people who'd just rather *not* use a fork and knife, why not try a Tre Sorelle Stromboli, a calzone-like turnover that wraps pizza dough around just about any kind of filling you want, though it's usually sauce, meat, and cheese. I was lucky enough to sample a sausage-and-peppers creation, which piled sautéed red peppers and onions in with Italian sausage, mozzarella, and Nonna's sauce—a warm, crispy, gooey, salty slice of heaven.

I guess that shouldn't come as too much of a surprise, though. When a family works together as well as this one does, paradise is never too far away. And what if the sisters have the odd spat? That just adds to Tre Sorelle's old-world charm.

Tre Sorelle started out small, with the sisters selling homemade pasta, meatballs, and sauce at a local farmers' market.

Stromboli

Makes: 4 stromboli

5 to 6 mild Italian sausages (preferably bought from Tre Sorelle!)
1/4 cup olive oil
3 to 4 large sweet red peppers, thinly sliced
2 onions (any type), thinly sliced
1 tablespoon minced roasted garlic
1/2 teaspoon Italian seasoning
Salt and freshly cracked black pepper
1 pound pizza dough (homemade or store-bought)
1 to 2 cups tomato sauce
3 cups shredded mozzarella cheese
2 cups grated Parmesan cheese
Olive oil
Egg wash (1 egg, beaten)

Preheat oven to 350°F.

In a large skillet over medium-high heat, cook the sausages in olive oil until browned and no longer pink inside. Cut the sausage into chunks and set aside.

Add the peppers and onions to the skillet; cook until they start to soften. Add the roasted garlic, Italian seasoning, and salt and pepper to taste; cook until the peppers and onions are tender.

Stir in the sausages and cook for 2 to 3 minutes. Remove from heat.

Divide pizza dough into 8 equal pieces and shape each piece into a ball. On a floured surface, roll out each ball into a 9-inch circle, about 1/8-inch thick.

Spread some of the tomato sauce down the middle of each circle. Sprinkle about 6 tablespoons of the mozzarella cheese over the line of sauce. Spoon a heaping pile of the sausage mixture over the middle of the stromboli. Top with another 6 tablespoons of mozzarella and 4 tablespoons of Parmesan.

Fold one end of the dough into the centre, and then fold down the opposite to meet it. Press the dough together to seal. Fill the remaining stromboli and transfer to 2 baking sheets. Spritz or lightly brush the stromboli with olive oil and brush with the egg wash.

Bake in two batches for 15 to 20 minutes or until golden brown.

Serve with marinara sauce on the side.

Tunnel Bar-B-Q

EST. 1941
58 PARK STREET EAST
WINDSOR · ON · N9A 3A7
WWW.TUNNELBARBQ.COM

The year was 1941. World War II raged in Europe, *Citizen Kane* was the movie everybody had to see, and the average price of a new house was less than $10,000. It was also the year Tunnel Bar-B-Q was born and hit upon a recipe that has stood the test of time. You see, this Windsor landmark has been preparing meaty ribs and juicy chicken the same way for more than seven decades, and given the devoted following it has among generations of locals and diehard fans from neighbouring Detroit, nothing will be changing any time soon.

One of the secrets to Tunnel's success is the custom rotisserie ovens they've been using since Day 1, which lock in flavour like nobody's business. This is only part of the equation, though, as you can't mention Tunnel Bar-B-Q without also mentioning their famous TBQ sauces, which have created a cult following among barbeque lovers the world over.

Some of the most unique meat toppers you'll ever sample, the sauces are based on the original recipes created by the founders of Tunnel Bar-B-Q, Harry and Helen Racovitis, and the tradition is continued to this day by their son Thom. The sauces come in two varieties, a sweet (which has a pretty good bite to it) and a hot (which has a *really* good bite to it), both of which begin with a base of ketchup, vinegar, molasses, smoked salt, brown sugar, and paprika, and are then jacked up on chef Lee Beneteau's secret sauce blend. TBQ sauce has become such an institution that the restaurant ships it all over the world.

Every good sauce needs a place to park itself, and Tunnel has loads of meaty options. The backbone of culinary offerings here is the ribs, a classic recipe that is as delicious as it is simple. Lee accordions two racks of Ontario pork side ribs onto a dangerously long skewer, then dusts them with smoked salt and paprika. Then they're offered to the gods of the rotisserie for close to an hour, all the while being basted in their own, well, *fat*! The

Just a stone's throw from Detroit, Michigan, the folks at Tunnel Bar-B-Q have one guiding principle: *don't give up value and quality for the sake of a dollar.*

Harry and Helen Racovitis opened Tunnel Bar-B-Q more than seventy years ago. Today it's son Thom—who started working at the restaurant when he was eleven—who continues the family legacy.

ribs are finished off on the charcoal broiler. What you're left with are some of the most delicious pieces of pork you'll ever have the pleasure of popping in your mouth: crispy on the outside, moist and meaty on the inside. In fact, these things are so damn good, they don't need any sauce at all . . . but you'll put it on, anyway.

No barbeque joint would be worth its smoke if it didn't offer up some chicken, and Tunnel does not disappoint with its quarter-chicken and half-chicken options. The birds, which come fresh from a local producer, are as juicy and tender as any you've ever tasted. As with the ribs, chickens are served with Tunnel's signature vinaigrette-based coleslaw (made fresh every morning), crinkle-cut fries, and a dinner roll.

But before you go thinking Tunnel Bar-B-Q is only a chicken-and-ribs joint, let me tell you that the menu here is truly a massive undertaking. Breakfast—served only on weekends—splashes out with frittatas, eggs Benedict, pancakes, omelettes, and breakfast sandwiches. But that's nothing compared to the dinner menu, which throws everything but the kitchen sink at you.

Soup and salad? They got 'em. Burgers and wraps? Got those, too. Seafood? Check. Chicken entrées? Yup. Steaks? Yessir! I was particularly enthralled with their sandwiches, especially the Pulled BBQ'd Pork. Lee starts with a bone-in pork butt, into which he lovingly rubs liquid smoke, smoked salt, and TBQ seasoning. Twelve oven-hours later, and you've got a piece of meat so moist and succulent you can pull it apart with a pair of tongs—which is exactly what he does.

When an order comes in, Lee tosses a portion of the freshly pulled pork into a pan with a heaping helping of TBQ sauce and serves it on a fresh bun the way the barbeque gods intended it to be: by itself! Meat and bread and sauce and . . . my, oh my! Don't ever change, baby.

I'm just happy knowing the taste will stay the same for the next seventy years.

This Windsor landmark has been preparing meaty ribs and juicy chicken the same way for more than seven decades.

5 pounds bone-in pork butt or shoulder with fat

2 tablespoons liquid smoke

2 tablespoons Tunnel BBQ Back Rib Rub (or your favourite dry rub)

2 tablespoons brown sugar

2 tablespoons coarse sea salt

Your favourite bread or rolls

Massage the meat with liquid smoke.

In a small bowl, stir together the rib rub, brown sugar, and salt. Rub mixture all over the meat. Place meat in a nonaluminum pan. Cover and refrigerate for 1 to 2 hours.

Preheat oven to 250°F.

Wrap the meat tightly in wax paper. Then wrap in layers of foil. Transfer to oven and cook for 10 to 12 hours or until a meat thermometer inserted in the centre of the meat registers 170 to 185°F.

Unwrap the meat and, with a pair of forks, pull the meat from the bone. Transfer the meat to a tray to cool.

Pile pulled pork into sandwiches.

Uncle Betty's Diner

EST. 2011
2590 YONGE STREET
TORONTO · ON · M4P 2J3
WWW.UNCLEBETTYS.COM

It may not be as spacious as the Taj Mahal in there, but Uncle Betty's makes use of every square inch. The front windows open entirely to a patio for open-air dining.

If fine dining, dim lighting, and a sophisticated atmosphere are your gig, stay away from Uncle Betty's! This Toronto joint has made a name for itself as a boisterous family eatery where kids are made to feel every bit at home as their parental units, and the food is as fun as the vibe.

I mean, where else can you get eggs Benedict served on a freshly made doughnut or a grilled cheese sandwich stuffed with a slice of meatloaf and some macaroni and cheese for good measure? If you answered "Nowhere else, John!," you're damn right! Uncle Betty's is a Canadian original.

Uncle Betty's is owned by Samara Melanson and her husband, Robert Lewocz, who moved back to Toronto from New York and couldn't resist their desire to open a great diner for people looking for a relaxed, fun meal out. The name comes from Samara's mom and her delicious home cooking. But Betty had a tough side, too, and when she became a bit of a father figure to the children of the extended family, they started calling her Uncle Betty. The name apparently stuck.

Yet Samara and Robert don't limit themselves to Betty's recipes, as one of their most well-known dishes—Betty's Benedict—attests. You're thinking you want breakfast, but you also want a doughnut. Could you have those two things together? Hey . . . substitute a freshly baked doughnut for the English muffin, then top with peameal bacon, poached eggs, and homemade hollandaise sauce. The result is a sweet and savoury combination that will knock your socks off.

You can always buy doughnuts as, well, just doughnuts (Uncle Betty's is the first place in Toronto to serve Dreesen's Donuts, which are hugely popular in the Hamptons), but why bother? When you can get something like Betty's Benedict or the Breakwich—an egg and cheese breakfast sandwich served on a doughnut—there's no reason to! If doughnuts aren't your thing, Uncle Betty's Stuffed French Toast jams mascarpone, ricotta cheese, and fresh blueberries between two slices of challah bread that have been egg-dipped and grilled to perfection.

Clever combinations also find themselves on the lunch menu at Uncle Betty's, where chef Paul Lampa concocts the mother of all comfort food, the Ultimate Grilled Cheese. The Ultimate is a breathtaking combo of a grilled cheese sandwich wrapped around a slice of Paul's homemade meatloaf and homemade mac and cheese. Happy munchers here call it a grilled cheese on steroids, the sandwich that combines all three food groups: gooey, meaty, and bready. If you're on a bread-and-meatloaf-free diet, order the Ultimate Macaroni and Cheese, a classic dish taken to the extreme with truffle oil and crispy pancetta.

For me, Uncle Betty's Ultimate Grilled Cheese is perfect. I love grilled cheese, meatloaf, and mac and cheese, but I don't have time to eat them separately. Problem solved!

Given Uncle Betty's young-at-heart personality, it's no surprise that desserts are a big part of what they do. Local ice cream seems to flow in buckets to customers' tables, in some of the most exciting flavours imaginable. Then there's the famous Twink "eh"—no relation to those mass-produced yellow things you buy at the corner store at three in the morning.

No sirree, the Twink "eh" is a finger-like cake that can be enjoyed in one of two varieties. The red velvet version is a spongy, fluffy red velvet cake stuffed with a roasted marshmallow filling. Chocoholics most definitely turn to the double chocolate joint, a chocolate cake injected with a decadent chocolate ganache.

So if you wanna feel like a kid again—or just give yourself a little belly hug after a long week on the job—there's no place like Uncle Betty's, where food and fun go hand in hand.

Shape and name aside, there is no common ground between Uncle Betty's ridiculously delicious homemade Twink "ehs" and those things that can reputedly survive a nuclear war.

Where else can you get eggs Benedict served on a freshly made doughnut?

Ricotta and Mascarpone Blueberry Stuffed French Toast

Makes: 4 to 6 servings

Filling

1 pkg (8 ounces/250 g) mascarpone
  cheese, softened
1 pkg (8 ounces/250 g) ricotta cheese
1/4 cup icing sugar
1 teaspoon vanilla extract
1/2 cup fresh or frozen blueberries

Assembly

Icing sugar
Seasonal berries
Butter
Maple syrup

French Toast

4 eggs
2 cups milk
1 tablespoon cinnamon
1 teaspoon sugar (optional)
Pinch of salt
Dash of vanilla extract
10 to 12 slices challah,
  cut 1/2 inch thick

Filling

In a medium bowl, beat together the mascarpone, ricotta, sugar, and vanilla until smooth; fold in the blueberries.

French Toast

Preheat oven to 150°F.

In a shallow dish, lightly beat the eggs. Stir in the milk, cinnamon, sugar (if using), salt, and vanilla.

Lightly coat a large skillet with a thin layer of butter, and heat over medium-low heat. Working only with as many slices as you will be cooking at one time, dunk the bread into the egg mixture, letting slices soak up the liquid for a few seconds, then turn to coat the other side.

Transfer bread to the skillet. Cook until the bottom is golden brown. Turn and brown the other side. Place French toast on a baking sheet, cover loosely with foil, and keep warm in the oven. Repeat with the remaining bread.

Assembly

Spread each slice of French toast with some of the filling. Fold over each slice on a diagonal. Place the French toast on plates; dust with icing sugar and garnish with seasonal berries. Serve hot with butter and maple syrup.

Chef Paul Lampa took a break from the high-stress world of fine cuisine to join the Uncle Betty family, and now his laugh often echoes through the kitchen.

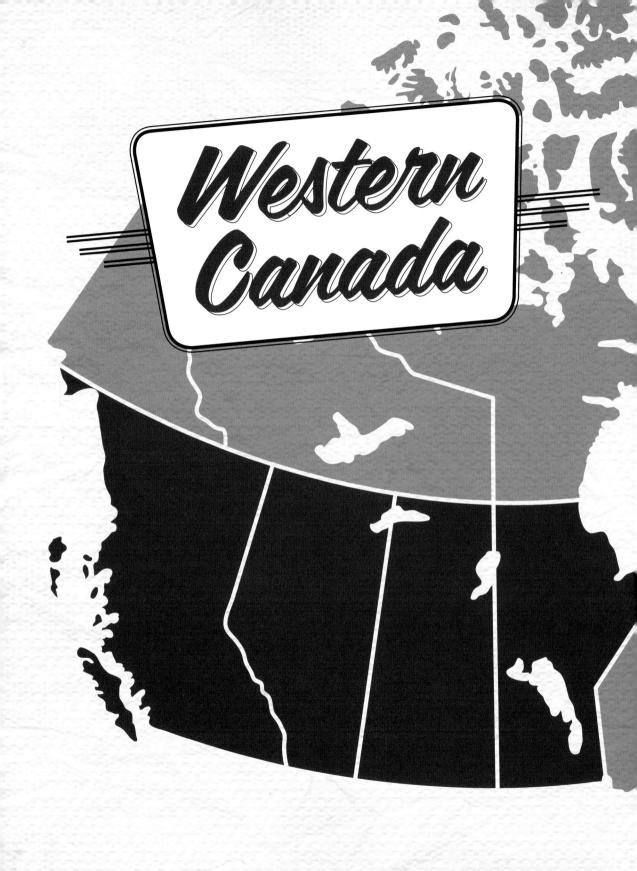

Western Canada

Argo Café

EST. 1954
1836 ONTARIO STREET
VANCOUVER · BC · V5T 2W6
WWW.ARGOCAFE.CA

The way I see it, there are out-of-the-way places that require lots of effort to reach, and then there are out-of-the-way places that you can walk by a million times without really noticing. The Argo Café falls into the latter category. Until you eat there, that is. Then you'll never forget.

The Argo is a neighbourhood institution that's developed a personality for serving gourmet food in a humble setting. Tiny and eclectic, the restaurant still looks much like it did when it opened fifty years ago, the original counter and swivel stools a focal point of its interior. Owners Denis Larouche (who's also the Argo's chef) and his brother-in-law Kirby Wong bought the Argo in 2004 from its original owner, though they hardly came to the restaurant business blindly: Kirby's family has been in restaurants for decades and Denis is a Quebec-trained chef. To add to the all-in-the-family theme, Denis's wife, Lynda (Kirby's sister), is also an executive chef, and their children are always helping out in one way or another.

Why does this man look so worried? Chef and Argo co-owner Denis Larouche makes sure I do the job just right.

Though the Argo features a full menu chock full of classic diner food, devotees of the eatery know to look first for the chalkboard specials Denis creates every day, for this is where the magic lies. Diner food, you say? How about Panko and Pistachio Crusted Halibut? Not your thing? A Grilled Chicken Cordon Bleu Burger, perhaps? Or maybe Seafood Pasta in Saffron Cream Sauce? How about Bacon-Wrapped Pork Tenderloin, which comes smothered in a spicy peppercorn sauce?

If you're really, really lucky, you may wander by the Argo when Denis is making his renowned Duck Confit, a cured duck leg that is poached in its own fat and finished on the griddle to crisp up the skin. When I was there, Denis topped the duck with a sweet and tangy mélange

Only forty-six people can fit inside the Argo Café at a time, but you can bet the farm they'll all be sporting ear-to-ear grins after sampling some of the best home-cooked meals money can buy!

of blueberries, lime juice, and honey, but he has been known to use a variety of sauces to accent the moist and tender bird.

On the everyday menu, the Argo's Spaghetti Carbonara is an unbelievably good combination of pasta, bacon, and prawns, topped with a perfect egg-and-cream sauce. I know I shouldn't say this in front of my Italian relatives, but I swear it was one of the best I've ever had.

Another everyday meal (if there is such a thing) at the Argo is their Mexican Poutine, which they also call Chicken con Queso on Fries. The dish is a delightful twist on poutine, with tender chunks of chicken breast, lime juice, and two types of cheese served over a mound of hand-cut fries. Yet like any good poutine, what makes the Argo's Mexican twist so special is its gravy, which uses three different types of chili peppers (ancho, Anaheim, and chipotle). Served with avocado slices on top (a $1 option), it's your own private fiesta, right inside your mouth.

Though it may all sound painfully exotic to gringos like me, these kinds of meals are just another day on the job for the men and women of the Argo, where diner classics and five-star fare coexist peacefully, side by side. As Denis, Kirby, and Lynda have been known to say, the Argo is *the* place in Vancouver for slow food . . . fast!

Though the Argo features a full menu chock full of classic diner food, devotees of the eatery know to look first for the chalkboard specials Denis creates every day, for this is where the magic lies.

Arriba! The Argo's Mexican Poutine is a beautiful thing to behold, yes, but even better to chow down on.

Duck Confit with Blueberry Gastrique

Makes: 4 servings

Timing note: The duck must marinate overnight.

Duck Confit

1/4 cup sea salt (or your favourite salt)

2 garlic cloves, minced

4 sprigs fresh thyme (or 2 teaspoons dried)

4 duck legs

4 cups duck fat (available at gourmet food stores)

Blueberry Gastrique

1/2 cup honey

1/4 cup lime juice

2 cups fresh or frozen blueberries

Duck Confit

Combine the salt, garlic, and thyme in a bowl. If using fresh thyme, rub the sprigs together to release the flavour. Add the duck legs and rub the salt mixture all over them. Place the duck legs in a baking dish and cover with plastic wrap. Refrigerate overnight.

Preheat oven to 300°F.

Melt the duck fat in a saucepan over medium-low heat. Pour the fat over the seasoned duck legs to cover them completely.

Cover with foil and bake for 2 hours. Check for doneness by poking a knife into the leg. If the knife slides easily into the meat, the duck is done; if not, continue to bake, testing every 30 minutes. The larger the legs, the longer they will need in the oven.

If not serving immediately, cool the duck in the fat to room temperature and then refrigerate, covered, for up to 2 weeks.

When ready to serve, remove legs from duck fat, place legs on a baking sheet, and bake at 325°F for 30 to 40 minutes, until the skin is brown and crispy.

Blueberry Gastrique

Heat blueberries in a saucepan over medium-high heat until they soften. Add honey and bring to a boil. Add lime juice and continue to boil for 3–5 minutes, until gastrique has the consistency of a runny jam.

Serve the duck legs drizzled with the blueberry gastrique.

Bacon-Wrapped Pork Tenderloin

Makes: 4 servings

2 pork tenderloins (12 ounces each), cut in half crosswise

4 slices bacon

2 tablespoons unsalted butter

1 tablespoon minced shallots

2 tablespoons green peppercorns in brine, drained

1 tablespoon cognac

1/2 cup demi-glace (available at gourmet grocery stores)

2 cups whipping cream

Salt and black pepper

Preheat oven to 400°F.

Wrap each tenderloin portion in a bacon strip; skewer with a toothpick to secure the bacon. Set aside.

In a medium saucepan over medium heat, melt 1 tablespoon of the butter. Add the shallots and cook until they begin to produce aromas. Add the peppercorns and cook for 1 to 2 minutes.

Add the cognac. Using a match, carefully light the cognac. Flambé the shallots and peppercorns until very little alcohol remains. Add the demi-glace, bring to a boil, and stir in the whipping cream. Simmer for 12 to 15 minutes or until the sauce coats a spoon thickly. Stir in the remaining 1 tablespoon butter. Remove from heat and set aside, keeping warm.

Heat a large ovenproof skillet over high heat. Sear the tenderloins, turning them to brown all sides. Season with salt and pepper to taste. Transfer the pan to the oven and roast the tenderloins for 12 to 15 minutes or until just a hint of pink remains inside and juices run clear.

To serve, pour the sauce over the pork tenderloins.

Bistro Dansk

EST. 1977
63 SHERBROOK STREET
WINNIPEG · MB · R3C 2B2
WWW.BISTRODANSK.COM

You know you've truly found your calling when you dance on the job . . . and you're not a dancer. That's Paul Vocadlo, the owner and chef at Bistro Dansk, which has been serving up Danish specialties since he was knee-high to his mother's apron strings. And it doesn't matter one stitch that Paul owes his heritage to the Czech Republic. He's been cooking Danish dishes like schnitzel, kylling, and frikadeller (hey, can we actually say that in print?) for more than twenty years, and he's damn good at it! Throw in a few Czech specialties and you've got an international range of reasons to stop by the Bistro Dansk.

Established in 1977 by a Danish couple, Bistro Dansk was purchased by Paul's parents just a year after it opened. Paul joined his mother in the kitchen when he was only thirteen and made a point of learning all her secrets. Ten years later, Paul and his wife, Pamela, took over; now Paul is a virtual one-man show in the kitchen, while Pamela manages the front of house.

Like he's done every morning for more than twenty years, Paul arrives at the restaurant by 6:30 to start baking French bread and get the stockpot boiling. Then it's off to the market to pick up the day's produce. Paul is back at the

Many of Bistro Dansk's regulars have been coming here for more than twenty years. As Pamela Vocadlo tells it, some who held her children as babies are now served by them.

Dansk by 10, flattening pork for schnitzel, frying crêpes for the lunch rush, and pulling warm baguettes out of the oven. Pamela is there almost as long, and their three children help out as servers, too.

One of Paul's specialties is Kylling, a Danish stuffed chicken recipe that's been handed down for generations. Paul gets his chickens delivered fresh every morning. Each half is lovingly laid over a mound of Paul's handmade stuffing, a sweet and savoury blend of sautéed onions, celery, dried apricots, walnuts, and spices. I couldn't believe how tender the chicken was under its won-

If eating these Palachinkas isn't enough to get you dancing, you just need to say it a few times. Pal-a-chink-a! Pal-a-chink-a! Pal-a-chink-a!

derfully crispy skin. For a guy whose favourite part of a turkey dinner is the stuffing, I was on Comfort Cloud 9.

You get the same feeling from Paul's pork schnitzel, which has been a customer fave since Day 1. Paul starts with rich pork tenderloin, which he beats flat with a tenderizing hammer before rubbing it with a special mix of spices. From there the schnitzel is dipped in batter, coated in bread crumbs, and fried until golden brown, ridiculously crispy, and tastier than any pig ever dreamt of being. Squirt on some fresh lemon juice and you'll swear you're dancing in the streets of Copenhagen with Paul at your side.

Yet what makes the schnitzel platter even more spectacular than the two gigantic pieces of fried goodness in front of you are the side dishes, Paul's lip-smacking Potato Salad and Sweet and Sour Cabbage.

The potato salad is rich and creamy, with lots of mayonnaise, green onions, lemon, and weighty chunks of chopped pickles. And if you think cabbage is just cabbage, you've never had the Bistro Dansk special, which is so popular that customers actually ask to substitute *for* it. Paul is happy to oblige, as he cooks up huge batches of the stuff. OK, so he dresses it up with pounds of chopped bacon, but I'm not holding that against him. As I always say, if you can add bacon to something . . . *then add bacon to something*!

Not everything is Danish at Bistro Dansk. Paul's Palachinkas are a tribute to his Czech heritage, and a delicious one at that! These crêpe-like pancakes are filled with a sautéed mélange that reminds me of the inside of a chicken pot pie, then rolled up and put in the oven to bake. Paul says the secret to the creamy filling is white wine, but I'm not interested in secrets . . . just hand me a fork and get out of the way!

Paul has been cooking Danish dishes like schnitzel, kylling, and frikadeller for more than twenty years, and he's damn good at it!

If being happy were an Olympic sport, Paul Vocadlo would be Canada's flag-bearer. This dude loves what he does . . . and it shows.

Kylling with
Potato Salad

Makes: 6 servings

Timing note: Boil the potatoes for the salad the night before and chill overnight.

Potato Salad

2 pounds Yukon Gold potatoes (unpeeled)

1 large kosher-style dill pickle, finely diced

1/2 cup thinly sliced green onions

1/4 cup mayonnaise

1/2 teaspoon each salt and pepper

Kylling

1/4 cup canola oil

1 cup chopped onion

1 cup chopped celery

1 heaping teaspoon poultry seasoning

1/2 cup slivered dried apricots

2 cups chicken stock

2 cups fine dry bread crumbs

1/2 cup coarsely chopped walnuts

2 eggs, beaten

1 teaspoon each salt and pepper

3 small roasting chickens

Potato Salad

Boil potatoes until tender. Drain, and refrigerate overnight.

Peel and dice the potatoes. Transfer to a large bowl and add the pickle (squeeze out a little of the juice), green onions (reserve some for garnish), mayonnaise, and salt and pepper. Mix together well, and chill until needed.

Garnish with reserved green onions.

Kylling

Preheat oven to 375°F. Line a baking sheet with parchment paper (or grease it).

In a large skillet, heat the oil over medium heat. Add the onions and celery and cook until softened, about 5 minutes. Stir in poultry seasoning and apricots, then add the chicken stock. Cover and simmer for 3 to 5 minutes, until the apricots are plump.

Transfer the mixture to a medium bowl and add the bread crumbs, walnuts, eggs, and salt and pepper. Mix together well, and then divide stuffing into 6 equal portions.

Cut chickens in half by cutting through the backbone and straight through the breastbone. Stuff 1 portion of the stuffing into each chicken half. Place on the baking sheet stuffing side down. Brush the chickens with canola oil and season with a little salt and pepper.

Roast for 45 minutes or until golden brown and juices run clear when pierced.

Serve with the potato salad.

Blondies

EST. 1990
1969 MAIN STREET
WINNIPEG · MB · R2V 2B7

The sign on the building might say Blondies, but to anyone who frequents this little diner, it's all Sandy's. And I mean *all*.

Sandy Doyle is the owner and chef at Blondies, a tiny joint that's been serving up big-time taste in Winnipeg for more than two decades. Opinionated, sharp, and quirky in an infinitely lovable way, Sandy is the life force behind what tons of people consider the best burger joint in the city. Just make sure you follow the rules. What rules, you ask? Open your eyes—they're written all over the walls. "If you order water, you might want to actually drink it!"

Such is life here at Blondies, where Sandy is not afraid to make her feelings known, no matter who might be dining there. She's one of those rare characters who can abuse people so lovingly that they keep coming back for more. In fact, it's on those days when you come into Blondies and *don't* get verbal whiplash that you start to wonder if something's wrong.

There's certainly nothing wrong with the food at Blondies, where burgers are the highlight of a menu that doesn't try to be anything it's not. Sandy gets freshly ground beef delivered daily by a local butcher, then adds Worcestershire sauce, seasoning salt, garlic powder, and fresh eggs. If this sounds overly simple to you, it's because you haven't considered the secret ingredient Sandy's been perfecting since Day 1: the grill. You see, Sandy is fiercely proud of the fact that her grill

You've got a looong way to go, boys! The Nine-Pound Burger is a ridiculous undertaking for two people, let alone the occasional lunatics who try it on their own.

has been seasoned with the juice of a million patties, and you can taste that history in every bite.

You can buy a Blondies burger with a patty as small as 2 ounces, though her quarter-pounders are most popular. From there, the sky's the limit, baby! You can enjoy burgers with

1/2-pound patties, but those are nothing compared to the 1-pound, 2-pound, 3-pound, 6-pound, and 9-pound monsters she also offers. At their core, Sandy's burgers are deliciously simple: Cheddar and bacon on a freshly baked bun with lettuce, tomato, mayonnaise, mustard, and sweet relish. But there's something about the taste that keeps you coming back for more. I'm guessing it's the grill.

That special Blondies taste is even evident in the Nine-Pound Burger, though you might lose the taste because you've got such a bad case of the meat sweats.

I don't care that Sandy learned how to cook on an old wood stove in the middle of the northern Ontario bush. Her food—like this massive Club House Sandwich—is world class.

This goliath bears a close resemblance to Sandy's other meat creations, just on steroids. The burger consists of two pizza-sized patties served on a custom-made bun. Each is covered in fifteen slices of processed cheese and about twenty strips of bacon. If your heart doesn't stop just thinking about it, you should perhaps pay heed to her customers, who like to call it a heart attack on a plate.

Maybe that's why only a few people have ever attempted the Nine-Pounder themselves, even if they get it for free (and their picture on the Wall of Fame) if they finish it in less than two hours (there may also be a free colonoscopy in there, but don't quote me on that). Not surprisingly, nobody ever has. Most patrons take a communal approach to the beast, cutting it like a cake and eating but a sliver. Just make sure you order it (and pay for it) in advance, or you'll get a good stern talking to!

Burgers aren't the only thing Sandy does. Blondies also serves up classic dishes like perogies (Sandy hates 'em!), hotdogs (10-inch European wieners served with bacon, cheese, mustard, relish, and fried or raw onions), sandwiches, homemade chili, and poutine.

But nothing—*nothing*—finishes off a Blondies meal like Sandy's universally famous milkshakes, which are made with *seven* scoops of ice cream, fresh fruit, and a dash of milk. You can choose from chocolate, strawberry, raspberry, banana, blueberry, mandarin orange, pineapple, cinnamon, peanut butter, or any combination you can dream up. I had the strawberry, which is brain-poppingly good. I sucked on that bad boy for all I was worth, but it was so thick I nearly ruptured a blood vessel.

Just make sure you've got the cash. As Sandy's rules state: "Best shakes you've ever tasted. $10 for plain and $2 for extras. If you can't afford it, don't order it!!!!"

Sandy is the life force behind what tons of people consider the best burger joint in the city. Just make sure you follow the rules.

Note: You will need an extra-large spatula to flip the burgers.

Patties

10 pounds ground beef (meat will shrink while cooking)

1 cup Worcestershire sauce

1/2 cup seasoning salt

1 teaspoon garlic salt

8 to 13 eggs, lightly beaten (depending on how thick the meat grind is)

Assembly

Large 3-layer bun

Mayonnaise

Ketchup

Mustard

Relish

Lettuce

Tomato slices

2 onions, sliced

Sliced mozzarella or Cheddar cheese

40 pieces of cooked bacon

Burgers

Preheat grill to medium.

Mix the beef, Worcestershire sauce, seasoning salt, and garlic salt together in a large bowl.
  Add 8 eggs to the mixture and mix together. Continue to add eggs, 1 at a time, until the meat
  holds together. Shape into 2 large patties.

Grill the patties, turning once, for 10 minutes on each side.

Microwave the patties on High for 10 minutes to ensure the meat is cooked through.

Assembly

Spread mayo, ketchup, mustard, and relish on the bottom bun. Top with half the lettuce,
  tomato, and onion. Top with one 4 1/2-pound burger. Place cheese and 20 pieces of bacon
  on top.

Place middle bun on top.

Spread mayo, ketchup, mustard, and relish on the middle bun and place it on top of the burger.
  Top with the remaining lettuce, tomato, and onion. Top with the other 4 1/2-pound burger.
  Place cheese and remaining bacon on top. Place remaining bun on top.

Boon Burger Café

EST. 2010
79 SHERBROOK STREET
WINNIPEG · MB · R3C 2B2
WWW.BOONBURGER.CA

Riddle me this: when is meat not meat? Answer: when it's a burger served at the Boon Burger Café, a vegan restaurant whose customers sometimes have to visit more than once before they realize the patty on their bun isn't meat at all! But when you whip up tasty, crispy, and exotic blends like Boon Burger does, it doesn't matter if you're a herbivore, omnivore, or carnivore. Nobody ever leaves dissatisfied . . . or hungry!

Boon Burger is the brainchild of wife-and-husband team Anneen duPlessis and Tomas Sohlberg, who were always big fans of North American burgers and fries, just not the ingredients. So they poured their passion (and restaurant experience) into creating their own version of the ubiquitous meal that can be enjoyed by everyone.

And they have! Today, their little eatery welcomes everyone with a taste for the extraordinary. Maybe that's why Boon was voted Winnipeg's Best Burger in 2010, a resounding victory for the underdog in a city that loves its ground beef.

The Boon offers customers a menu of thirteen burgers. One of the most popular is the Thanksgiving Burger, which some describe as a family dinner in every bite. The foundation is Boon's White Patty (one of four vegan patty styles featured here), a blend of grated tofu, brown rice, oats, onions, garlic, mustard, and a secret spice mix that looks suspiciously like salt and pepper. The patty is then coated in crispy potato crumbs and baked.

The surprisingly crispy burger is served on a freshly baked (in house, of course) organic whole-grain bun, topped with homemade vegan mayonnaise, cranberry sauce, caramelized onions, maple-glazed yams, and lettuce. But what brings you right back to the dinner table at your grandmother's house is the vegan brown gravy, which tastes as good as any beef-based one you've ever eaten.

This is a place of open-mindedness and inclusion. Owners Tomas and Anneen welcome everyone to their vegan restaurant, and have been overwhelmed by the influx of customers since opening day.

Burgers take on an Eastern flair with Boon's Bombay Talkie Burger, which features the funky fresh Buddha Patty, a soy-free groove perfect for burger lovers with gluten allergies. Then comes sweet and tangy Bombay Sauce, lettuce, tomatoes, cucumbers, and red onions, followed by vegan cheese and tofu bacon.

Hold on there, Johnny boy . . . did you just say tofu *bacon*?

Indeed I did! "Bacun," to be exact. You see, Tomas realized a long time ago that it's the smoky flavour and saltiness that makes bacon what it is. So he thinly slices extra-firm tofu, then marinates it in soy sauce, liquid smoke, chili, sugar, nutritional yeast, and oil. And OK, so it's missing the pig part of the recipe, but put it on a burger and you'd swear you were eating the "real" thing.

If it's a meaty bite you crave, the signature Boon Burger uses Tomas's genius and what I'm sure is a little bit of black magic to transform a blend of brown rice, oats, tofu, spices, and buckets of cremini mushrooms into beef's stunt double:

The master at work! Tomas Sohlberg watches carefully and the cameraman documents the action as I prepare a baking tray for yet another batch of Boon Burger delights.

the Boon Beefy Patty. The Boon Burger is served on a freshly baked bun with homemade vegan mayonnaise (no eggs), Dijon mustard, caramelized onions, sliced cucumber, lettuce, and tomatoes. The final touch is Tomas's homemade peach chutney, which wraps the burger in a package so tasty you'll wonder how you got hooked on beef in the first place.

The vegan genius of Tomas and Anneen doesn't stop with their burgers: they also fool unsuspecting diners with a Chili Cheese Dog (a jumbo vegan dog topped with smoky bean chili and vegan cheese), Fries (tossed with sesame seeds and baked), Not the Same Ol' Poutine (no dairy in this cheese and no meat in this gravy!), and even Chili Cheese Fries. And if you thought dessert was out of the question, you haven't tried the Boon's soft-serve coconut milk ice cream.

It's just another day on the job at the Boon Burger Café, where the unexpected is expected.

Boon Burger uses Tomas's genius and what I'm sure is a little bit of black magic to transform a blend of brown rice, oats, tofu, spices, and buckets of cremini mushrooms into beef's stunt double.

1 tablespoon olive oil

1 large onion, sliced

2 tablespoons minced fresh ginger

1 tablespoon minced garlic

1/4 cube vegetable bouillon

2 tablespoons curry powder

1 tablespoon turmeric

1 teaspoon ground cumin

1 teaspoon hot pepper flakes

1/4 cup tomato paste

2 tablespoons water

2 cans (19 ounces/540 mL each) chickpeas, drained and rinsed

2 cups cooked brown rice

1 cup potato crumbs or dry bread crumbs

1/4 cup brown rice flour

1/2 cup chopped fresh cilantro

2 tablespoons lemon juice

1 tablespoon salt

Preheat oven to 375°F. Line a baking sheet with parchment paper and oil the paper.

In a large saucepan, combine the olive oil, onion, ginger, garlic, bouillon cube, curry powder, turmeric, cumin, hot pepper flakes, tomato paste, and water. Cook over medium heat for 45 minutes, stirring often, as spices will burn easily.

Remove from heat and add the chickpeas, brown rice, potato crumbs, rice flour, cilantro, lemon juice, and salt. Stir well.

Process 3 cups of the mixture in a food processor until smooth. Stir the processed mixture back into the rest of the burger mix. This is the "glue" that holds everything together.

Shape into 12 burgers and arrange on the baking sheet. Drizzle with olive oil. Bake for 30 minutes, flipping patties halfway. When done, the patties will have started to set and become firm, like a cookie, and the edges will be slightly golden.

Serve burgers right out of the oven or reheat on a panini press.

Assembly Recommendation

Spread sweet tangy Bombay sauce (mayo, ketchup, garlic, barbeque sauce, mustard) on a bun and top burger with vegetarian bacon, Daiya brand cheddar (or other vegetarian cheese), tomatoes, cucumbers, red onions, and lettuce.

Chuckwagon Cafe & Cattle Company

EST. 1973
105 SUNSET BOULEVARD
TURNER VALLEY · AB · TOL 2A0
WWW.CHUCKWAGONCAFE.CA

The Chuckwagon Cafe has had several incarnations since it first opened in 1973, but it took current owner Terry Myhre to put it on the map. Terry bought the Chuckwagon in 1998, dropped the Korean fare it was serving at the time, and focused on his bread and butter: here in cowboy country, classic western dishes are the food du jour.

It wasn't long before Terry became dissatisfied with the quality of beef he was getting, though. Not the kind of man to sit around, he decided to do something about it. Now Terry owns a ranch near the restaurant, where he raises his own cattle. Terry doesn't have to wonder where the Chuckwagon's meat is coming from anymore, because he raises it himself!

In case you haven't figured it out, the Chuckwagon is all about the beef. And although they're open only for breakfast and lunch, burgers and steaks are king, no matter what time of day you're enjoying your meal.

There's no cattle inside that barn, though owner Terry Myhre's ranch isn't far off, as the saddles, ropes, and cowboy hats inside attest.

Take, for example, the Chuckwagon's spin on a breakfast classic: the Flat Iron Steak Benedict.

Sure, you get your poached eggs and hollandaise sauce (Terry serves them on a nice soft croissant instead of an English muffin), but what makes this dish extraordinary is the layer that comes between the two: four slices of gently fried beef tenderloin (it's a muscle the cows don't use that often, Terry says). The meat is so tender that the knife just floats through it, and the taste is out of this world.

Speaking of beef (hey, did I mention beef?), the Chuckwagon also serves up a classic Steak and Eggs that makes everything else out there seem downright ordinary. Terry's beef is dry-aged for twenty-four days, compared with the one day of aging that grocery-store beef sees, and never

The meat is so tender that the knife just floats through it, and the taste is out of this world.

gets growth hormones. At 8 or 9 ounces, these steaks are enough to fill any cowboy's boots. For those of you who really, really don't want steak with your breakfast, though, the Chuckwagon can accommodate with omelettes, breakfast burritos, huevos rancheros, or pancakes.

Lunch at the Chuckwagon is a beefy affair, where Terry's burgers are as homemade as any you'll find anywhere. That's because he uses chuck roast and top sirloin from his own herd and grinds it himself. Then he adds mustard, Worces-
tershire sauce, onion powder, chopped garlic, a few secret spices, and a little bit of honey. As if the meat alone wasn't enough to give you the most suc-culent burger that's ever passed your lips—and it is—Chuckwagon's patties are mixed and formed by hand, which is said to keep the meat as tender as possible.

Rather than throw hundreds of burger options at his customers, Terry chooses to let the meat do the talkin'. So you can get the Regular Burger (a traditional array of relish, mustard, mayo, lettuce, and tomato), or splash out with the House Burger, which adds bacon, mushrooms, onions, and cheese to the operation. The Mushroom and Swiss Burger is your only other choice, but no matter which you go for, get ready for an explosion of beef taste in your mouth like you've never experienced before.

One guy in this picture is a Member of the Order of Canada, the other likes pasta. Now . . . can you guess which one is legendary singer Ian Tyson and which one is me?

And in case you're wondering, yes, there are items on the menu that *don't* include beef—such as the Chicken Club and Grilled Cheese sandwiches. But not the soup. It's a Beef Barley that Terry's been perfecting for years. He knows that the key to any good soup is the stock, and when you're tossing hunks of your own sliced chuck roast into the pot, you know it's going to be good. And hot damn! It is!

When all is said and done, the tongue is hankering for something sweet, and the Chuckwagon does not disappoint with its Beef-Filled Doughnuts and Steak Cupcakes.

OK, I was kidding about the dessert part. But if Terry ever does decide to throw some beef inside a deep-fried dough ball, I'll be the first one in line.

Beef and Barley Soup

Makes: 12 servings

1 tablespoon canola oil

1 tablespoon unsalted butter

3 pounds chuck roast or blade steaks,
  sliced 1 inch thick

2 pounds beef bones (shank, neck,
  or oxtail)

2 onions, chopped

3 stalks celery, chopped

3 carrots, chopped

4 garlic cloves, finely chopped

1 cup dry red wine

2 quarts low-sodium beef stock

1/2 teaspoon dried thyme

2 bay leaves

1/2 cup pearl barley

Salt and pepper

Preheat oven to 300°F.

Heat the oil and butter in a Dutch oven over medium heat. Working in batches so you don't crowd the pot, brown the beef and bones all over. Transfer as browned to a plate.

Add half of the onions, celery, carrots, and garlic; sauté for 10 minutes. Add the red wine and reduce by half or until syrupy.

Return the beef and bones to the pot and add the beef stock, thyme, and bay leaves. Cover, transfer to the oven, and cook for 3 1/2 hours.

Skim off any fat that may have risen to the top. Discard the bones. Remove the meat, shred it, and return it to the pot. Add the barley and the remaining onions, celery, carrots, and garlic. Cover and return to the oven for another 1 1/2 hours or until the barley is cooked and the meat and vegetables are tender.

Skim off any fat that may have risen to the top and season with salt and pepper to taste.

Huevos Rancheros

Makes: 4 servings

4 (8-inch) flour tortillas

1/3 cup tomato salsa

1 tablespoon unsalted butter

4 eggs

2 cups refried beans (optional)

1 1/2 cups diced fresh tomatoes

1/3 cup sliced green onions

1 cup shredded mixed Cheddar and
   Monterey Jack cheese

Sliced banana peppers (optional)

Chopped fresh cilantro (optional)

Salt and black pepper

Preheat broiler.

Warm the tortillas in the microwave.

Warm the salsa in a small saucepan over medium-low heat. Warm the refried beans (if using)
   in a second small saucepan over medium-low heat.

In a nonstick skillet, melt the butter, then fry the eggs sunny side up (although any style will do).

Arrange the tortillas on a baking sheet. Top each tortilla with some of the warm salsa and
   refried beans (if using); top with an egg. Top with tomatoes, green onions, cheeses, and banana
   peppers and cilantro to taste (if using).

Broil until the cheese melts. Season with salt and pepper to taste.

Deja Vu Cafe

EST. 2007
16 HIGH STREET EAST
MOOSE JAW · SK · S6H 0B7
WWW.DEJAVUCAFE.CA

What is it about the combination of a deep-fryer and, well, just about anything you can drop into it that keeps people coming back for more? At Moose Jaw's Deja Vu Cafe, owner Brandon Richardson has one approach when it comes to food: let's deep-fry this sucker! And judging by the devout following he's built in a relatively short time, it's a philosophy that fellow Moose Javians believe in, too. (C'mon, people. You *did* know that a person from Moose Jaw is called a Moose Javian, right? What were you expecting? Moose Jawite? Moose Jawon?)

After almost twenty years at a local cable company, Brandon woke up one morning to find out he was being laid off. Just a few weeks later, he heard of a restaurant for sale. Being the spontaneous and carefree guy that he is, Brandon bought it, and Moose Jaw's new favourite deep-fried destination was born.

Chicken is the highlight of a menu that never takes itself too seriously. Deja Vu's Strip Dinner is a ridiculously huge basketful of love, with six chicken breast strips served alongside a second basket of freshly cut russet potato fries and a dish of homemade coleslaw. Yet unlike similar meals at other eateries, this one lets the meat do the talking; each strip is lightly coated in a seasoned flour mix before it hits the oil.

If choosing your entrée is easy at Deja Vu, selecting your dipping sauce is anything but. The reason? Brandon offers more than seventy of them. And the sauce menu is always growing, thanks to Brandon's seemingly infinite creativity. Whether he's trying out new combinations or simply tweaking old

That's a lotta sauce! The folks at Deja Vu offer more than seventy different dipping sauces to accompany their deep-fried delights.

favourites, Brandon's sauces are legendary around these parts.

Exotic sauce creations also come home to roost in the Wing Dinner, another in a long litany of deep-fried Deja Vu delights. The massive wings come twelve to an order (good luck finishing them!), and are battered the same way as the strips. When done, they're tossed in the customer's choice of sauce or dry toppings (Déjà Vu has fifteen dry flavours on its sauce menu) and served alongside a basket of fries. Tender, juicy, and über-meaty, these wings are the biggest and baddest around!

It seems everything at Deja Vu is the product of Brandon's preferred method of food preparation. The Kebob Basket is chicken on a stick, yes, but Brandon first batters the chicken breast pieces and then deep-fries them! Think chicken tenders on a skewer. The Rib Dinner starts with a full pound of boneless pork riblets, battered and tossed in the deep-fryer. Locals in the know say they're best with the Sweet Heat (Thai sweet chili) or Passion (honey garlic with extra heat) sauce. If you're feeling a distinct lack of vegetable matter in your Deja Vu diet, fear not! Brandon's Deep Fried Pickle is loaded with all the vitamins and minerals you need.

It should come as no surprise to learn that Brandon's frying fetish makes its way onto the dessert menu, and his (deep-fried) Cheesecake Bites are truly a wonder to consume. The chocolate-covered cheesecake balls are dipped back and forth between powdered pancake mix and milk, building up a substantial coating. They're served three or six to a plate, surrounded by mounds of whipped cream and drizzled with chocolate sauce. They are incredible! The cool and creamy cheesecake inside is set off beautifully by the warm, crispy exterior. You can get Brownie Bites, Mini Chocolate Bars, and bananas all served the same way.

Fun, casual, and homey, Deja Vu Cafe is as popular with families as it is with groups of young guys looking to out-eat one another.

I'm going to pass on dessert, though, and go straight for one of Deja Vu's signature milkshakes. Don't know if I'll be able to choose from the fifty flavours, though . . . I'm fried.

Deep-Fried Cheesecake Bites

Makes: 4 to 6 servings

Cheesecake Bites

1 pkg (8 ounces/250 g) cream cheese, softened

1 can (300 mL) sweetened condensed milk

1 teaspoon vanilla extract

1 teaspoon lemon juice

Chocolate Dipping Sauce

2 cups semisweet chocolate chips

1/3 cup grated edible paraffin wax

1/3 cup margarine

Assembly

Vegetable oil for deep-frying

2 cups prepared pancake batter (homemade or store-bought)

2 cups 2% milk

Chocolate sauce

Cheesecake Bites

In a large bowl, beat the cream cheese with the condensed milk until frothy. Add the vanilla and lemon juice; beat to combine. Refrigerate for 1 hour.

Line a baking sheet with wax paper. Roll the cheese mixture into 8 to 12 balls (about the size of a golf ball) and place on the baking sheet. Freeze for 2 hours.

Chocolate Dipping Sauce

In a medium saucepan, combine the chocolate chips, wax, and margarine. Stir over medium-low heat until melted and smooth.

Assembly

Dip the cheesecake balls into the chocolate dipping sauce and place back on the baking sheet. Freeze for 2 hours.

Pour 2 to 3 inches of oil into a large, heavy pot and heat over medium-high heat to 350°F (or use a deep-fryer).

Have the pancake batter ready in a bowl. Pour the milk into a second bowl.

Working in batches if necessary, dip the cheesecake balls in the milk, then in the pancake batter. Repeat until a substantial coating is built, and fry the cheesecake balls until golden brown.

Serve with whipped cream and chocolate sauce.

Diner Deluxe

EST. 2001
804 EDMONTON TRAIL NE
CALGARY · AB · T2E 3J6
WWW.DINERDELUXE.COM

I f good things come to those who wait, then you can add Maple Fried Oatmeal, Meatloaf Hash, Chocolate Sourdough French Toast, and Eggs Benedict with fresh basil hollandaise sauce to the official list of Good Things. Because at Calgary's Diner Deluxe, the lines start early and last long, especially during its famous brunch. But it's worth every second, even if you're outside in the bone-chilling cold.

Meals at the Deluxe are synonymous with brunch, and their menu boasts some of the most delicious morning inventions you'll find anywhere. Near the top of that list is the eggs Benedict, which is made extra special with chef James Waters's addition of a fresh basil paste that gives the hollandaise a freshness and taste I've never experienced before. Always looking for a new twist on an old standby, James substitutes freshly baked apple flax sourdough bread—baked next door at the Urban Bakery,

> *If this sounds like the dessert you've always dreamed of . . . you're right. But here's the great news: it's breakfast!*

the Deluxe's partner in crime—for English muffins. Choose between grilled chorizo and spinach, Canadian bacon, or smoked salmon on your Benny, and add a side of hash browns (yellow and sweet potatoes) to complete the culinary tour de force.

If it's dinner you crave in the morning, fear not. The Deluxe's Meatloaf Hash is a breakfast version of their popular Veal Meatloaf dinner plate, which daring customers will tell you is better than their granny ever made. The hash is served in a cast-iron skillet, and starts with a bed of fresh spinach buried under homemade hash browns. A thick slice of meatloaf is then laid on top and drizzled with red pepper jelly. Add two perfectly poached eggs to the skillet, and you've got a messy merger of yolk, meatloaf, potatoes, and wilted spinach—a little bit of magic on your plate.

Feeling more sweet than sassy this morning? Put the Maple Fried Oatmeal—a Diner Deluxe breakfast favourite—on your must-eat list. James starts by making a traditional oatmeal, then adds sun-dried cranberries, brown sugar, nutmeg, and butter. But it's not ready for your bowl yet. In fact, this oatmeal never sees a bowl! James then spreads the oatmeal thick in a baking sheet to cool and firm up, cuts it into hefty squares, and fries each square in a cast-iron skillet. Once it's crispy and delicious, James drizzles on a generous amount of maple syrup, pours on a ridiculously rich homemade vanilla bean cream sauce, and plops in a weighty dollop of lemon curd. If this sounds like the dessert you've always dreamed of . . . you're right. But here's

the great news: it's breakfast! Two words: *ridiculously good.*

Other awe-inspiring delights on the brunch menu include Chocolate Sourdough French Toast with grilled banana, courtesy of the Urban Bakery's chocolate sourdough bread. A savoury twist on an old favourite comes courtesy of the Stuffed French Toast: apple flax sourdough that's stuffed with Canadian bacon and a locally made Gouda. Topped with rosemary-infused syrup, it's one of James's all-time faves.

But don't you go thinking there's nothing but breakfast at the Diner Deluxe. Brunch may have put this place on the map,

An instant classic, Diner Deluxe opened in 2001 to rave reviews and soon became the go-to breakfast/brunch spot in Calgary.

but lunch and dinner have kept it there. The Rangeland Burger makes the ordinary extraordinary with ground Alberta bison, jalapeño Jack cheese, caramelized apple, and caramelized onions. The Salmon BLT coats two pieces of apple flax sourdough with Dijon dill dressing,

followed by butter lettuce, tomato, strip bacon, a 6-ounce fillet of wild sockeye salmon, and Oka cheese. Deluxe Mac & Cheese becomes distinctive courtesy of green onions, sun-dried tomatoes, and basil paste.

So put on your down parka, take a number, and settle in. Foodie nirvana is waiting . . . if you're willing.

Nothing says breakfast to this guy like a monster slice of meatloaf and a couple of poached eggs! Diner Deluxe's Meatloaf Hash is a classic part of what has been voted Calgary's best brunch for years.

Maple Fried Oatmeal

Makes: 8 servings

Lemon Curd

1 cup sugar

2 eggs

5 egg yolks

Zest and juice of 5 lemons

1/2 pound cold butter, cubed

Vanilla Cream

2 cups apple juice

1/2 cup real maple syrup

1/4 cup lemon juice

2 vanilla beans (or 3 tablespoons
   pure vanilla extract)

2 quarts whipping cream

Oatmeal Squares

4 cups quick-cooking rolled oats

1/4 cup brown sugar

3 tablespoons unsalted butter

2 tablespoons salt

1 teaspoon cinnamon

1/2 teaspoon nutmeg

1/2 cup dried cranberries

Assembly

1 tablespoon unsalted butter

1/2 cup real maple syrup

Lemon Curd

In the top of a double boiler (or in a heatproof bowl), whisk together the sugar, eggs, egg yolks, and lemon zest and juice until well combined. Whisk over simmering water until a ribbon of the mixture is visible for a few seconds after the whisk is lifted.

Remove from heat and whisk in the cold butter, a few pieces at a time, whisking until the butter is melted and the mixture is smooth and cool.

Cover the surface with plastic wrap and refrigerate until needed.

Vanilla Cream

In a medium saucepan, combine the apple juice, maple syrup, and lemon juice. Split the vanilla bean lengthwise and scrape the seeds into the pot. Add the vanilla beans. Simmer over medium heat for 8 to 10 minutes.

Stir in the whipping cream and return to a gentle simmer. Do not boil or the cream will curdle. Simmer until reduced by half, approximately 20 minutes.

Let cool. Cover the surface with plastic wrap and refrigerate until needed.

Oatmeal Squares

Lightly butter or line with parchment paper a 9- × 6-inch baking pan.

In a medium saucepan, bring 4 cups of water to a boil. Stir in the oats, brown sugar, butter, salt, cinnamon, and nutmeg. Bring the mixture back to a boil, then reduce heat and simmer, stirring occasionally, until the oats are cooked, 7 to 10 minutes.

Stir in the dried cranberries, then spread the mixture in the baking pan. Let cool. Slice into 8 equal bars.

Assembly

Melt the butter in a large nonstick skillet over medium heat. Gently fry the oatmeal squares until lightly browned on the bottom. Flip the squares and cook until golden on the second side. Transfer to plates and top each square with 1 tablespoon maple syrup, 1/2 cup vanilla cream, and 1 tablespoon lemon curd.

Evelyn's Memory Lane Cafe

EST. 1996
118 4TH AVENUE SW
HIGH RIVER · AB · T1V 1P7
WWW.MEMORYLANEICECREAM.CA

Here's how you know a café is special: new owners—who have previous restaurant experience—buy an existing eatery. They move hundreds of miles to run their new café, and the chef who used to cook for them asks if she can come, too!

That's the tale of husband-and-wife team Evelyn and Don Zabloski and their chef and very close friend Dörte Gensky. In 2003, when Don and Evelyn bought an ice cream parlour in the small town of High River, Alberta, and Dörte asked to be part of it, a '50s-style diner was born. Today Evelyn's serves hearty home-cooked meals to go along with forty-five different flavours of famous homemade ice cream.

You might think that people are drawn to Evelyn's for the decor, where red vinyl booths boast their own mini-jukeboxes and the black-and-white checkered floor recalls a simpler time. But devout customers will tell you that while the interior design certainly adds to the Evelyn's experience, it's food like their Chicken Sandwich that keeps people coming back for more.

The sandwich—by far the most popular item sold here—starts with a massive Hutterite chicken (they grow everything big here in Alberta!) that Evelyn roasts and then pulls apart by hand. Evelyn slathers two fresh slices

A trip to Evelyn's is exactly what you'd expect from a place that calls itself the Memory Lane Cafe. Retro decor and boundless hospitality make you feel as if you've stepped back in time.

of homemade seven-grain bread with mayonnaise (she will tell you that the mayo acts as a barrier, preventing the profuse chicken juices from making the sandwich soggy). Then comes fresh lettuce, a spoonful of cranberries, and a heaping mound of the most tender chicken a piece of bread has ever seen.

There are loads of ever-changing sandwich options at Evelyn's, so you never quite know what's going to be on the menu. You might be lucky enough one day to stumble upon a vegetarian mélange of tomato, cucumber, hummus, avocado, and Monterey Jack cheese, and a more carnivorous pesto, provolone, salami, and ham number the next. Either way, you're bound to be wowed by the fresh ingredients and sheer girth of Evelyn's sandwiches.

Evelyn's serves up a bevy of hot meals, too. The Hearty Beef Stew is a long-time crowd-pleaser that Dörte starts with seasoned chunks of stewing beef, seared to seal the juices and flavours inside. Meanwhile, a stockpot sees onions, celery, and carrots sautéed together, followed by the addition of the meat, its rich juices, and water. After a few hours of stewing, potatoes are added, and soon the stew has reached a fusion of flavours and textures that feels like your granny's kitchen. Dip the bread into the thick, rich juice and you'll make Dörte happy, too!

If stew's not your brew, then you can always try things like Chicken, Sweet Potato and Broccoli Casserole (it's yummy!), the Tuna Noodle Casserole (the one customers keep asking for), Chicken Chili (with sweet potato and black beans), or a variety of homemade quiches.

And what better way to finish off a hearty Alberta meal than with some of the eye-popping desserts at Evelyn's? The Bakeshop features an ever-changing selection of bars, squares, pies, and cakes. The Rhubarb Meringue Ecstasy Square is perhaps the most popular dessert Evelyn serves, but the Cinnamon Buns—which are made from scratch every day—are not to be missed, either. Of course you could always go for a Cranberry and White Chocolate Scone or the Banana Cake, a classic banana bread loaded with chocolate and covered with dark and white chocolate icing. Just make sure you ask for a side dish of Don's delicious homemade ice cream. It's made with pure pasteurized cream, and you'll find a continually changing menu where sixteen of the forty-five flavours are offered at any time. The most popular is Medicine Tree (praline, butterscotch, and chocolate flakes), named after a local tree that Aboriginals believed to have special powers.

Me, I'm putting my faith in Evelyn, Don, and Dörte.

Devout customers will tell you that while the interior design certainly adds to the Evelyn's experience, it's food like their Chicken Sandwich that keeps people coming back for more.

Hearty Beef Stew

Makes: 6 servings

1/3 cup all-purpose flour

1 teaspoon salt

1/4 teaspoon freshly ground pepper

2 pounds stewing beef, cut into 1-inch cubes

1/4 cup vegetable oil

4 cups boiling water

2 stalks celery, chopped

1 large onion, cut into 1-inch cubes

2 bay leaves

4 to 6 cups beef stock

12 small carrots, trimmed

8 to 10 small new potatoes, peeled

On a sheet of wax paper, mix together the flour, salt, and pepper. Roll the beef cubes in the seasoned flour to coat. Shake off excess flour.

In a medium Dutch oven, heat the vegetable oil over high heat. Working in batches, add the beef and cook until browned all over. As each batch is finished, transfer to a plate.

Return all the beef to the pot. Carefully add the boiling water—stand back, as it will splatter. Stir, then add the celery, onions, bay leaves, and enough beef stock to cover the beef. Reduce heat, cover, and simmer until the meat is tender, 1 1/2 to 2 hours.

Add the carrots and potatoes. Cover and continue to simmer for 45 minutes or until the vegetables are tender when pierced with the tip of a knife.

Cranberry and White Chocolate Scones

Makes: 4 to 8 servings

1 3/4 cups all-purpose flour

1/4 cup sugar

2 1/2 teaspoons baking powder

1/2 teaspoon salt

5 tablespoons butter, frozen

6 tablespoons buttermilk, plus additional for brushing

1 large egg, beaten

1/2 cup dried cranberries

1/2 cup coarsely chopped white Callebaut chocolate (or white chocolate chips)

Preheat oven to 400°F. Grease a baking sheet with vegetable oil or line with parchment paper.

In a large bowl, whisk together the flour, sugar, baking powder, and salt. Grate the butter over the flour mixture and toss to combine. Add the buttermilk, egg, cranberries, and chocolate; stir until the dough holds together.

Turn the dough out onto a lightly floured surface and knead gently about 10 times; don't over-knead, or the scones won't be fluffy and light. Pat the dough into a round 1/2 inch thick; cut the round into 8 wedges. (For smaller scones, shape the dough into 2 smaller rounds and cut each round into 8 wedges.) Transfer the wedges to the baking sheet with a spatula, leaving at least 2 inches between the scones. Brush with buttermilk.

Bake for 10 to 14 minutes or until golden brown.

Fat City Franks

EST. 2005
#3 2015 4 STREET SW
CALGARY · AB · T2S 1W6
WWW.FATCITYFRANKS.COM

Think hotdogs are just for the ballpark? Think again, dog hater! This is Fat City Franks, the place where dogs come home to roost in gourmet style. (I know I just mixed metaphors, OK? But when you *know* you've done it, it's allowed.)

The real mom-and-pop hotdog shop, Franks attracts customers of all ages, whether they're one or ninety. If you're dedicated to the dog, this is the place for you.

What else would you expect from a "retired" couple who just couldn't stomach a life of leisure and opened a hotdog stand at a local farmers' market to fill their time? Response was so overwhelming that Bob and Jane Steckle gave their dogs a permanent home. Now they're enjoying what they like to call their second childhood, living the dream of running a mom-and-pop hotdog shop in a city that can't seem to get enough of them.

As for the quality of their dogs, each wiener is made to order by a local producer, with no additives, fillers, by-products, or chemicals. Choose between pork/beef (their most popular mutt), all beef, farmer's sausage, bratwurst, and vegetarian dogs. As if choosing the wiener wasn't enough, your next decision is even more challenging: deciding from among thirteen gourmet options.

Rating pretty high on the uniqueness scale is the Breakfast Dog, which isn't just a morning food at Franks. As with all dogs here, the Breakfast Dog starts with a bakery-fresh, crusty-soft Italian bun and your choice of dog, topped with a layer of chive-dotted eggs scrambled with cream cheese and butter. Sprinkled with shredded Cheddar and real bacon bits, it reminded me of my childhood, when my dad used to scramble eggs and chopped hotdogs together and serve them for breakfast. Who would have thought someone else could dream up such a delicious combination?

Cultural melting pots are nothing new at Franks, and Bob and Jane are willing to throw pretty much anything on a dog. Take, for example, the Mediterranean Dog, which first lines the bun with creamy hummus, then tops its dog with chopped artichoke hearts, green olives, feta,

Figuring out how to jam it in your mouth is the trick, but a worthwhile challenge. Because once you do, you're hooked.

and parsley. I'm pretty sure Homer wasn't eating like this, but he'd wax poetic if he had!

Yet the dog that made my borscht bubble at Fat City Franks had to be their classic Ukrainian Dog—a deconstructed perogy on top of a frank. It's everything you love about a perogy, without the wrapping to get in your way. The secret is in the mashed potato blend, where Jane combines russet potatoes, sautéed onions, and shredded Cheddar. This is piled high on the dog, followed by a generous helping of sautéed onions, sour cream, and bacon. Figuring out how to jam it in your mouth is the trick, but a worthwhile challenge. Because once you do, you're hooked.

In addition to the other masterpieces on the everyday menu at Franks—such as the Chilean Completo Dog, the French Dog, and the San Antonio Black Bean Chili Dog—Bob and Jane are proud to boast a Dog of the Month, an extra-special combination that many customers yearn for year-round. The Louisiana Po' Boy adds homemade pulled pork and Cajun spice to the mix, while the Colombian tops its wiener with ham, pineapple, mayo, onions, mozzarella, and crushed potato chips. Feeling a little cross-border love? Then you've got to try the Yankee Noodle, which lays in homemade macaroni and cheese on top of its dog, followed by ketchup and bacon.

Dog enthusiasts though they are, Bob and Jane are cosmopolitan enough to offer side dishes with their meat-and-bun pairings . . .

Retirement, schmetirement! Owners Bob and Jane Steckle have built the fun family restaurant they always wanted. Hey . . . where's *my* T-shirt?

well three of them, anyway. I was a big fan of the chunks of dill pickle and radishes in the homemade potato salad, while the coleslaw (finished with Italian dressing instead of mayonnaise) was light and fresh.

If it's sweets you're after, don't go away! Franks satisfies with desserts such as cookies and homemade butter tarts, courtesy of Jane's mother's recipe. The showstoppers, though, are the Vintage Malted Milkshakes, which are available in vanilla, chocolate, and strawberry.

And no, you *can't* get a milkshake hotdog, though I understand why you'd ask.

Fat City Franks
Ukrainian Perogy Hotdog

Makes: 3 cups perogy topping, enough for 10 hotdogs

Ukrainian Perogy Topping

2 tablespoons unsalted butter

3/4 cup finely chopped onion

2 pounds russet potatoes

1 1/2 teaspoons salt

1 teaspoon pepper

1 cup shredded Cheddar cheese

Assembly (for each serving)

Cooked hotdog

Hotdog bun

Sour cream

1 teaspoon bacon bits

Perogy Topping

Melt the butter in a skillet over medium heat. Add the onion and cook, stirring, until translucent. Remove and set aside 1 tablespoon of onions per hotdog; reserve remaining onions.

Peel and quarter the potatoes. Place in a large saucepan. Add enough cold water to just cover. Bring to a boil over medium heat; cook until potatoes are tender. Drain and return to the pot. Add salt, pepper, and reserved remaining onions. Mash thoroughly until all ingredients are combined. Add the Cheddar cheese and mash until the cheese has melted and is combined.

Assembly

Place a hot dog in a bun and top with a heaping 1/4 cup of Ukrainian Perogy Topping. Sprinkle with 1 tablespoon of the reserved onions. Finish with a dollop of sour cream and bacon bits.

Note: Perogy topping may be frozen.

Floyd's Diner

EST. 2006
866 YATES STREET
VICTORIA · BC · V8W IL8
WWW.FLOYDSDINER.CA

The building has housed a few different restaurants over the years, but since it became Floyd's in 2006, it's been a local favourite.

So you're on a bit of a diet, right, watching the old waistline, but you *just* don't feel like cooking today. My advice to you? Don't go to Floyd's! Sure, you're gonna get some of the best damn diner eats you've ever stuffed in your mouth, but this place is not for the faint of heart . . . or stomach! In other words, the only prerequisite for a visit to Floyd's is a hearty appetite.

A Victoria institution, Floyd's has made a name for itself by serving up massive all-day breakfasts and lunches in a funky and eclectic '80s-style mishmash decor that speaks to its unique culinary personality. For here the meals are as heavy on humour as they are on calories. Where else can you gamble on a meal? Flip a coin and it's either free . . . or pay double!

This is the place where you will find such dishes as the Berlin Wall Omelette—"When you knock this down, you'll feel liberated"—which features spinach, sun-dried tomatoes, bacon, roasted garlic, and feta cheese topped with homemade herb-pesto hollandaise. Or there's always the Lumberjack breakfast: "You'll either want to nap or go build something after this one," the menu says.

If you're truly Paul Bunyan-sized, go straight for the BC Hash, a gargantuan breakfast that starts with a layer of scallop-cut fries dusted in an addictive herb-and-spice

Would you hire this bunch? Owner Petr Prusa (*third from left*) would, and that's what makes Floyd's so cool.

Grab some friends and dive into the insanely massive Mahoney. Feelin' lucky, punk? Try Lady Luck and see if you can snag your meal for free!

blend that chef Jamie Patterson says keeps customers lined up outside the door. But that's just the beginning. Jamie then fries together a panful of sausages, bacon, scrambled eggs, and salsa, and piles it on the fries. Topped with shredded cheese and green onions, the BC Hash is a mountain of flavour.

For lunch, the First Kiss Burger is "sorta wet, sloppy and awkward at first, but ultimately something you'll remember forever." And if you think nothin' says French toast like chipotle mayonnaise does, the Tommy Gun Open-Faced Beef Sandwich is for you. It's a house-made burger patty served on an improbably thick chunk of savoury French toast, then buried in sautéed mushrooms, red onions, thick gravy, and diced fresh tomatoes. It's served with fries, too.

But if there's one dish that defines the true character of Floyd's Diner, it has to be the Mahoney, which you can order for breakfast or lunch. Now, I'd like to be able to tell you what the Mahoney is, but I can't. You see, if you order the Mahoney, you get whatever the chef dreams up at that particular moment. Of course, if you're not happy with what you get, you can always flip for it . . . double or nothin'!

The one thing I *can* tell you about the Mahoney is that like everything else on the menu at Floyd's, it's massive! Jamie made me a double-stacked meal of two pizza-sized flour tortillas piled high with sautéed chicken breasts (*six!* in total), cheese, garlic, green onions, mushrooms, peppers, chorizo sausage, and bacon. Add some salsa and pop it in the oven and . . . invite a few friends to try to finish it!

If anything, the funky groove at Floyd's is the product of owner Petr Prusa's personality. A laid-back dude with a sharp sense of humour, Petr is proud of the fact that his tattooed employees were once described in a magazine as looking more like a prison gang than a kitchen crew. The way Petr sees it, that kind of individuality can only mean big things for Floyd's.

Just like the portions.

Here the meals are as heavy on humour as they are on calories. Where else can you gamble on a meal? Flip a coin and it's free . . . or pay double!

Tommy Gun Open-Faced Beef Sandwich

Makes: 4 servings

Chipotle Mayo

1 to 3 chipotle peppers, coarsely chopped

1/2 red onion, coarsely chopped

1 cup mayonnaise

1/2 cup sour cream

Hamburger Patties

2 pounds ground beef

1 garlic clove, minced

4 dashes Worcestershire sauce

1/2 cup chopped fresh parsley

1 teaspoon ground cumin

1 teaspoon pepper

1 tablespoon salt

2 eggs, lightly beaten

1 cup dry bread crumbs

Gravy

1 1/2 cups water

1 tablespoon beef bouillon powder

1/4 cup all-purpose flour

1/4 cup butter, melted

Salt and pepper

Assembly

5 eggs

4 slices French bread

2 tablespoons unsalted butter

1 cup chopped mushrooms

1 cup chopped red onions

1 cup diced tomatoes, not seeded

Chopped fresh parsley

Chipotle Mayo

Purée the chipotle peppers and red onion in a food processor. Add mayo and sour cream; process to thoroughly mix. Taste the mayo and add extra chipotle peppers for more spice, if you wish. Refrigerate until needed.

Hamburger Patties

In a large bowl, combine the ground beef, garlic, Worcestershire sauce, parsley, cumin, pepper, salt, and eggs; mix thoroughly. Add the bread crumbs and mix again. Pat into 4 burger patties. Refrigerate until needed.

Gravy

Combine all ingredients in a saucepanover medium heat; whisk until smooth. Bring to a boil, then reduce heat and simmer, stirring frequently, until thickened. Set aside, keeping warm.

Assembly

Preheat grill. Grill burgers for 4 minutes on each side.

Start your French toast once the burger patties have been cooking for 4 minutes. Whisk the eggs. Dip French bread in eggs, then grill on both sides.

While French toast is cooking, melt the butter in a skillet on the grill over medium heat. Add the mushrooms and onions; sauté for 2 1/2 to 3 minutes, until the mushrooms are softened and brown and the onions are starting to brown.

Spread the chipotle mayo on the French toast and place a burger patty on top. Top with onions and mushrooms. Drizzle with gravy and top with tomatoes and parsley.

Serve with a side of curly fries if desired.

BC Hash

Makes: 4 servings

6 cups finely chopped all-purpose potatoes
Olive oil, salt, and pepper
1 pound bacon
1 pound breakfast sausage
10 eggs
1/3 cup milk
Salt and pepper
1 tablespoon unsalted butter
2 cups shredded Cheddar cheese
1/2 cup fresh salsa
1/2 cup sliced green onions

Preheat oven to 375°F. Toss potatoes with olive oil, salt, and pepper to taste. Spread evenly on a baking sheet and bake for 15 minutes. Stir, then bake for another 15 minutes or until hash browns are soft in the middle and golden.

Slice the bacon and sausages into 1/2-inch pieces and cook in a large skillet over medium heat until cooked. Transfer to a plate and drain off excess fat.

In a medium bowl, whisk together the eggs, milk, and salt and pepper to taste.

Melt the butter in the same skillet over medium-low heat. Add the egg mixture and begin to scramble. When eggs are almost cooked, remove from heat and add the sausage mixture, 1 cup of the cheese, and the salsa. Mix well.

Place cooked hash browns in the middle of each plate. Top with scrambled eggs and sprinkle with the remaining cheese. Sprinkle with green onions and serve with toast.

Fraser Park Restaurant

EST. 1996
4663 BYRNE ROAD, #103
BURNABY · BC · V5J 3H6

Anton, Sylvia (far right), and her two daughters keep their devoted clientele abreast of happenings at the restaurant with their weekly "Deli News" newsletter.

Getting to the Fraser Park Restaurant is easy. Get yourself to Burnaby, BC. Rent a car. Drive to the Middle of Nowhere, make a left, and drive a few more kilometres. It's on the right.

Yet as devoted customers of this quirky, fun, and irrepressibly down-to-earth eatery will tell you, making the trip to the Fraser Park is well worth the effort. They don't come for the decor, for there's nothing fancy here: red-and-white checkered tablecloths mark a cafeteria-style interior that hasn't changed much since the day the restaurant opened. What makes this place a true destination is the delicious home-cooked meals whipped up every day by chefs and owners Anton and Sylvia Heggen.

For Anton, the love of food has been a life-long journey, one that literally began at his mother's apron strings. He learned to cook by her side as a boy, and cherishes his mother's handwritten recipe book, which he uses to this day. Anton went on to study food science, and honed his meat-carving skills in Berlin.

As devoted customers of this quirky, fun, and irrepressibly down-to-earth eatery will tell you, making the trip to the Fraser Park is well worth the effort.

Anton moved to BC to work as the head of product development at a sausage company, which is why he now stands as the only master sausage maker I've ever met. He opened Fraser Park in 1996, and working side by side with Sylvia and their four children, serves locals who know exactly where to go for "quality homemade foods and generous portions," as the Heggens like to say. Here is where you'll find authentic family fare, served by family who consider Fraser Park not a restaurant but an extension of their home kitchen.

Anton's butchering expertise is what makes the Fraser Park special (not to mention the fact that the guy plays the double bass and has been known to break into impromptu jams in the dining room!). He makes his own sausage, bacon, and home-cured meats on site every day. And almost everything else that hits the plate is made from scratch, whether it's the baked goods, dressings, sauerkraut, or Sylvia's hand-crafted soups.

Many of these items find their way onto one of the most popular items at Fraser Park, the German Breakfast, which is big enough to feed a lumberjack. The breakfast combines a three-egg omelette, Anton's homemade sausage, bacon, home-cured ham, pan-fries, and potato pancakes.

You'll get a similar belly-warming experience from the German Deluxe, a dinner entrée that includes the homemade bacon, sausage, and ham, then adds a pork schnitzel

As if one savoury, hand-carved roast beef sandwich isn't enough, you get two with the Fraser Park's Beef Dip plate.

to a plate already loaded with homemade sauerkraut and potato salad. Top the entire dish with caramelized onions and a rich, dark gravy, and you're going to have to fight the urge to yodel.

Anton's meat expertise also gets its due in his famous Beef Dip plate, the dish that patrons say is worth not being vegetarian for! Order this and you get two Portuguese buns coated with paprika mayonnaise, stuffed full of marinated, slow-roasted beef, and served with a bowl of rich, homemade gravy. Pile a sizzling mound of hand-cut fries on the plate and it's simple yet delicious home-cooked food that has a way of making you smile from the inside out.

But that's the kind of place Fraser Park is. People are happy to be here, happy to work here. And if you find yourself hopelessly lost in Burnaby, chances are you're just about there.

Deutschland on a plate: Anton's German Deluxe dinner entrée features a variety of his famous meats, which are all made on site and double roasted for maximum flavour.

Highlands Kitchen

EST. 2008
6509 112TH AVENUE NW
EDMONTON · AB · T5W 4K3
WWW.HIGHLANDSKITCHEN.CA

When Cindy Lazarenko and her husband, Geoff Lilge, opened the Highlands Kitchen in 2008, Edmonton was already home to Canada's largest Ukrainian population. But if word gets out about the Ukrainian specialties on offer here, someone better notify Kiev. Just don't mention that Cindy likes to add her own twists and turns to otherwise classic meals, OK?

A self-taught chef, Cindy is the culinary heart of the Highlands. Almost every meal she creates is a modern-day tribute to her Ukrainian heritage, beginning with hand-pulled pork shoulder crêpes, and Cindy's interpretation of *nalysnyky*, traditional crêpes filled with cottage cheese and dill.

Cindy's crêpes start with a giant pork shoulder rubbed with an exotic blend of spices and seared in a very hot oven. Then the shoulder is doused in a braising liquid of sautéed onions, garlic, and celery, tomatoes, red wine, soy sauce, and water. After five or six hours in the oven, the shoulder is so tender that it can be pulled apart by hand, after which it's left to soak up the flavours of the braising liquid and its own juices.

Then the meat is heaped upon a homemade crêpe—itself a simple recipe of flour, eggs, and milk—sprinkled with shredded Gouda and drizzled with homemade saskatoon berry barbeque sauce. Rolled and served three to a plate, the crêpes are offered under a heaping dollop of sour cream and a mound of marinated onions. I love this dish! There was an intriguing distinction between the textures and flavours of each part, from the sweet sauce to the feel of the pork to the soft, warm crêpe. Sign me up, Kiev . . . I'm coming!

Perched in the northeast Edmonton neighbourhood of the same name, the Highlands Kitchen strives to support local suppliers as much as possible.

If you can't get enough of Cindy's bison short ribs, you're not alone. This house specialty also appears in the Highlands' Pulled Bison Sandwich.

I also had the pleasure of feasting upon the Highlands' Smoked Paprika Chicken Stew, a wonderfully comforting dish that starts with chicken chunks dusted with flour and smoked paprika, then browned in a pan with garlic. The chicken is then simmered with sautéed celery, leeks, garlic, spices, and white wine. Then comes chicken stock, sour cream, Dijon mustard, and cubed potatoes, after which it's into the oven. The finished stew is served in its own cast-iron skillet and topped with homemade sauerkraut. My belly was warm and my heart was full after eating this one.

I don't know how many buffalo are roaming Ukraine, but Cindy's slow-braised bison short ribs (which to my untrained eye don't seem that short at all!) feel like home nonetheless. Customers rave about this house specialty, which starts with a rub of cumin, coriander, and guajillo peppers. After the ribs are dry-seared on both sides, they're immersed in a braising liquid of onions, garlic, tomatoes, balsamic vinegar, red wine, Worcestershire sauce, brown sugar, ketchup, and water.

After three hours in the oven, the über-tender ribs are served with Cindy's homemade roasted potato salad. I was floored by how she managed to keep the meat crispy on the outside but melt-in-your-mouth tender on the inside. And that potato salad was perfected by the homemade dressing, a combination of roasted garlic, chilies, cumin, yogurt, buttermilk, and green onions.

Of course it's not *all* Ukraine at the Highlands, though I can understand why you'd think so—there are, after all, few other places you can get Braised Rabbit with Nachynka (Ukrainian cornmeal stuffing) or a Kalyna Platter, which includes locally made *pyrohy* (perogies), handmade bacon gremolata, a lazy cabbage roll, and grilled local kubasa. Cindy's brunch menu actually includes dishes like Buttermilk Waffles, eggs Benedict, and Steak and Eggs; the vegetarian quiche lunch seems downright continental; and the beef tenderloin dinner entrée could be served in any fine Alberta steak house.

But I wouldn't put that call to the Ukrainian Consulate on hold just yet. After one taste of Cindy's classics, immigration can't be far behind.

Cindy is the culinary heart of the Highlands. Almost every meal she creates is a modern-day tribute to her Ukrainian heritage.

Chicken Stew

1 tablespoon + 1 teaspoon olive oil

1 tablespoon + 1 teaspoon unsalted butter

1/2 cup chopped leeks (white and pale green part only)

1/2 cup chopped celery

1/2 teaspoon minced garlic

1/2 teaspoon chili flakes

1/4 cup all-purpose flour

1 tablespoon smoked paprika

1/2 teaspoon each salt and pepper

4 boneless, skinless chicken thighs, cut into bite-size pieces

2 boneless, skinless chicken breasts, cut into bite-size pieces

2 tablespoons dry white wine

1 1/2 cups chicken stock

2 tablespoons sour cream

1 tablespoon Dijon mustard

2 cups new potatoes, cut in half

2 cups chopped kale

Chicken Stew

Heat 1 teaspoon of oil and 1 teaspoon of butter in a large saucepan over medium-high heat. Add the leeks and celery and cook for 10 to 12 minutes or until tender and golden brown. Add the garlic and chili flakes and cook for 1 minute. Transfer to a large bowl.

In a shallow dish, combine the flour, paprika, and salt and pepper. Dredge the chicken pieces in the flour, shaking off the excess.

Heat the remaining tablespoon of oil and butter in the same saucepan over medium-high heat. Add half of the chicken thigh pieces and half of the chicken breast pieces. Cook for 5 to 6 minutes or until browned on all sides.

Add the browned chicken to the leek mixture. Repeat with the remaining chicken.

Add the wine to the skillet and stir to loosen the brown bits. Add the stock, sour cream, and mustard. Bring to a boil.

Stir in the chicken mixture and potatoes. Cover, reduce heat, and simmer for 30 minutes or until potatoes are fork-tender. Add more stock if necessary.

Stir in the kale and simmer for 10 minutes.

Season with salt and pepper to taste, and serve with sauerkraut if desired.

Jelly Modern Doughnuts

EST. 2011
100 1414 8TH STREET SW
CALGARY · AB · T2R 1J6
WWW.JELLYMODERNDOUGHNUTS.COM

Say what you want about maple syrup, back bacon, and poutine, we Canucks are tried-and-true doughnut eaters. So much so, in fact, that these mighty cakes of fried dough have been called our unofficial national food.

But for sisters Rita and Roseanne Tripathy, something was missing from the mass-produced versions they got from the drive-through window. It wasn't until they took a trip south of the border that they experienced true mom-and-pop doughnut shops, and the inspiration for Jelly Modern Doughnuts was born.

After recruiting gifted pastry chef Grayson Sherman, their dreams turned into reality. Now Jelly Modern is turning what was once an every-day food into edible art, with more than twenty-five varieties of the most

Don't be fooled by the clean modern lines and minimalist decor: over-the-top indulgence is waiting behind the glass.

sumptuous doughnut creations imaginable. From a hand-fried Apple Fritter to Whoopie Pie with homemade marshmallow, Jelly Modern is reinventing the wheel . . . Canadian style.

Jelly Modern makes two kinds of doughnuts: cake and raised (or yeast). Cake doughnuts are fairly straightforward: flour, sugar, egg powder, water, baking powder, and baking soda. After various ingredients are added to individualize them, the doughnuts make their way to the hopper for shaping and are dropped into hot oil for frying.

Raised doughnuts begin with a mix of flour, yeast, and a touch of sugar. After rising, the dough is run through a sheeter (a double-action rolling pin) and a cutter, then sent to a humid proofer, where the doughnuts double in size before heading for the fryer. After cooling, it's time for Grayson to work his magic, transforming the doughnuts from fried bread into edible art.

If there's one doughnut on Jelly Modern's menu that demonstrates Grayson's love of country, respect for family, and culinary genius, it may be the Maple Bacon, a raised doughnut glazed with brown butter icing (his mother's recipe), squirted with maple syrup, and covered with a heap of real bacon bits. Skeptical about bacon on your doughnut? Then perhaps you haven't learned what Grayson did long ago: bacon on anything is good; bacon on a doughnut is better. It's like Canada in your mouth—without the rocks and wood.

Jelly Modern Doughnuts is awash in the sweet scent of freshly fried marvels, and customers walk around in a doughnut-induced daze.

If you insist on staying in your box and staunchly refuse to combine the words *bacon* and *doughnut*, Jelly Modern will not let you down. The S'mores doughnut coats one side of a raised doughnut with milk chocolate glaze, then fills the divot in the middle (where the hole would normally be) with Grayson's homemade marshmallow fluff. The S'mores is then topped with a homemade marshmallow and toasted with a blowtorch before being sprinkled with a liberal helping of graham wafer crumbs. If you're feeling old and crotchety, this one makes you feel like a kid again.

Grayson also pays homage to his mom's cooking prowess with the Lemon Curd doughnut, which stuffs a raised doughnut full of hand-crafted lemon curd, then tops it with fresh lemon glaze and a dollop of even more curd.

What, you're craving something a bit more savoury and think Jelly Modern can't accommodate you? In case you haven't noticed, Grayson is the kind of guy who likes to colour outside the lines, and his Doughnut Sandwiches fit the bill. Freshly fried raised doughnuts make a pillowy nest for Grayson's homemade fillings, such as ham and Brie, egg salad (his grandmother's recipe), roast beef, veggie, and peanut butter and jelly.

And if there was any part of me that ever considered doughnuts to be ordinary, it evaporated the day I walked through the doors at Jelly Modern Doughnuts. National food or not, every Canadian should be lucky enough to eat these at least once in their life. Or even once every week.

Bacon on anything is good; bacon on a doughnut is better. It's like Canada in your mouth—without the rocks and wood.

Cinnamon Sugar Beignets

Makes: 24 beignets

Beignets

Oil for deep-frying
1 egg
1/2 cup 10% cream
1 tablespoon canola oil
1 1/2 cups all-purpose flour
1/4 cup sugar
2 1/2 teaspoons baking powder
1 teaspoon cinnamon
Pinch of salt

Coating

2 cups fruit sugar (also known as superfine sugar and available at specialty food shops)
1 tablespoon cinnamon

Beignets

Pour about an inch of oil into a large heavy pot and heat to 350°F.

In a medium bowl, whisk together the egg, cream, and canola oil.

Sift the flour, sugar, baking powder, cinnamon, and salt over the wet ingredients. Stir until just combined.

Drop by the tablespoon into the hot oil and fry until brown. Drain on paper towels and let cool slightly.

Coating

Whisk together the fruit sugar and cinnamon. Toss the beignets in the cinnamon sugar while still warm.

Nenshi Brown Butter Fondant Drizzle

Makes: Enough to ice a 10-inch cake

6 cups icing sugar
1 cup unsalted butter
2/3 cup warm milk
1/2 teaspoon vanilla extract
1/4 teaspoon sea salt

Sift the icing sugar into a large bowl.

Melt the butter in a small saucepan over medium-low heat. When it starts to foam, reduce heat and cook, without stirring, until dark particles form on the bottom of the pan and the foaming subsides. Strain the butter through a fine-mesh sieve into the icing sugar. Whisk slightly.

Add the warm milk, vanilla, and salt; whisk until smooth. Let cool.

Spoon fondant into a microwave-safe squeeze bottle and store in the fridge.

To use fondant drizzle, microwave in 5-second increments until desired thickness.

Serve on ice cream, or use to ice a cake or cupcakes.

The Nenshi Brown Butter Fondant Drizzle is a sweet-and-salty tribute to the dietary laws of Calgary mayor Naheed Nenshi.

John's Place Restaurant

EST. 1984
723 PANDORA AVENUE
VICTORIA · BC · V8W 1N9
WWW.JOHNSPLACE.CA

John Cantin says the secret to his success is his work ethic. When the restaurant first opened, John lived in his office, working from 6 a.m. to 9 p.m. seven days a week.

I mean, really, is there anything but good to say about a restaurant that goes through *600 pounds* of butter every week?

That's John's Place, a Victoria institution that's been serving up a mind-boggling array of breakfast, lunch, and dinner specialties since 1984. But if you ask the dozens of people who always seem to be lined up outside John's what brings them coming back for more (and more and more and . . .), it's the breakfasts. And at John's, breakfast means eggs Benedict.

Owner and master chef John Cantin (the guy represented Canada at the 1976 World Culinary Olympics!) knows that the key to a great eggs Benny is the hollandaise sauce. The man is crafting liquid gold back there in the kitchen.

Of course John will serve you the classic eggs Benedict—two poached eggs and lightly seared Virginia ham served on toasted English muffin halves and buried in hollandaise—but he's just getting started. There are nine other eggs Benny varieties at John's, each as tempting as the next. One of my favourites was the Chorizo Sausage, which substitutes John's homemade cornbread for the English muffins. Then come two succulent patties of grilled chorizo (John makes his own), eggs poached to perfection, and oh yeah . . . liquid gold, baby!

John also does a to-die-for Belgian Waffle breakfast that starts with a yeast batter that makes the waffles huge, fluffy, and delicately soft inside. As if that wasn't enough (and for me it was!), John then tops the Belgian with layers of fresh whipped cream, berries, bananas, and what I like to call white gold: his maple cream cheese syrup. Tastes like you have died and gone to heaven, my brothers and sisters. Can I get an *amen*?

As fantastic as the food is at John's, there's so much more here than just eating. John knows that the essence

Is there anything but good to say about a restaurant that goes through 600 pounds of butter every week?

of a great restaurant is that it brings food and people together, and his place does just that. John's feel-good energy is everywhere, from the menu to the interior design. The restaurant is decorated much like a traditional '50s diner, and virtually every square inch of the wood-panelled walls is plastered with photos of John's life and passions: movie stars, musicians, travel, concerts, and of course the people who have eaten there.

Gotta get that! Liquid gold (John's hollandaise sauce), chorizo sausage, and cornbread make this a truly memorable eggs Benny.

And John has fed *lots* of people in his day! One local favourite dish is Cloudy with a Chance of Meatloaf (yes, John has a way with words, too!), a southwestern groove that takes your mom's best comfort food and adds a few twists and turns that leave your mouth begging for more. Instead of bread crumbs, John adds crumbled cornbread to the meat mix. For zip and zing, he throws in fresh cilantro and salsa. By the time the meatloaf comes out of the oven, is turned on the grill for a few seconds, and smothered in rich mushroom Marsala gravy, it's out of this world.

John also delighted me with a stuffed blue-cheese burger topped with crispy fried onions. It was so good, I broke the Put Down the Fork Rule and devoured my meal in a matter of seconds. (What's the Put Down the Fork Rule, you ask? It's the only way this guy can protect his waistline from reaching epic proportions. Before shooting an episode, I beg my director and field producer to not let me eat an entire dish. I tell them, "Even if it's the most delicious dish in the world, *do not* let me finish it. Let me take a few bites and describe how amazing it is, but make sure you tell me to put down the fork so I don't end up lying around all day like a sea lion." Count the

Always packed with happy customers, John's Place is as much about the friendly atmosphere as it is about the food. When the restaurant first opened and money was tight, John invited local artists to submit pictures, then started adding his own.

rule broken on this one, though.) And if I seemed just a wee bit maniacal hunched over the burger with my elbows thrown out to prevent anyone from getting close, I apologize. But it was mine . . . all mine! (Cue the evil laugh.)

Watching me eat made John happy. Come to think of it, everything seems to make John happy, but nothing more than when people enjoy the food he and his staff so lovingly prepare.

Ultimately, that's what makes John's Place so special.

Belgian Waffles

2 1/4 teaspoons active dry yeast

3 cups warm milk

3 eggs, separated

1/2 cup unsalted butter, melted

1/4 cup vegetable oil

2 teaspoons vanilla extract

1/2 teaspoon salt

4 cups all-purpose flour

1/2 cup sugar

Cream Cheese Syrup

1 pkg (8 ounces/250 g) cream cheese, at room temperature

Zest of 1 small orange

1 teaspoon salt

1 teaspoon vanilla extract

2 cups maple syrup

Belgian Waffles

In a small bowl, stir the yeast into 1/4 cup of the warm milk. Let sit for 5 minutes, until foamy.

In a large bowl, combine the remaining warm milk, egg yolks, melted butter, vegetable oil, vanilla, and salt. Beat on low speed for 1 minute.

Add the flour and the yeast mixture; beat on medium speed until smooth.

In a separate bowl, whip the egg whites on high speed, adding the sugar a spoonful at a time, until soft peaks form. Fold egg whites into the flour mixture. Cover and set aside in a warm place from half an hour to two hours. (Meanwhile, make the cream cheese syrup.)

Pour batter into a preheated waffle iron and cook until the waffles are golden and the lid lifts easily.

Cream Cheese Syrup

In a large bowl with an electric mixer (or using a stand mixer), beat the cream cheese, orange zest, salt, and vanilla on high speed for 3 minutes, stopping and scraping the bottom occasionally. Slowly add the maple syrup, stopping and scraping the bowl as you go. Set aside.

Serve waffles with whipped cream, the cream cheese syrup, and mixed berries.

Meatloaf

1 tablespoon oil
1/2 onion, diced
2 1/4 pounds lean (80/20) ground beef
12 ounces ground pork
1 3/4 cups cornbread crumbs
3/4 cup salsa
1 1/2 teaspoons chopped garlic
Leaves from 1/4 bunch fresh cilantro, chopped
4 eggs, lightly beaten
1 tablespoon each salt and pepper

Marsala Sauce

1 tablespoon clarified butter
1 onion, chopped
12 mushrooms, sliced
1/3 cup Marsala
1/2 cup demi-glace (available at gourmet grocery stores)
Salt and pepper
1/3 cup whipping cream

Meatloaf

Preheat oven to 350°F.

Heat the oil in a medium skillet over medium heat. Add the onion and cook until soft and translucent.

Transfer the onion to a large bowl. Add the ground beef, ground pork, cornbread crumbs, salsa, garlic, cilantro, eggs, and salt and pepper. Mix well.

Shape the mixture into a loaf and wrap in plastic wrap, then wrap in foil with the shiny side in; twist the ends of the foil and place the meatloaf on a baking sheet.

Bake for 50 minutes. When you unwrap the meatloaf, juices should run clear.

Marsala Sauce

While the meatloaf is baking, heat the clarified butter in a medium skillet over medium heat. Add the onions and mushrooms; cook, stirring, until the mushrooms are tender. Add the Marsala and reduce the sauce, stirring, for 30 seconds. Stir in the demi-glace and season with salt and pepper to taste. Pour in the cream and gently simmer until the sauce is thickened to your taste.

Cut meatloaf into slices. Pour Marsala sauce over the slices and serve with mashed potatoes.

Mrs. Riches Restaurant

EST. 1985
199 FRASER STREET
NANAIMO · BC · V9R 5CI
WWW.MRSRICHES.CA

Nothing—and I mean nothing—on the dessert menu compares with the Monster Mocha Pie, an ice cream dessert so thick it's hard to imagine anyone finishing it in one sitting.

We all have mountains to climb in our lives, right? Whether real or imagined, there's always a challenge out there we have to conquer. Well, at Mrs. Riches, the challenge is the food, especially their Original Mountain Burger, which is so big you may have to invite a few friends to help you finish it.

The Mountain Burger is the brainchild of brothers Gerry, Ron, and Rich Wong, the third-generation restaurateurs who created Mrs. Riches to offer the people of Nanaimo a fun and creative dining experience. The burger starts with a custom bun the size of a small pizza, upon which they slap a 1-pound patty of prime ground beef. Follow that with slice after slice of processed cheese (for creaminess), Cheddar cheese, piles of ham and back bacon, a fried egg, an entire sliced tomato, heaps of lettuce, handfuls of onions, plenty of pickles, and . . . oh yeah, mayo!

As if it wasn't challenging enough to fit all this food into your gut, the Wongs make it more difficult by giving you just one hour to do it. If you want the T-shirt, that is. Did I mention the sides? If you really want the shirt, eating the burger alone isn't enough. You also have to finish the heap of fries or onion rings they pile on your plate. Finish it or not (and Gerry says 99.9 percent of those who attempt the Mountain never make the cut), you'll at least get your picture on the Wall of Fame, an ever-growing collage of photos that assumes a fairly prominent position at Mrs. Riches. The way I see it, invite a few friends, cut it into pieces like a birthday cake, and go buy your own T-shirt! A quarter of a Mountain Burger? That's something I can do!

But Mrs. Riches isn't all about the Mountain, of course. They offer a delicious selection of other burgers, too (the restaurant actually started as a classic burger joint), and a huge variety of other dishes, from sandwiches to seafood, Chinese soups to steaks, pasta to rice bowls. One particularly good dish here is their half rack of Maui Ribs (look for the Oink section on the menu), which start with good ol' Canadian pork back ribs, to which Gerry adds add a rub of sugar, salt, and rosemary before baking them in a pan with a splash of water to keep the ribs moist.

Yet what makes the Maui Ribs so incredible is the Mrs. Riches Honey Garlic Pineapple Chunked barbeque sauce, a perfect balance of sweet, tangy, and salty. Gerry starts the sauce with a base of garlic, soy sauce, and honey, but it's the fresh pineapple chunks that make it truly delectable. If that's not enough to get your taste buds doing backflips, the homemade scalloped potatoes will set you right over the edge.

If there's any room in your belly after feasting upon a Mrs. Riches main course, the brothers Wong offer several decadent desserts, including a Mixed Berry Cake, Key Lime Cheesecake, Brownie Blaster, and Deep Caramel Pecan Flan. But nothing—and I mean nothing—on the dessert menu compares with their Monster Mocha Pie, an ice cream dessert so thick it's hard to imagine anyone finishing it in one sitting. Then you taste it, though, and as wave after wave of ice cream (vanilla and chocolate), peanut butter, chocolate cookie crumbles, whipped cream, caramel and chocolate sauce wash down your throat, you realize it's just another one of those worthwhile challenges that Mrs. Riches throws at you.

Like brother Rich, Gerry (*left*) and Ron Wong are third-generation restaurateurs. Their grandfather ran a Chinese restaurant in Nanaimo, and their parents also owned a restaurant. Maybe that's why their mother can't stay out of the kitchen!

Mrs. Riches Monster Mocha Pie

Makes: 6 to 8 servings

Timing note: Make the pie a day ahead, because it must freeze overnight.

Pie Crust

5 cups crushed chocolate sandwich cookies

1/4 cup unsalted butter, melted

1/4 cup sugar

Candied Peanuts and Almonds

1 egg white

1/2 cup sugar

2 cups honey-roasted peanuts

2 cups slivered almonds

Pie Filling

4 quarts chocolate ice cream

1/2 cup warm brewed coffee

1/4 cup instant coffee powder

Bottled chocolate syrup (optional)

Assembly

1 quart vanilla ice cream, softened

Bottled chocolate syrup

Whipped Cream

1 cup whipping cream

1/4 cup sugar

1 teaspoon vanilla extract

Serving

Vanilla ice cream

6 to 8 teaspoons peanut butter

1/2 cup bottled chocolate syrup

Caramel syrup

Maraschino cherries (optional)

Pie Crust

Preheat oven to 275°F.

Mix together the cookie crumbs, melted butter, and sugar in a bowl until well combined. Spread 3 cups of the crumb mixture in an 8-inch springform pan, pressing down to form an even crust across the bottom. (Set aside remaining crumb mixture.)

Bake crust for 7 minutes or until crust appears a little bit glossy and softened. Set aside to cool.

Candied Peanuts and Almonds

Preheat oven to 275°F.

In a medium bowl, whisk together the egg white and sugar. Add the peanuts and almonds; stir together until nuts are thoroughly coated. Spread the nuts on a parchment-lined baking sheet.

Bake for 7 to 10 minutes, rotating the pan once, until lightly golden. Set aside to cool.

Pie Filling

Refrigerate the chocolate ice cream for 1 hour to soften.

Stir together the warm coffee and instant coffee to make a coffee syrup.

In a large bowl, combine the softened chocolate ice cream and coffee syrup. (Add chocolate syrup if desired to intensify the chocolate flavour.) Mix until smooth. Keep refrigerated.

Assembly

Spread half of the pie filling over the crust. Spread the vanilla ice cream over the outer three-quarters of the filling to resemble a doughnut. Fill the hole with some of the pie filling.

Sprinkle the ice cream with the remaining 2 cups of crushed chocolate cookies. Generously drizzle cookies with chocolate syrup. Top with the remaining pie filling, spreading evenly. Freeze the pie overnight.

Whipped Cream

Shortly before serving, beat the cream with a whisk or an electric mixer until soft mounds form. Beat in the sugar until it is all incorporated. Add the vanilla and whip until stiff peaks form.

Serving

Wrap a warm, damp cloth around the sides of the springform pan to loosen the crust. Remove sides of the pan and cut the pie into wedges.

Top each wedge with a large scoop of vanilla ice cream. Add a teaspoon of peanut butter. Drizzle with chocolate syrup. Top with a dollop of whipped cream and caramel syrup. Sprinkle with a tablespoon of candied nuts. Top with a maraschino cherry (if using).

Neighbour's Restaurant

EST. 1982
6493 VICTORIA DRIVE
VANCOUVER · BC · V5P 3X5
WWW.NEIGHBOURSRESTAURANT.CA

When you put as much love, heart, and soul into your restaurant and your food as the Tsoukas family does, the result is bound to be special. And that's exactly what you get here at Neighbour's Restaurant, which George and his wife, Niki, have forged into a local landmark for more than thirty years. Now it's children Mitsy, Evelyn, and Johnny—who essentially grew up at Neighbour's—who make this one of the most welcoming, caring, and friendly restaurants you'll ever set foot in.

A lot of that feeling comes from Papa George, the lovable patriarch of the Tsoukas family who

George and Niki Tsoukas once ran food stands in local food fairs and malls. When the couple decided to offer more menu options in a permanent location, Neighbour's was born.

feels like everyone's dad. George has a magical way of instantly connecting with people, whether it's by rubbing their shoulders after a long day at work—like he did to me—or by warming their bellies with his signature Greek and Italian recipes. Either way, a visit to Neighbour's is a trip to a kinder, gentler, simpler time.

George's pizza evokes the same feeling, probably because of what he calls the primary ingredient in every pie he makes: love. That's a whole lotta love considering Papa has been making homemade dough for about forty years. George says his secret is the pockets he pushes into the dough with his fingers, which leaves room for the heat to travel underneath the

This man knows his dough! When you've been making pizza for more than four decades like Papa George has, you know the secret to a good crust.

Athens, here I come! Neighbour's Lamb Dinner features a 22-ounce piece of the most tender shoulder meat imaginable.

crust when it's baking. George is also a master sauce maker, and his tomato creation is as good as any I've tasted.

Once the foundation has been built, the pizza party begins! There are thirty-five (that's right, Toto, we're not in Kansas anymore!) varieties at Neighbour's, though the Neighbour's Deluxe is the one that caught my eye . . . and my mouth. This wonder starts with a layer of George's sauce topped with mozzarella, Edam, Canadian bacon, ham, pepperoni, mushrooms, green peppers, onions, and another pile of cheese. Top it all off with black olives, shrimp, and sliced fresh tomatoes, and you'll see why anyone who eats it considers George a good neighbour!

Spanakopita (spinach pie) is Niki's territory. A simple yet exotic Greek dish, the pie begins with a filling of fresh spinach, dill, onion, parsley, eggs, and lots of feta cheese. The trick to making spanakopita comes in assembling the little pockets of love. Sheets of phyllo are cut into strips, then brushed lightly with olive oil. The spinach filling is laid on the phyllo, wrapped, and baked until golden and perfectly crispy. Served with homemade tzatziki, rice, roasted potatoes, Greek salad, and pita bread, it's like a trip back to the old country with every bite.

Neighbour's delights with tons of other classic Greek dishes, including souvlaki, kalamari, and Ribs à la Greka. But the dish that sent me on a one-way ride to the Acropolis was George's Roast Lamb, which was the most tender piece of meat I've ever put in my mouth. After George trims the lamb to his standards, he cuts hunks of it into a massive baking tray along with a cinnamon stick, then covers it with seasoning salt and black pepper. Then he mixes up dry mustard, yellow mustard, chicken stock, and lots of lemon juice and pours it in with the lamb. Three hours of baking later, you've got a fall-off-the-bone dish that Socrates himself would love!

No trip to Neighbour's would be complete without dessert, and there are loads of tasty selections. You can try cheesecake (White Chocolate Amaretto, Chocolate Coffee Chunk, or New York), Deep Dish Caramel Pecan Flan, or Apple Pie, but I'm staying in the old country, thank you very much, and ordering the baklava. Niki still makes every piece of this classic by hand, which sees strips of crispy phyllo layered between almonds and walnuts, then drenched in cinnamon honey syrup and served warm.

You can taste the love in every bite.

The dish that sent me on a one-way ride to the Acropolis was George's Roast Lamb, which was the most tender piece of meat I've ever put in my mouth.

Spanakopita

Makes: Approx. 50

Filling

1 1/2 bunches fresh spinach, rinsed well, drained, and chopped

Leaves from 1 bunch fresh parsley, finely chopped

1 bunch fresh dill, finely chopped

1 red onion, finely chopped

3/4 teaspoon pepper

1/2 teaspoon salt

1 1/2 pounds feta cheese, crumbled (4 cups; use more if preferred)

2 eggs, lightly beaten

Assembly

1/2 pkg (16 ounces/454 g) phyllo pastry, thawed

3/4 cup vegetable oil

Filling

In a large bowl, combine the spinach, parsley, dill, onions, pepper, salt, and feta. Mix well with your hands. Add the eggs and mix well.

Assembly

Preheat oven to 350°F.

Carefully unroll phyllo, and use a sharp knife to cut the stack lengthwise into strips 2 1/2 inches wide. Keep phyllo covered with a dampened kitchen towel because it dries out quickly.

For each triangle, remove 2 strips of phyllo and stack them with a short end facing you. Lightly brush top with oil. Put 1 heaping tablespoon of filling 1 inch from the end closest to you. Fold the bottom right corner up over the filling to the left edge to form a triangle. Fold the triangle up, bringing the point at the bottom left to rest along the left edge. Fold the lower left corner over to touch the right edge. Continue folding in this manner until you reach the end of the strip. Transfer to a baking sheet.

Repeat until you have the desired number of spanakopitas. (You can save extra filling and phyllo in the fridge for up to 3 days.)

Poke 3 or 4 holes in each spanakopita to allow steam to release, and lightly brush the tops with oil.

Bake for 30 minutes or until golden.

Serve with tzatziki for dipping.

Pagliacci's

EST. 1979
1011 BROAD STREET
VICTORIA · BC · V8W 2A1
WWW.PAGLIACCIS.CA

OK, I admit it that I'm just a teensy-weensy bit biased when it comes to pasta (what else do you expect from an Italian kid whose parents served him the best of the best?). So when I say Pagliacci's is hands-down one of the best Italian joints I've ever eaten in, you might raise a skeptical eyebrow . . . or perhaps two, if you've that kind of skill. But don't take my word for it, you cynics. Just ask the throngs of people lined up outside the door. They'll set you straight. And if they don't, there's always Howie.

Along with brother David, Howie Siegel launched Pagliacci's back in 1979 in an effort to save Victoria from becoming what he described as a culinary wasteland. Now Howie is the front man for one of the most renowned restaurants in the city (if not all of Canada), a flamboyant character whose voice rings loudly throughout the halls of this jam-packed piece of pasta heaven.

Over the years, Howie has become as much of a Victoria institution as has the restaurant he and David run to this day. (Howie likes to say that he is the face of Pagliacci's, while his brother is the backside.) Cocky, loud, abrasive, and full of bluster, this native Brooklynite certainly didn't leave his New York attitude behind when he got to Canada. The place is loud, boisterous, and dripping with people,

Count yourself among celebrities like Peter C. Newman, Bob Dylan, and Mel Gibson when you come for a meal at Pagliacci's.

people who know that when they come here they're transported to a bygone era, where the only things larger than the portions are the characters who run the joint.

Here the names of the dishes are as authentic as the food itself, and everything is made from scratch under the direction of chef Sukhvinder "Sook" Basra, who has been a fixture at Pagliacci's for almost its entire history. Sook started me off with something he calls the Big Easy, a Cajun-inspired penne dish that features prawns, chicken, Italian sausage, bell peppers, and mushrooms in a spicy marinara sauce.

Made fresh every day using the same recipe they've had since Day 1, focaccia at Pagliacci's is like religion. Customers here expect it to come early and often, and if the restaurant runs out . . . mutiny!

But what really warmed my heart at Pagliacci's was the Hemingway Short Story, a simple yet perfectly crafted meat-and-cheese tortellini dish served in a cream sauce with bacon and green onions that reminded me of meals at home as a kid. Sook cooked the tortellini perfectly, leaving it al dente enough to still have a bite.

And nothing goes better with a plate of pasta than a piece of crusty, buttery, salty, fresh-out-of-the-oven focaccia, a Pagliacci's institution and a loaf my dad would be proud of. Made fresh every day using the same recipe they've had since Day 1, focaccia at Pagliacci's is like religion. Customers here expect it to come early and often, and if the restaurant runs out . . . mutiny! No wonder they go through almost a hundred loaves every day.

If pasta's not your thing (what's *wrong* with you?), then there are loads of other options at Pagliacci's, including a host of steak, chicken, lamb, fish, and veal dishes. The Damon Runyon steak is a top seller, a 10-ounce AAA Angus steak drenched in a Kentucky bourbon marinade and char-grilled with mushrooms and garlic. The brunch menu is just as witty, and features such items as the Jayne Mansfield ("two large, round, firm, voluptuous, delectable, creamy lemon ricotta cheese pancakes"), Breakfast at Tiffany's (a riff on eggs Benedict), and the Cool Hand Luke Brunch Special.

Finding a place to sit at jam-packed Pagliacci's isn't always easy, but don't worry: Howie (in the grey fedora) will tell you where to go!

Dessert lovers have several options at Pagliacci's, but the place is famous for its homemade New York Cheesecake ("the dish that made us . . . and Manhattan"). Of course, you could always go for the Marble, the Chocolate, or the Espresso cheesecake, too.

And if that's not enough, there are always things like Carrot Cake and Turtle Pie.

Just don't let Howie catch you eating 'em. After all, you can take the boy out of New York, but you can't take the New Yorker out of the boy.

Pagliacci's New York Cheesecake

Makes: 10 to 12 servings

1 1/4 cups graham cracker crumbs

2 cups sugar

1/4 cup unsalted butter, softened

5 pkg (8 ounces/250 g each) cream cheese, softened

2 tablespoons fresh lemon juice

Seeds scraped from 4 vanilla beans (or 2 teaspoons vanilla extract)

2 tablespoons all-purpose flour

1/4 teaspoon salt

5 eggs

2 egg yolks

1/4 cup whipping cream

Preheat oven to 500°F.

Stir together the graham cracker crumbs, 1/4 cup of the sugar, and the butter until well blended. Press mixture firmly into the bottom and 1/2 inch up the sides of an ungreased 9-inch springform pan. Refrigerate until ready to use.

In a large bowl, beat the cream cheese until smooth. Beat in the lemon juice and vanilla.

Sift the flour with the salt and remaining 1 3/4 cups sugar. Add to the cream cheese mixture and beat until light and smooth, approximately 5 minutes. Beat in eggs, 1 at a time, and then the egg yolks, 1 at a time, beating well after each addition. Beat in the whipping cream.

Pour mixture into the crust and bake for 12 minutes. Reduce heat to 200°F and bake for 45 minutes, or until a knife inserted in the centre comes out clean.

Cool on a rack. Refrigerate for 24 hours before serving.

Focaccia

Makes: 1 focaccia

4 cups all-purpose flour

1 tablespoon salt

2 teaspoons sugar

2 teaspoons instant yeast

1 cup warm water

1/4 cup olive oil, plus additional
    for brushing

Coarse salt

Coarsely ground pepper

Preheat oven to 450°F. Coat the bottom and sides of a baking sheet with olive oil.

In a large bowl, stir together the flour, salt, sugar, and yeast. Add the water and olive oil; stir until a soft, sticky dough forms.

Knead the dough for 2 or 3 folds on a floured surface. Dig a knuckle into the dough. If it sticks, work in a little more flour until the dough is no longer sticky.

Let the dough rise, covered with a cloth, for 30 minutes.

Turn the dough into the pan and stretch it out to fill the pan. With your fingertips, make imprints all over the dough. Brush the dough all over with olive oil; sprinkle with coarse salt and pepper to taste.

Bake for 18 minutes or until golden brown.

Let focaccia sit for 5 minutes before slicing and serving.

Pfanntastic Pannenkoek Haus

EST. 1997
2439 54TH AVENUE SW
CALGARY · AB · T3E IM4
WWW.DUTCHPANCAKES.CA

In a city that prides itself on pancakes—particularly during the Stampede—a small, unassuming restaurant is bucking the trend in a big way. At the Pfanntastic Pannenkoek Haus, fluffy flapjacks are verboten. Instead, the Pannenkoek Haus is home to the giant crêpes the Dutch have been eating for centuries. Only here, the party doesn't end with breakfast.

Actually, in the Netherlands a pannenkoek is traditionally eaten for lunch or dinner. Owner Denice Greenwald serves them up for breakfast, too, because she knows how fond we Canadians are of eating cake-like products in the morning. I'm not sure what they'd think of that in the traditional Dutch pannenkoek house where Denice did her training, but given the fact that she's serving up dishes like Philly Cheesesteak and Cinnamon Bun pannenkoeks, I get the feeling she's quite willing to add her own flair.

The Pfanntastic Pannenkoek Haus was born when owner Denice Greenwald quit her job with a big Calgary oil company in pursuit of something more meaningful.

Joe Payne is the pannenkoek handyman behind Denice's creative genius. A fixture at the Pannenkoek Haus since the day it opened, Joe knows that the foundation of a good pannenkoek is the batter, simple though it may be. Water, eggs, milk powder, salt, and baking powder are mixed together, followed by cake flour, enriched flour, and malt flour, which keeps the pannenkoeks sweet and smooth and allows them to rise a bit higher as well.

It's one thing to know how a pannenkoek is made. Deciding which one you want is another thing altogether, especially because they offer eighty different kinds. There are sweet pannenkoeks, savoury pannenkoeks, and (for those of you who can't make up your minds), sweet *and* savoury pannenkoeks. There are breakfast pannenkoeks, lunch pannenkoeks, and (you guessed it!) dinner pannenkoeks, too. Then—just when you thought a decision was in sight—there's always the build-your-own-pannenkoek option!

One of my favourites on the savoury side of the ledger is the Steak Met Smeerkaas (Philly cheesesteak), which starts with a giant panful (pannenkoek pans are 12 inches in diameter) of sautéed mushrooms, onions, red peppers, green peppers, and chopped flank steak. The batter is poured directly onto this mixture, swirled around the pan to keep the cake even, and topped with mozzarella, Cheddar, and Edam cheeses. After a masterful flip of the cake to grill everything together, the pannenkoek is served in all its flattened beauty.

The Potato, Onion, Bacon, and Cheese Pannenkoek is one of the most popular items on the menu, and with little wonder. Topped with sour cream, it's like a giant perogy.

The chicken Parmesan is another savoury lunch/dinner treat, which starts with a panful of sautéed double-smoked bacon, mushrooms, and thick pieces of chicken breast. After the batter has been added and the pannenkoek starts to firm up, Joe adds shredded leeks, flips the unit on its head, and serves it with a whole lot of Parmesan. How did I like it? How does the word *perfect* sound?

The pannenkoek is also the perfect platform for desserts, and Joe is happy to oblige with a classic combination of banana and chocolate sauce. Not your thing? How about the Kaneel Rol (Cinnamon Roll, which coats a cooked pannenkoek with brown sugar, cinnamon, and cream cheese icing)? You well-mannered folk might reach for your fork and knife, but I roll it up and eat it with my hands. Pannenkoek desserts hit the big time with the Zwarte Woud (Black Forest), which tops its cake with a dusting of icing sugar, then places three scoops of French vanilla ice cream right in the middle of it all. A wall of warm cherries is then laid around the edge of the pannenkoek, punctuated by three heaping mounds of whipped cream. As a final touch, a homemade chocolate cup is perched atop the ice cream and filled with kirsch, a cherry brandy. A few squirts of chocolate sauce later and you've got what tastes like a Black Forest cake . . . Dutch style.

Try finding something like *that* in your Stampede breakfast!

It's one thing to know how a pannenkoek is made.
Deciding which one you want is another thing altogether.

1 1/3 cups all-purpose flour

1/3 cup cake-and-pastry flour

1/2 teaspoon baking powder

1/2 teaspoon salt

2 cups buttermilk

2 eggs

1/2 cup water

5 tablespoons unsalted butter, melted

1 1/2 teaspoons molasses

Preheat oven to 200°F.

Sift together the all-purpose flour, pastry flour, baking powder, and salt.

In a large bowl, combine the buttermilk, eggs, and water; beat slowly with an electric beater, adding the flour mixture as you go. There should be no dry ingredients on the sides of the bowl when the batter is mixed well.

At high speed, beat in 3 tablespoons of the melted butter and the molasses just until mixed. Do not over-mix, as air pockets will ruin the batter. The batter should be golden brown and thin enough to pour.

Heat a crêpe pan or medium skillet over medium heat. (Using a few pans simultaneously will reduce cooking time.) When the pan is warm, use a pastry brush to coat it with some of the remaining melted butter. Use only as much butter as is needed for the pannenkoek to slide with ease in the pan. If the batter does not easily spread across the pan when tipped, use less butter.

Lift the pan off the heat and ladle some batter into the pan; the pan should sizzle when the batter hits it. Do not load the pan with too much batter; instead, tip the pan to spread the batter.

Cook until the pannenkoek is golden brown on the bottom. Flip the pannenkoek in the air or slide it onto the bottom of a flat lid; brush pan with butter and invert the pannenkoek back into the pan.

When the bottom is golden brown, flip the pannenkoek back to the first side and let rest for a minute before serving; do not leave in the pan for too long because the pannenkoek will overcook easily. Place pannenkoek on a baking sheet and keep warm in the oven. Repeat with the remaining batter.

Load with your favourite toppings. Recommended are sliced bananas, shredded coconut, and a drizzle of warm chocolate sauce.

Red Top Drive-Inn Restaurant

EST. 1960
219 ST. MARY'S ROAD
WINNIPEG · MB · R2H1J2

There may not be waitresses in roller skates and poodle skirts bringing your food out to your car anymore, but when it comes to eating at the Red Top Drive-Inn, the traditions that have established this place as a Winnipeg dining institution are alive and well. From the wood-panelled walls to the red vinyl booths, from the fried chicken to the burgers, eating at the Red Top is a delicious and comforting trip back in time.

The Red Top Drive-Inn was started in 1960 at the hands of Gus Scouras and quickly became a late-night gathering place for hundreds of Winnipeg teens craving a homemade burger and a root beer. Gus soon partnered with brother John, and when Gus retired in 1996, John and his wife, Vicky, kept the Red Top's history alive.

John passed away suddenly in 2007, leaving his son Pete, who literally grew up in the business, to take over. Pete works hard to keep the quality, made-from-scratch standard that his ancestors built. For just as it was more than fifty years ago, the Red Top remains a great place to get some of the best diner food you'll ever want to sample.

And while Georgia might seem like half a world away, the folks at the Red Top sure know how to whip up some of the best fried chicken

It may be more than five decades young, but the Red Top still sees many of its original patrons coming in for their favourites.

I've ever tasted. I'm not sure what the exact secret is, but I suspect it has something to do with the pressure fryer, a device that combines a pressure cooker with a deep-fryer. Red Top's Fried Chicken is improbably crispy on the outside (it's coated in a bread crumb spice mix), hot and juicy on the inside. And the best part? It was almost impossible to find a drip of grease anywhere. Just crispy, tender, tasty. Choose from coleslaw, salad, fries, or spaghetti with chili on the side.

When you go through about a hundred pounds of chili every week, you need big pots and bowls! Red Top's chili is a staple item, and it's served atop everything from burgers to spaghetti.

Yet as good as the Red Top's fried chicken is, there's something about a drive-in that says burgers, and this joint does them up *right*. All Red Top patties start with freshly ground beef brought in daily by a butcher down the street who's been supplying the restaurant since the '60s. The meat is then mixed with a simple blend of eggs, diced onion, and homemade bread crumbs.

The Red Top revels in its simplicity, so you won't find a mindbending array of burger options here. They're all fried in their own fat on the flattop grill, housed in a fresh bun, and dressed with mustard, onions, chili, and pickles. But if there's one burger that stands out, it's the aptly named Monster Burger, a six-patty colossus that comes in at almost three pounds when the condiments, all-beef chili, and fresh sub bun are tallied with the meat. Not for the faint of heart or small of belly, the Monster is as delicious as it is messy.

Pete is not one to turn his back on his heritage (having his mom there helps, too), so it should come as no surprise that there are lots of Greek dishes at the Red Top. Gyros come in beef, lamb, chicken, or vegetarian varieties; each is awash in homemade tzatziki. Greek salad is made extra special by the Red Top's signature dressing, and Vicky's homemade baklava is enough to get an *opa!* out of anyone. And if you're looking to wash all that goodness down, there's nothing more classic than an old-fashioned Red Top Milkshake—vanilla, chocolate, or strawberry.

If it's your first time at the Red Top, just remember that you may be starting a family tradition. For if you're anything like the thousands of people who flock here, you'll probably be coming back with your children and their children and their children . . .

Just as it was more than fifty years ago, the Red Top remains a great place to get some of the best diner food.

Red Top Burger

Makes: 10 burgers

2 pounds lean ground beef
1 Spanish onion, finely chopped
1 1/2 cups fresh bread crumbs
2 eggs, lightly beaten
2 tablespoons pepper
Salt to taste

In a large bowl, combine all ingredients. Mix well with your hands. Shape into 10 burgers. Cook burgers on the barbeque or a griddle and serve with your favourite condiments.

Rock Cod Café

EST. 1990
1759 COWICHAN BAY ROAD
COWICHAN BAY · BC · VOR 1NO
WWW.ROCKCODCAFE.COM

When a restaurant is as close to the Pacific Ocean as Cowichan Bay's Rock Cod Café, there's little doubt what they're offering on the menu. Seafood, seafood, and oh . . . did I mention seafood?

A local favourite for more than two decades, the Rock Cod Café has made a name for itself by serving up what devoted customers say are the best fish and chips on Vancouver Island, if not in all of British Columbia. And the numbers don't lie: the Rock Cod goes through hundreds of pounds of fresh halibut, cod, and salmon every week. That's nothing compared to the potatoes, though. Chef Brian Hemstalk says they can burn through 500 pounds of them in a single day . . . and every one is hand cut.

Ask owner Jacob Hokanson what distinguishes his fish and chips and he'll tell you it's the batter they smother the fish in, a recipe passed on to Jacob from the restaurant's previous owner, who himself bought it from the owner before him. Yes, it's that good. Brian says it's also their use of premium fish, plus a whole lotta love and care.

Rock Cod Café customers enjoy its nautical decor and come-as-you-are mentality. Inside, you're sure to find lots of quirky treasures among the marine nets and floats that festoon the walls.

Each fish-and-chips order comes with two gigantic pieces dipped in batter before being introduced to the deep-fryer. But rather than just drop his fish in the oil, Brian swims it across the top until it floats, then sets the piece free. This gives the fish its trademark crispy-but-tender consistency, which happy guests say keeps them coming back for more. The fish is served on a heap of fries, accompanied by coleslaw and tartar sauce.

Not enough for you? Then get ready for the Captain's Plate, a slice of deep-fried heaven overflowing with halibut, prawns, scallops, and calamari. Throw in a couple of grilled oysters to finish it off and serve on a mound of fries. I wasn't feeling quite so, well, *hungry*, so I opted for the R.C. Fish Tacos, hard-shelled tacos filled with a piece of deep-fried halibut, then buried under what chef Chelsea Tiemer calls Savoury Slaw, a cross between homemade salsa and coleslaw.

Taste buds take note: the R.C. Fish Tacos will delight you with a flood of flavour, but they're saving some butt-kicking heat for the end, when the Mango Habanero Sauce kicks in.

But what makes the R.C. Fish Tacos super-duper special is Chelsea's Mango Habanero Sauce. The sauce starts with diced onions sautéed in olive oil, followed by minced garlic, mangoes, pineapple juice, and roasted habanero peppers (minus the seeds, which are the hottest part). The mixture cooks until reduced and is then blended until smooth, making a beautiful yellow sauce that gives the tacos a sweet yee-ha! blast of heat before the savoury slaw kicks in and cools it all off again.

Come all the way to Cowichan Bay and fancy a burger? No problem. The Rock Cod offers nearly a dozen burgers and hot sandwiches, four of which—the Wild Sockeye Burger, Halibut Burger, Rock Cod Café Burger, and Oyster Burger—feature seafood. There's even a veggie burger—the West Coast Garden Burger—for those of you who would prefer to avoid both meat and fish.

For those of you who *want* both meat and fish, there's an option, too. The Surf & Turf combines a 6-ounce AAA steak with jumbo tiger prawns. Accompanied by steamed vegetables, seasoned potato wedges, and a choice of Rock Cod or Caesar salad, it's a deliciously sophisticated alternative to the beautiful simplicity of fish and chips. The Rock Cod's Asian Bowls are the menu's international twist, and each one—the Asian Crispy Halibut Bowl, Teriyaki Salmon Bowl, Sweet Thai Prawn Bowl, and Asian Fusion Torpedo Prawn Bowl—capitalizes on gifts from the sea.

Desserts are many and varied, and the Sex in a Pan is sure to pique your curiosity. I mean, how big do they make pans in Cowichan Bay, anyway?

Ask owner Jacob Hokanson what distinguishes his fish and chips and he'll tell you it's the batter, a recipe passed on to him from the restaurant's previous owner.

Halibut and Chips

Makes: 4 servings

Batter

2 cups all-purpose flour

1 tablespoon baking powder

1 tablespoon salt

1/2 teaspoon cayenne pepper

2 1/2 cups water

1 tablespoon lemon juice

Tartar Sauce

1 1/2 cups mayonnaise

3/4 cup sweet green relish

1 tablespoon lemon juice (or to taste)

Grill Flour

1 1/2 cups all-purpose flour

2 tablespoons dried dillweed

1 tablespoon each lemon pepper, garlic salt, and paprika

Assembly

Oil for deep-frying

3 pounds Kennebec or russet potatoes, cut into 1/2-inch fries

16 ounces halibut fillet, cut into 4-ounce pieces

Coleslaw

Lemon wedges for garnish

Batter

In a medium bowl, whisk together the flour, baking powder, salt, cayenne, water, and lemon juice; set aside.

Tartar Sauce

In a small bowl, stir together the mayonnaise, relish, and lemon juice; set aside.

Grill Flour

In a small bowl, stir together the flour, dillweed, lemon pepper, garlic salt, and paprika; set aside.

Assembly

Preheat oven to 325°F.

Pour 2 or 3 inches of oil into a large heavy pot and heat over medium-high heat (or use a deep-fryer). Deep-fry the potatoes in the hot oil for 7 to 10 minutes or until golden. Drain fries on paper towels, then transfer to a baking sheet and keep warm in the oven.

Dredge the halibut in the grill flour, then in the batter. Deep-fry the fish until golden brown.

Serve the fish with the fries, coleslaw, and tartar sauce. Garnish with lemon wedges.

SugarBowl

EST. 1942
10922 88TH AVENUE
EDMONTON · AB · T6G 0Z1
WWW.THESUGARBOWL.ORG

omeone call Charles Darwin, because evolution is alive and well, and it's happening right here in Edmonton.

The SugarBowl opened its doors back in 1942, serving homemade burgers and fries. New owners redefined the restaurant in 1987, transforming it into a relaxed, Belgian-style café. And the evolution has continued since 1995, when owner Abel Shiferaw reinvented the SugarBowl as one of Edmonton's premier comfort restaurants, offering a full menu of inventive and heart-warming food, a variety

The SugarBowl's dining room is large, relaxed, and inviting, and its two glass garage doors stay open all summer long.

of beer, and an extensive wine list. Whether you're coming for breakfast, lunch, dinner, or weekend brunch—or are just making a special trip for what some have called the best damn cinnamon buns on Earth—you're bound to be happier after a trip to the SugarBowl.

And who wouldn't be after digging into Abel's cinnamon buns? Lauded by local media who consistently rate them as one of the best reasons to visit Edmonton, Abel's steamy buns are so popular they frequently sell out before noon. In fact, loving parents will often buy boxes of the things to ship to their kids away at university.

Gigantic, sticky, sweet, and melt-in-your-mouth amazing, the buns start with a buttery, sweet, cinnamony yeast dough that is shaped into rolls, submerged in a bowl of melted butter, coated in cinnamon sugar, then twisted and shaped by Abel's masterful hands into giant knots of love and affection. They almost double in size when they bake, after which they're brushed with more butter and sprinkled with yet more cinnamon sugar. I don't know if Darwin ever tasted anything as heavenly as this, but he would have been a happier man if he did.

Abel takes great pride in his food, and it's evident in everything he sells, particularly his house specialty, Chicken and Waffles. The dish starts with a classic Belgian waffle batter flavoured with buttermilk, brown sugar, and vanilla. Meanwhile, Abel cooks up a couple of big chicken breasts that have spent the night getting intimate with a buttermilk marinade. The breasts are breaded,

Take my advice and order your Sugar-Bowl cinnamon buns to go. If you stay and eat them, you may never leave!

fried, and baked to a perfect golden-brown finish, laid gently on the soft, spongy waffles, then topped with homemade maple butter. The sweet and savoury result is unforgettable. And sure, you can be genteel and use a fork and knife, but I prefer to slam the chicken between the waffles and make a sandwich out of it . . . easier and faster! And messier. Definitely messier.

Every item on the SugarBowl's menu seems to have that special combination of inventiveness, size, warmth, and love. The Bison Chili gives a blast of flavours in every bite, and is hugely popular with the large, friendly crowds that fill the SugarBowl's inviting dining room. Steak and Frites uses fresh local flank steak smothered in homemade blue cheese butter and chipotle mayo. Espresso BBQ Riblets cover roasted pork ribs in the house-made Espresso BBQ Sauce, while Hoegaarden and Bacon Mussels steam PEI mussels in bacon, garlic, butter, and Hoegaarden beer.

Abel knocked me on my ass with his signature Lamb and Goat Cheese Burger, a ridiculously thick and juicy sandwich that starts with ground lamb seasoned with a mind-boggling array of onion, garlic, jalapeños, eggs, rosemary, mint, parsley, lemon juice, allspice, cumin, and coriander. The grilled patty is served on a fresh brioche bun coated in Guinness mustard and weighed down by an improbably thick slab of goat cheese and a mound of caramelized onions. This was one of the best burgers I've ever eaten, and the marriage of its many flavours was love at first bite.

Like so many who are drawn to the restaurant business, SugarBowl owner Abel Shiferaw is happiest when people are gorging themselves on his restaurant's offerings.

Desserts? Yes. It's called the SugarBowl, after all. Each is delicious in its own right, but the Bread Pudding—made with their cinnamon buns—is a treat you won't want to miss. You may never want to leave the place after a bowl of this, and something tells me Darwin would have a theory about that, too.

Every item on the SugarBowl's menu seems to have that special combination of inventiveness, size, warmth, and love.

Lamb and Goat Cheese Burger with Stout Mustard and Garlic Aïoli

Makes: 6 or 8 burgers

Lamb Burgers

2 eggs

1/4 cup lemon juice

1 onion, finely chopped

4 garlic cloves, minced

2 jalapeño peppers (with or without seeds), minced

1/2 cup each minced fresh mint, parsley, and rosemary

2 tablespoons ground coriander

1 tablespoon each crumbled dried oregano and ground cumin

1 1/2 teaspoons ground allspice

2 1/2 tablespoons each salt and pepper

3 pounds lean ground organic lamb

Stout Mustard

3 tablespoons brown mustard seeds

1/4 cup stout beer such as Guinness

2 tablespoons balsamic vinegar

1 1/2 teaspoons salt

Garlic Aïoli

1/2 cup mayonnaise

1 garlic clove, minced

2 tablespoons lemon juice

1 tablespoon minced fresh parsley

1 1/2 teaspoons each salt and pepper

Caramelized Onions

2 tablespoons unsalted butter

1 large onion, sliced

1/2 teaspoon salt

Assembly

2 tablespoons canola oil

1 pound goat cheese

6 or 8 brioche buns or kaiser rolls

Lettuce leaves

2 tomatoes, sliced

Timing note: Start the stout mustard 1 or 2 days ahead.

Stout Mustard

In a small bowl, combine the mustard seeds, stout, balsamic vinegar, and salt. Cover and refrigerate overnight.

In a blender, process mustard mixture for 2 minutes. Refrigerate for 24 to 48 hours.

Garlic Aïoli

In a small bowl, combine the mayonnaise, garlic, lemon juice, parsley, and salt and pepper. Stir until well combined. Refrigerate until needed.

Lamb Burgers

In a large bowl, beat together the eggs and lemon juice. Stir in the onion, garlic, jalapeños, mint, parsley, rosemary, coriander, oregano, cumin, allspice, and salt and pepper. Add the ground lamb and mix until well combined. Shape into 6 or 8 patties. Refrigerate.

Caramelized Onions

Melt the butter in a large skillet over low heat. Add the onions and salt; cook, stirring occasionally, until golden, 15 to 20 minutes. Remove from heat.

Assembly

Heat the canola oil in a large nonstick skillet over medium heat. Add the burgers and fry for 4 minutes. Flip the burgers and fry for another 3 minutes or until juices run clear.

Sprinkle a generous amount of goat cheese over the burgers and cook for another 2 minutes. Meanwhile, warm the buns in the microwave.

Slice the buns in half. Spread garlic aïoli on one half of each bun. Spread the Stout Mustard on the other half. Assemble the burger as desired, adding the lettuce, tomatoes, and caramelized onions.

The Tallest Poppy

EST. 2007
631 MAIN STREET
WINNIPEG · MB · R3B 1E1
WWW.THETALLESTPOPPY.COM

When Talia Syrie's catering business found the kitchen space it needed in Winnipeg's recently renovated Occidental Hotel, little did she know there would be a catch: open a restaurant out front, too. It didn't matter to Talia that she had no restaurant experience. With recipes from her sister, mother, and grandmother in hand, she opened the Tallest Poppy, a retro-chic café where classic Jewish cooking gets new life.

Since its opening in 2007, the Tallest Poppy has developed a reputation for serving delicious comfort food made from scratch. And if people are nervous about the old neighbourhood's reputation, that apparently doesn't stop them from making the pilgrimage to the North Main Strip for a bowl of borscht and some blintzes.

The Poppy's breakfast menu offers a wide selection, from the pulled pork Po' Boy sandwich to the Breakfast Burrito. But what made my mouth water in the morning was Talia's Chicken Fried Steak and Eggs, which features her mother's brisket recipe. The beef is braised in red wine, Worcestershire sauce, garlic, and onions, then slow-cooked for at least six hours on a bed of onions.

Talia then breads improbably thick slices of the brisket and fries them in a pan of vegetable oil. Top with a couple of fried eggs, surround with two slices of delicious cheese-and-onion fougasse bread, drown in homemade gravy and . . . Bubbie! This is good eating! The brisket is melt-in-your mouth tender beneath its crispy coating, and the creamy eggs and crunchy toast all combine for a meal you'll be craving for a long time to come.

The lunch menu at the Poppy is an ever-changing affair, and you never quite know what you're going to get. One thing's for sure, though: Talia is not afraid

The Tallest Poppy plays host to an eclectic clientele, from rock bands to ladies who lunch. Weekend brunches are served family style, with platters of food placed at the centre of the table for sharing.

of tinkering with her ancestors' recipes, as her Corned Elk Reuben Sandwich attests. Talia corns her own meat, whether it's beef, bison, or elk. The meat is brined for at least a week in a corning solution flavoured with peppercorns, bay leaves, mustard seeds, caraway, fennel, cinnamon, dried peppers, oregano, and lots of fresh garlic.

After it's been slow-cooked for hours, the corned elk is sliced and fried on the flattop grill in a heaping mound covered with homemade sauerkraut and mozzarella cheese. Pile high on fougasse that's been coated in homemade Thousand Island dressing and Talia's signature poppy butter, throw in some lettuce and tomatoes for good measure, and you've got a sandwich that will barely fit in your mouth. But once it does, it's well worth the effort, my little *chaver*. Tender, drip-down-your-face juicy, this is big-time munching!

Call your baba and tell her to take the morning off. Talia's Chicken Fried Steak and Eggs is as good as homemade . . . only you don't have to make it!

And if you're wondering why Talia's right there scrutinizing your reaction to her homemade creations, it's probably because she puts a little bit of her heart into every meal she makes. Customers here say you can taste the love that goes into the food. I know I did. Whether it's the Poppy's Hybrid Burgers (which combine ground beef, pork, bison, and elk), homemade meatloaf (wrapped in bacon!), or even tongue (a cured delicacy that Talia plans to force on her customers . . . whether they like it or not!), every dish here comes with an extra-special ingredient you can't find everywhere.

Talia's challah bread is the product of her great-grandmother's recipe. She'll also stuff you full of blintzes, traditional Jewish crêpes that she'll happily serve you with a classic cottage cheese filling. But given her non-traditional side, Talia also whips up blintzes stuffed thick with butternut squash and Parmesan, bacon and blue cheese, sheep's feta and spinach, mushrooms, kasha (buckwheat) and onions, sweet potato and walnut, and even pulled pork.

So what if Talia's granny may cringe at having her cottage cheese filling violated? The customers can't get enough. It's that combination of old and new that keeps people coming back. For in the end, it's just like Saturday afternoon at your Jewish grandmother's house . . . minus the guilt trip for not visiting more often.

With recipes from her sister, mother, and grandmother in hand, Talia opened the Tallest Poppy, a retro-chic café where classic Jewish cooking gets new life.

Sweet Potato Blintzes

Makes: 28 blintzes

Blintz Crêpes

4 eggs

3 tablespoons vegetable oil

1 teaspoon salt

1 3/4 cups all-purpose flour

1 3/4 cups water

Sweet Potato Filling

1 1/2 cups mashed boiled sweet potato

1 pkg (16 ounces/454 g) dry curd cottage cheese

1 egg

1 tablespoon margarine, melted

1 tablespoon sugar

1 teaspoon pepper

3/4 teaspoon salt

1 handful walnuts, roughly chopped

Assembly

1 tablespoon unsalted butter

Blintz Crêpes

In a large bowl, combine the eggs, vegetable oil, and salt. Beat with an electric mixer on low speed. Add flour and water, alternating 1/4 cup of each at a time, beating well after each addition.

Heat a 6-inch skillet over medium heat. Brush the pan with a little oil.

Pour 1/4 cup of the batter into the centre of the pan, lift off the heat, and tilt the pan so the batter coats the bottom evenly. Return pan to the heat and cook the crêpe for 3 minutes or until the edges turn light brown.

Gently loosen the crêpe with a spatula and flip it over. Cook for another 2 minutes or until lightly browned. Transfer to a plate.

Repeat with remaining batter, stacking finished crêpes on top of each other.

Sweet Potato Filling

In a large bowl, combine the sweet potato, cottage cheese, egg, margarine, sugar, pepper, and salt. Beat with an electric mixer on low speed. Stir in walnuts.

Assembly

Place 2 tablespoons of the filling on each crêpe. Roll up like a burrito, tucking in the sides.

Melt the butter in a large skillet over medium heat. Brown the blintzes lightly on both sides.

Serve with sour cream and fresh fruit or compote.

My Great-Grandmother's Challah

Makes: 2 loaves

1 1/2 teaspoons active dry yeast

1 teaspoon sugar

1/2 cup lukewarm water

7 cups all-purpose flour

1 tablespoon salt

4 eggs

1/2 cup sugar

1/2 cup vegetable oil

1 1/2 cups warm water

Egg wash (1 egg, beaten)

In a medium bowl, stir together the yeast, sugar, and lukewarm water. Let sit until foamy, about 10 minutes.

In a large bowl, combine the flour and salt.

Add the eggs, sugar, and vegetable oil to the yeast mixture; mix well. Add to the flour mixture and stir until the dough comes together.

Knead the dough on a floured surface for about 10 minutes, or until it is smooth and elastic (Grandma used to say "smooth as a baby's tush").

Place the dough in a large oiled bowl and cover with a kitchen cloth. Let rise until it has doubled in size, about 2 1/2 hours.

Turn the dough out onto a floured surface and gently knead it to deflate it. Return to the bowl, cover, and let rise again, about 2 1/2 hours.

Preheat oven to 350°F. Line a baking sheet with parchment paper.

Divide the dough into 6 equal pieces. Roll and pull each piece into a rope about 1 1/2 feet long. Braid 3 ropes together to make a loaf, pinching and tucking under the ends. Repeat to make a second loaf.

Place loaves on the baking sheet and brush with the egg wash.

Bake for 30 to 40 minutes, or until golden brown. Cool on racks.

The Tomahawk Barbecue

EST. 1926
1550 PHILIP AVENUE
NORTH VANCOUVER · BC · V7P 2V8
WWW.TOMAHAWKRESTAURANT.COM

I know I'm in for a rare treat when a restaurant owner introduces me to everybody in the restaurant by name. And that's exactly what happened at the Tomahawk, which has assumed legendary status in North Vancouver.

How else can you describe an eatery that traces its roots back to 1926, when founder Chick Chamberlain opened the Tomahawk as Vancouver's first drive-in restaurant? Back then, diners would park in front and wait patiently for Chick to emerge and take their orders. Then he would go back inside, cook the order, and deliver it to the car. For those who didn't have the luxury of an automobile (or arrived on horseback), there were fourteen stools and a counter inside, wrapped in a neat horseshoe around the grill where Chick plied his trade and kept the conversation flowing.

In the eighty-plus years since, the Tomahawk has built a reputation for delicious, belly-warming food, mountainous portions, and an interior design that straddles the fine line between museum and urban kitsch. The decor is testimony to the Chamberlain family's fascination with the culture of First Nations people of the West Coast. It's little surprise, really: when money was tight during the Depression, Chick would often trade food for objects with local First Nations bands.

A Tlingit tribal totem stands watch over the Tomahawk's entrance. Known as the Fog Woman Totem, it depicts the legend of the creation of the Salmon.

But as quirky as the restaurant's style might be, the secret to its success lies in its strict adherence to rock-solid principles: keep it in the family and cook delicious food. Chick's son Chuck is the current owner and the brains behind the menu, the foundation of which is breakfast. And while the breakfast choices are many and varied at the Tomahawk, you can give me the Yukon-Style Bacon and Eggs any time, one of its biggest all-time sellers.

The Yukon is a rustic combination of four toast wedges buried under hand-cut hash browns and framed by two fried eggs. But the highlight of the Yukon breakfast—and many breakfasts at

the Tomahawk, for that matter—is the five slices of Yukon-style bacon piled on the plate. I don't know what kind of pigs they grow in the Yukon, but I want one! This is bacon like I've never eaten before: round like pancetta, succulent and meaty, but far less greasy and salty than traditional strip bacon. Ask head chef Natalie Davis where the bacon comes from, and she clams up. The source is top secret, she says. So just eat and enjoy.

The party doesn't stop with breakfast. The Tomahawk offers tons of lunch and dinner choices, though their burgers garner the highest ranking on the Wow! scale. The hallmark of Tomahawk burgers is certified organic beef sourced from a local producer. As if that wasn't enough, Natalie adds mountains of toppings, transforming her burgers from sublime to . . . sublimer!

I dug into two of these mouth-stretching bad boys, each of which was named after a local First Nations chief from years gone by. The Chief Simon Baker Burger is a skyscraper of bacon, mushrooms, cheese, patty, bacon, mushrooms, and cheese. The Skookum Chief Burger is a goliath that starts with special sauce and a mound of let-

You don't have to have a gold miner's appetite to forge your way through the Yukon Breakfast's heaps of deliciousness . . . but it sure helps!

tuce, followed by bacon, Cheddar, a split hotdog, a fried egg, more bacon, more Cheddar, tomatoes, a pickle . . . and oh yeah, the burger, too! Eating it is a two-step process: (1) squish; (2) open wide!

For those who prefer not to dislocate their jaws during a meal, there are more manageable options. The Steak and Mushroom Pie is a succulent concoction of organic Angus beef chunks and sautéed mushrooms, served dripping with gravy in a buttery homemade pastry shell. Any day of the year you can dive into the Roasted Turkey Dinner, a massive plate of slow-roasted meat topped with homemade stuffing and cranberry relish, with mashed potatoes and veg, all smothered in the Tomahawk's thick gravy. And what's a turkey dinner without a slice of pie . . . as in the Tomahawk's Mincemeat Pumpkin Pie, which fuses two holiday classics into one damn good dessert.

If you're anywhere near North Vancouver and want to sample a taste of a living legend, the Tomahawk should be high on your list of must-see restaurants. And even though it might be your first visit, expect to be treated like family. As Chuck likes to say, the community is as much a part of the Tomahawk as the Tomahawk is part of the community.

As quirky as the restaurant's style might be, the secret to its success lies in its strict adherence to rock-solid principles.

3 eggs
1 can (28 ounces/796 mL) pumpkin purée
1 cup sugar
1 cup canned evaporated milk
1/2 teaspoon each cinnamon and ground ginger
Pinch each of nutmeg, ground cloves, and salt
1 cup mincemeat filling (homemade or store-bought)
9-inch uncooked pie shell

Preheat oven to 350°F.

In a stand mixer fitted with the paddle attachment (or using an electric mixer), combine the eggs, pumpkin, sugar, evaporated milk, cinnamon, ginger, nutmeg, cloves, and salt; mix together on low speed for 10 minutes.

Spread the mincemeat filling evenly in the pie shell. Pour the pumpkin filling evenly over the mincemeat.

Bake for 1 hour or until filling is no longer jiggly. Cool for 15 minutes.

Serve warm with vanilla ice cream or whipped cream.

Topanga Cafe

EST. 1978
2904 WEST 4TH AVENUE
VANCOUVER · BC · V6K 4A9
WWW.TOPANGACAFE.COM

I f the secret to good Mexican cooking is the freshness of the ingredients, then the folks at the Topanga Cafe know exactly what they're doing. A Kitsilano favourite for more than three decades, the Topanga combines a funky atmosphere with creative cooking and friendly staff to give Vancouverites a south-of-the-border experience in their own backyard.

The vibe at Topanga is warm and friendly, and evident as soon as you walk through the door. The walls are covered in what seems like hundreds of framed placemats, all of which have been ingeniously coloured by visitors over the years. Boisterous and busy, the Topanga has a dedicated local following and is popular with families and university students alike. They come for the huge portions, reasonable prices, and extensive menu. At the Topanga, you're guaranteed a superb meal every time.

Of course it's California style: the Topanga's original owners moved from California to Vancouver and brought recipes with them.

And if that meal includes the Wet Prawn Burrito, all the better! This classic starts with a pile of prawns marinated in a tangy mixture of oil, cilantro, onions, garlic, roasted jalapeños, spices, and lemon juice, then fried on the flattop until they're deliciously pink. But this is just the beginning. The prawns are added to a buttered and lightly fried flour tortilla, covered in chili relleno sauce, then rolled and placed on a massive plate between piles of refried beans and rice.

Hold your horses, pardner, there's more! The burrito is then doused in enchilada sauce (it's a *wet* burrito, remember?), covered in a mound of Monterey Jack cheese, and popped in the oven. When the dish comes out, all sticky and gooey with cheesy deliciousness, the finishing touch goes on: a hefty smothering of the Topanga's avocado sauce, a scoop of sour cream, and a black olive for good measure. It's so garlicky, fresh, and delicious, you'll have a hard time putting your fork down. Just remember to freshen your breath before that hot date or business meeting!

The Topanga Cafe's current owner is Andrew Pyatt, who started out as the restaurant's dishwasher back in 1988.

In addition to other classic Mexican fare like tacos, enchiladas, nachos, chimichangas, flautas, quesadillas, and tostadas, the Topanga serves a number of specialties. Here you can dine on exotic meals like Mexican Pizza or Chile Papa, but one of my favourites was the Carne Norteña (Meat of the North), which arrives at your table like a fajita, with a warm tortilla on the side.

Like many other Topanga dishes, the Carne Norteña is served on a platter framed by refried beans and rice. In the middle of this picture is the focus of the meal, a heap of tender, tangy marinated pork tenderloin hunks that have been fried on the flattop grill with a mixture of onions, bell peppers, and tomatoes. Smothered in fresh salsa, sour cream, green onions, Cheddar cheese, fresh tomatoes, and lettuce, it is a perfect combination. The meat is moist and juicy, and cooked to perfection.

Need a little sugar to set you free? Try the Homemade Chocolate Cake, a dense, moist delight that's covered in rich chocolate icing. OK, so it's not covered in avocado sauce, but I think I'll let them slide on this one.

A Kitsilano favourite for more than three decades, the Topanga gives Vancouverites a south-of-the-border experience in their own backyard.

Wet Prawn Burritos

Makes: 4 to 6 servings

Timing note: Make the chili relleno sauce, enchilada sauce, and avocado sauce while the shrimp are marinating. If you're roasting your own jalapeño peppers, roast 4 at once.

Marinated Prawns

1/2 cup canola oil

1/4 bunch fresh cilantro

2 garlic cloves

1 small roasted jalapeño pepper (home-roasted or bottled)

1/4 cup finely chopped onion

1 1/2 teaspoons lemon juice

1/2 teaspoon black pepper

1/4 teaspoon salt

1/4 teaspoon paprika

1/4 teaspoon dry mustard

2 pounds large prawns or shrimp (unpeeled)

Chili Relleno Sauce

1 can (14 ounces/398 mL) whole tomatoes, slightly drained

1/2 can (12 ounces/340 g) crushed tomatillos

3 garlic cloves

2 1/2 cups finely chopped onions

1 small roasted jalapeño pepper (home-roasted or bottled)

1 tablespoon vegetable oil

1 teaspoon salt

1/4 cup diced green chili pepper

Enchilada Sauce

1 can (14 ounces/398 mL) stewed tomatoes

3 garlic cloves

1/2 cup finely chopped onion

1 teaspoon hot pepper flakes

1/2 cup chili powder

Vegetable oil

Pinch of salt

Avocado Sauce

2 avocados

2 small roasted jalapeño peppers (home-roasted or bottled), finely chopped

1 or 2 garlic cloves, minced

1/2 cup chopped fresh cilantro

1/2 cup sour cream

1/4 cup finely chopped onion

1/4 cup diced tomato

1 tablespoon lemon juice

1/2 teaspoon black pepper

1/4 teaspoon dry mustard

1/4 teaspoon paprika

Pinch of salt

Assembly

4 to 6 flour tortillas

Refried beans

4 ounces Monterey Jack cheese, shredded

Sour cream for garnish

4 to 6 olives for garnish

Marinated Prawns

Place all ingredients except the prawns in a blender and purée. In a bowl or resealable plastic bag, combine the prawns and the marinade. Marinate prawns, refrigerated, for 2 to 4 hours.

Chili Relleno Sauce

In a blender, combine the tomatoes, tomatillos, garlic, 1/2 cup of the onions, and the jalapeño. Blend until smooth. Set aside.

In a large saucepan, heat the oil over medium-high heat. Add the remaining 2 cups onions and the salt. Sauté until mostly caramelized.

Add the tomato mixture, reduce heat, and simmer for 1 hour. Stir in the green chili. Remove from heat.

Enchilada Sauce

In a blender, combine the tomatoes, garlic, onion, and hot pepper flakes. Blend until smooth. Set aside.

Place the chili powder in a large saucepan. Stir in just enough oil to dampen the chili powder. Heat slightly. Add the tomato mixture and salt; bring to a boil, stirring often. Reduce heat and simmer, stirring occasionally, for 1 hour.

Avocado Sauce

In a medium bowl, coarsely mash the avocados with a fork. Add the jalapeño peppers, garlic, cilantro, sour cream, onion, tomato, lemon juice, black pepper, mustard, paprika, and salt. Taste and adjust seasonings.

Assembly

Preheat grill. Preheat oven to 350°F.

Grill the prawns until the inside is white and the peel is orange. Set aside.

Warm the tortillas. Place 10 to 12 prawns down the centre of each tortilla. Top with your desired amount of chili relleno sauce and loosely roll the tortillas up. Transfer burritos to a shallow baking dish along with the refried beans. Cover each burrito with enchilada sauce and a few ounces of Monterey Jack cheese.

Bake until the cheese starts to lightly brown.

Cover each burrito with avocado sauce. Garnish with a dab of sour cream and an olive.

Tres Carnales Taquería

EST. 2011
10119 100A STREET NW
EDMONTON · AB · T5J 0R5
WWW.TRESCARNALES.COM

How do you know a city is ready for a dietary change? Open a Mexican restaurant, put beef tongue tacos (did you get the *tongue* part?) on the menu, and watch them fly out the door! That's exactly what happened with Tres Carnales Taquería, the authentic Mexican restaurant Edmonton apparently was waiting for.

Tres Carnales is the brainchild of Edgar Gutierrez, Daniel Braun, and Chris Sills, three amigos who met in Edmonton with a common dream of owning their own restaurant. Although the eatery hasn't been open very long, it's already made a huge impact on the Edmonton food scene. Vibrant, lively, and welcoming, Tres Carnales feels as much like Mexico as it tastes, from the open kitchen to the Mexican hip-hop.

Tres Carnales keeps things simple, wowing its customers with authenticity rather than a dizzying array of menu items. The foundation of the menu are the eight different fillings that can be put on tacos, quesadillas, or tortas. The tacos and quesadillas are founded upon tortillas brought in fresh every day from a nearby Mexican family; tortas are warm sandwiches served on fresh buns from a local bakery.

Before opening Tres Carnales, co-owners Daniel, Edgar, and Chris set out on a research vacation to Mexico, sampling food from every taco stand and restaurant they could find.

I've eaten lots of sandwiches in my day, but the Chorizo Torta that chef Edgar made for me was not your typical Canadian bread-and-meat affair. It starts with chorizo, a house-made Mexican ground sausage and one of the eight Tres Carnales fillings. Edgar's special recipe is a combination of ground pork, chilies, onions, garlic, cloves, cinnamon, vinegar, dried ginger, allspice, oregano, chili powder, and achiote (a popular Mexican spice blend that gives food a distinctive red hue).

Tres Carnales feels as much like Mexico as it tastes, from the open kitchen to the Mexican hip-hop.

But it's not just the meat that gives the torta its one-of-a-kind taste. Edgar throws a pile of shredded cheese on the flattop grill, then lays one side of the split bun on top. When the cheese has melted to a nice brown crisp, he scoops it off the flattop, piles on the meat, then tops it all off with guacamole, cabbage, and two of their six homemade salsas: Mexicana (traditional salsa) and Aguacatillo (a mix between salsa verde and guacamole). I love this sandwich! The blend of meat and sauces was a non-stop party on my tongue, and the melted cheese was crispy but still gooey.

Other than the chorizo quesadilla, Tres Carnales offers seven other fillings for its tacos, quesadillas, and tortas. The Arrachera is made with marinated flank steak, grilled and cut into strips. When an order comes in, the meat is sautéed on the flattop. I had the Arrachera on three soft tacos stuffed with shredded cheese and drizzled with Salsa Mexicana, served with homemade Salsa Roja, a traditional red salsa made with tomatoes, onions, garlic, and chilies. The meat was cooked to perfection; the heat from the salsa cleared my nasal passages.

No, *lucha libre* isn't a new dish at Tres Carnales. It's Mexican wrestling, and if the folks at *You Gotta Eat Here!* ever show me the door, I'm hitting the mat in Tijuana.

Other fillings at Tres Carnales include the Pollo Asado (marinated and grilled chicken), Carnitas (pulled pork shoulder slow-cooked in its own fat), Pescado (lightly battered and fried Pacific red snapper), Rajas con Crema (a creamy blend of grilled poblano chilies, corn, and onions), and Vegetariano (poblanos and vegetables in adobo sauce). But the one that set my heart a-skippin' was the Al Pastor, marinated pork loin steaks piled on a vertical spit then slow-roasted, shwarma style. The pork is shaved off for each meal, which in my case was tacos, and served with a homemade fire-roasted Pineapple and Habanero Salsa.

And if you're still waiting for a beef tongue taco, you may have to hold your breath. It's a special item that makes its way onto the weekly features board only once in a while. Just don't be surprised if they're sold out.

Arrachera Marinade

3 cups soy sauce
1/2 cup lime juice
1/4 cup granulated garlic
1/4 cup pepper
1/4 cup vegetable oil
1/4 cup Worcestershire sauce

Arrachera Steak

4 1/2 pounds flank steak
1 to 2 tablespoons vegetable oil

Salsa Verde

2 pounds tomatillos
5 serrano chilies
Leaves from 1 bunch fresh cilantro
1 onion, cut into quarters
2 cups water
1 teaspoon salt

Assembly

Corn tortillas
Vegetable oil
Chopped onion
Chopped fresh cilantro
Lime wedges

Salsa Verde

Combine the tomatillos and serrano chilies in a pot and cover with cold water. Bring to a boil over high heat; turn off the heat and let stand for 20 minutes.

Drain the tomatillos and chilies. Working in batches if necessary, in a blender combine the tomatillos, chilies, cilantro, onion, and 2 cups water. Blend at medium speed for 3 minutes. Season with the salt. Set aside.

Arrachera Marinade

In a shallow dish large enough to hold the flank steak, combine all marinade ingredients and whisk together until blended.

Arrachera Steak

Place the flank steak in the marinade and cover with plastic wrap. Let it sit in the refrigerator for at least 4 hours and up to 24 hours.

Preheat grill to medium-low (or heat a grill pan over medium heat).

Grill the flank steak for 7 to 8 minutes on each side or to desired doneness. Once cooked, remove from heat and let sit for 15 minutes.

Slice the steak into 1/2-inch-thick strips. Chop the strips into cubes.

Heat the oil in a large skillet over medium-high heat. Add the cubed steak and fry, stirring constantly, until the meat gets crispy edges and caramelizes, 5 to 10 minutes.

Assembly (for each serving)

To assemble tacos, lightly toast 2 corn tortillas on a griddle or in a large skillet with 1 tablespoon vegetable oil.

Stack tortillas on a plate and spoon on a heaping mound of flank steak.

Top with a tablespoon of salsa verde, and garnish with chopped onion, cilantro, and a wedge of lime.

Note: To turn this into a Tres Carnales quesadilla, stuff with cheese like Oaxaca, Gouda, or mozzarella and fold your tortilla in half.

Tubby Dog

EST. 2005
1022 17TH AVENUE SW
CALGARY · AB · T2T 0A5
WWW.TUBBYDOG.COM

Art-school student by day and bartender by night, Jon Truch couldn't figure out how to kick-start business on those long, slow Tuesday nights when nobody seemed interested in having a drink. Until someone gave him a hotdog rotisserie, that is. That's when the light bulb in his head started blinking, and Jon began to give away dogs to accompany the drafts he was pouring. Well, bar business went through the roof, and pretty soon more people came for the wieners than for the drinks. The cult was building.

When demand would not let up, Jon knew that his future was in the art of the dog, and Tubby Dog was born. Now the restaurant is nothing short of a Calgary phenomenon, and Jon sculpts meat-and-bread creations that Michelangelo himself would be proud to eat.

Tubby Dog changes personality depending on the evening. On Tuesdays it's a taquería, while gamers converge on Wednesdays for Street Fighter. Fridays feature a DJ spinning '60s garage, soul, and R&B tunes.

In case you haven't picked up on what I'm putting down, Tubby Dogs does hotdogs, more hotdogs, and only hotdogs. Sure, you can snag a side of yam fries, T-rings, Tubby chips, Anna's pickled eggs, or big pickles, but that's where the non-canine variety comes to a screeching halt. Unless you order a beer, that is. Then you can choose from domestic, imported, or a Big Beer. Woo-hoo!

To the dogs, sir! Tubby serves up several different 1/3-pound wieners, including the Classic Dog (beef-chicken mix), the Turkey Dog, the Not Dog (veggie), and the monstrous 1/2-pound Ukey, a Ukrainian sausage made by a local butcher according to Jon's grandfather's family recipe. Smaller appetites can opt for the more demure Jr. Dog, a 1/4-pound version of any wiener on the menu.

But if you think choosing the type of dog is a challenge, you have yet to set eyes upon the menu, where Jon assembles some of the most mind-bogglingly delicious wiener combinations this side of Frankfurt. Want proof? Then try the Sumo, the cowboy sushi of the Tubby Dog menu. A soft, freshly steamed bun is lined with wasabi, upon which the dog is lovingly placed. Next comes the Japanese mayonnaise, seaweed salad (known as wakame), pickled ginger, and a sprinkle of lightly toasted sesame seeds. In other words, take everything you love about sushi, then add meat. *Banzai!*

The A-bomb dog tries to stuff a Ukey into a bun, but there's a lot of meat sticking out either end. Squirt on some mustard (which Jon says is the foundation of any great dog), then add ketchup, mayo, and heaps of bacon bits. But Jon's just getting started. Now he piles on mounds of potato chips, a blend of all-dressed, sour cream and onion, barbeque, ketchup, and salt and vinegar. Then comes a generous squirt of what Jon calls Space Cheese, liquefied cheese he keeps warm all day in the steamer. One bite and you'll realize why this is Tubby's best seller. Chips on a dog? Killer!

Owner Jon Truch may be the shock jock of the hotdog world, but his food is all about the quality. He makes many of his condiments from scratch and uses double-smoked butcher bacon as often as he can.

If you really want to test the limits of hotdogdom, then dive into Sherm's Ultimate Gripper, which starts with a bacon-wrapped dog that meets the deep-fryer. But the dog doesn't hit the bun until the bread is doused in a heap of homemade chili, after which it's topped with a squirt of mustard (the foundation, remember?), piles of banana peppers, sautéed onions, and bacon bits. Done? I think not. Pile on fried ham, a fried egg, and some Space Cheese and you've got a dog that's as challenging to describe as it is to get in your mouth.

Ah, but you say you're walking by Tubby Dog one morning and want something more breakfasty? Jon has just the thing: his insanely inventive Cap'n Dog, which lines the bun with creamy peanut butter, pops in a signature bacon-wrapped dog, then slathers it all in grape jelly and Cap'n Crunch cereal. Who needs oatmeal? This is every kid's fantasy breakfast!

If the regular menu isn't out there enough for you, Tubby's features weekly and monthly special dogs that make use of even more labour-intensive ingredients. Although these specials know only the limit of Jon's vast imagination, you might encounter things like the Gobbler (a garlic turkey dog on a bed of homemade mashed potatoes topped with stuffing, gravy, and cranberry and apple sauce, and served with a slice of pumpkin pie), or the Cinco de Mayo (Spanish chorizo on a crispy taco in a bun with guacamole, topped with raw white onion, pico de gallo, Space Cheese, crème fraîche, taco sauce, and green onions).

And if you're waiting in line and that wrinkled bearded guy in front of you can't make up his mind, cut him a little slack, OK? That's Michelangelo, and he's in awe.

Jon sculpts meat-and-bread creations that Michelangelo himself would be proud to eat.

4 hotdogs
4 hotdog buns
Wasabi
Japanese mayonnaise
Seasoned seaweed salad (wakame)
Pickled ginger (Tubby Dog uses white ginger)
Toasted sesame seeds

Grill, boil, or steam the hotdogs.

Spread the desired amount of wasabi on the buns. Place hotdogs in the buns and spread with
Japanese mayonnaise. Top with seasoned seaweed salad and pickled ginger. Finish with a
light sprinkling of sesame seeds.

Urban Diner

EST. 2004
12427 102 AVENUE NW
EDMONTON · AB · T5N 0M2
WWW.URBANDINER.COM

When a classically trained Dutch chef moves to Edmonton and sees a lack of his native cuisine, he's got two options: move back to Holland or do something about it. For Cyrilles Koppert, the choice was clear. So back in 2004, he and partner Lisa Dungale opened the Urban Diner in downtown Edmonton. The place was such a hit that Cyrilles opened a second location, near the University of Alberta. Now both are booming, with people braving ungodly temperatures to stand in line just to get a taste of Cyrilles's recipes.

And what keeps 'em lined up out the Urban's door are the ridiculously delicious breakfasts, including my personal favourite, the teensy-weensy pancakes known as poffertjes, a traditional Dutch treat that takes everything you love about pancakes and shrinks it down into a tiny package.

The Urban mixes the best of the past with current food trends. In summer, diners can eat under a canopy of elm trees on the large patio at the back of the restaurant.

Beginning with a yeast pancake batter, the secret to poffertjes is the dimpled griddle they're cooked on, not an easy thing to find! In fact, Cyrilles had to import his from Australia. Who knew that the Aussies were such poffertjes fans? Each order gets a dozen of these little puffs of joy, which are sprinkled with icing sugar and served alongside maple syrup, chocolate sauce, and homemade raspberry compote.

In keeping with their reputation of serving up to-die-for breakfasts, the Urban's Huevos Wrap is an international twist that starts with Cyrilles's homemade slow-cooked vegetarian chili laid gently across a tomato-flavoured flour tortilla with a squirt of sweet chili sauce. Pile in scrambled eggs and aged Cheddar, then fold! But Cyrilles isn't ready to serve it to you until after he's baked it in the oven for a few minutes, a trick that helps firm up the tortilla enough that it won't fall apart in your hands when you start tearing into it with animal-like fervour. (OK, so maybe only guys like me tear into food with

Whoa, keep your drool to yourself! The Urban's Huevos Wrap packs a surprising back-end boot of heat, thanks to a squirt of sweet chili sauce.

animal-like fervour . . .) Add a little back-end heat from the chili, serve with homemade hash browns, and you've got a meal that sings with southern delight.

If you can't decide whether it's breakfast or lunch you ache for, why not go for the sandwich that straddles the line between both? The Breakfast Burger starts with a fresh onion kaiser smothered in garlic aïoli and buried under a thick piece of homemade meatloaf, itself a taste sensation thanks to the caramelized vegetables, roasted garlic, herbs, and spices Cyrilles includes in the meat blend. Then he adds just a bit more heft (just a bit) by piling on back bacon, strip bacon, shaved ham, and a fried egg (this is a *breakfast* sandwich, after all).

In case you haven't guessed, the trickiest part of eating this monster is wrapping your mouth around it. But once you do . . . the joy! Like me—and the buckets of other people who start their day with this colossus—you'll be messy but happy.

There's more to the Urban than just breakfast, and Cyrilles will even serve you his meatloaf as a dinner entrée with homemade cranberry chutney, mushroom gravy, and mashed potatoes. The Reuben and Beef Brisket sandwiches are delicious hand-held classics, while the Diner Mac N' Cheese tosses corkscrew cavatappi noodles in a homemade Cheddar sauce that contains secret spices and herbs to give it an unexpected kick. Feeling quirky? Throw in grilled chicken, chicken apple sausage, or hamburger mix.

Dessert at the Urban follows Cyrilles's mantra of honest food with a gourmet twist. Like cheesecake? Try the Cheesecake Balls, which takes chunks of peanut butter and banana cheesecake, moulds them into golf balls, and covers them in chocolate. As a finishing touch, they're rolled in a praline-nut mixture to add an addictive outer layer of crunchiness.

Surprised? Don't be. It's just what you'd expect from a Dutch chef on a mission.

What keeps 'em lined up out the Urban's door are the ridiculously delicious breakfasts, including my personal favourite, the teensy-weensy pancakes known as poffertjes.

Dutch Poffertjes

Makes: 60 pancakes, serving 4 to 5

1 teaspoon active dry yeast

1 tablespoon warm milk

2 cups all-purpose flour

2 large eggs, beaten

1 teaspoon sugar

1/2 teaspoon salt

2 tablespoons unsalted butter, melted

2 tablespoons liquid honey

3 drops vanilla extract

1 cup + 2 tablespoons cold milk

Butter

Garnishes

Icing sugar

Softened butter

Chocolate sauce, maple syrup, or berry compote

Dissolve the yeast in the warm milk. Let sit until foamy, about 10 minutes.

In a large bowl, combine the yeast mixture, flour, eggs, sugar, salt, melted butter, honey, and vanilla. Stir well to combine.

Whisk in 1/2 cup of the cold milk until smooth. Stir in the remaining milk. The batter should fall from the whisk in ribbons. Cover with plastic wrap and let sit in a warm place until thickened and starting to bubble, about an hour.

Optional: Pour the batter into a large squeeze bottle.

Heat a little butter in a large nonstick skillet. Squeeze small dollar-sized dollops of batter into the pan (or drop in teaspoonfuls of the batter in circular movements) and cook until the poffertjes are golden brown and firm. Flip, and cook until golden brown on the bottom.

Dust poffertjes with icing sugar and serve with butter and chocolate sauce, maple syrup, or berry compote.

Acknowledgements

O f the many people who work on *You Gotta Eat Here!*, I have the easiest job. I stuff my face and smile. But there are lots of people who work incredibly hard behind the scenes to make the show a success. Without them, *You Gotta Eat Here!* would not exist, let alone thrive. So this is my humble, talking-with-my-mouth-full way of expressing my gratitude to those who don't get the chance to have their faces shown on TV or in the pages of a book. Thank you to:

❏ Diamondfield Entertainment, particularly my manager, Lorne Perlmutar, and my agent, Morgan Flood, who have always believed in me
❏ Everyone at Shaw Media and Food Network Canada, especially Holly Gillanders and Leslie Merklinger
❏ All the amazing people at Lone Eagle Entertainment:
  • Michael Geddes and Sheldon Teicher for having had the foresight (or lack of judgment) to hire a comedian to host a food show
  • The incredibly talented producers, Rachel Horvath, Steven Mitchell, and Sarah Nixey
  • The hard-working folks of the research department, who helped find all these delicious restaurants: Morgan Leech, Rachel Wagner, Dila Velazquez, Matt Murray, and Kristen Boychuk
  • Bridget Lee, Sylvia van Helden, Margie Shields, and Gabriela Skubincan
  • D'Arcy Butler, Richard Hughes, Chuck Kraft, Russell Gienapp, and all the talented crew members who worked on the first season
  • All the amazingly gifted editors who have worked on the show
  • Everyone at Fearless Post and VO2 Mix Audio Post
❏ My road family, including Jim Morrison, Monique Douek, Scott Chappel, Steve Lindsay, and Josh Henderson: thank you for always having my back and for making fun of me when I deserve it
❏ My co-writer, Mike Vlessides: you made this experience one to remember
❏ Brad Wilson and everyone at HarperCollins
❏ Michael, Sheldon, Rachel, and Sarah Hewitt at Lone Eagle: I really appreciate how effortlessly you added a book to your busy schedules and so skillfully wrangled recipes, research, and photographs for this project; this book wouldn't have been possible without you—or at least it wouldn't have been published on time

❏ My mom, Diana, my sisters, Marta and Rose, and the beautiful extended family that comes along with them, Kathy, Jay, Deanna, and Katherine: thank you for your constant love and support

Finally, to my wife, Shawne, and my daughters, Ruby and Claire: I want you to know that the hardest part of this job is being away from you guys. Thank you for being amazing. I love you lots.

And thanks to you. I hope you enjoy.

John Catucci

Producing a book is a lot like producing a TV show. A few of us are lucky enough to see our names in print, but for every writer, there are a dozen people beavering away in their offices late at night. These folks don't get the glory, but their contribution is no less vital. In the end, *You Gotta Eat Here!* is one hell of a good read, and that blue ribbon belongs as much to the people behind the scenes as it does to John and me.

Of all those folks, though, none played as integral a role as Brad Wilson at HarperCollins. He is as good as editors get, on both sides of the ledger. Not only does he have an uncanny knack for moulding the roughest text into some pretty damn good prose, but he is always there to lend an ear, a hand, or whatever else a frustrated scribe might need. If I were the kind of guy who wore a hat, I'd take it off to him.

Then, of course, there's my boy Johnny C., who (for some bizarre reason) I now count among my friends. I don't know exactly when it happened, but somewhere along the way John and I morphed from total strangers into amigos. And while that association may have dropped his value on the stock market of life, I am a better man for it. Easygoing, dangerously witty, smart, and funny (like . . . really funny), John made me feel like a brother from the first time we spoke. I hope this book reflects our new-found kinship; it's a gift to me.

My miraculous children, Dawson and Teya, are as much a part of this book as I am. They were there with me in every chapter and had to suffer through my dangerous obsession with diner food for a large part of 2012. And I value their collective dedication to being authentically themselves, no small feat for teenagers these days.

Finally, this book is dedicated to my best friend, Carolyn, whose unwavering support and encouragement are of universal proportions.

Michael Vlessides

Lone Eagle Entertainment want to thank the people who make *You Gotta Eat Here!* possible. To our fantastic crew, our production team, and all those who contribute to the show: we appreciate your hard work. Your dedication is what makes the show great.

To Barbara Williams, Christine Shipton, Emily Morgan, Leslie Merklinger, Holly Gillanders, and all of our friends at Shaw Television and Food Network Canada: thank you for giving us an opportunity to showcase Canada's incredible food culture.

And a special thank you to all the great owners and chefs of the restaurants across the country that welcomed us into their kitchens and shared with us their recipes and passions. We love what you are doing, so keep doing it right.

Finally, thanks to the viewers and readers who are fans of the show. We appreciate your support. Now get in the kitchen and cook something great from this book, or get in the car and drive to your favourite hidden gem of a restaurant and order your favourite meal. Go on . . . you deserve it.

Lone Eagle Entertainment

Recipe Index

BREAKFAST

BC Hash, 264
Belgian Waffles with Cream Cheese Syrup, 280
Coastal Cinnamon Skillet, 24
Finnish Pancakes, 150
Huevos Rancheros, 243
Maple Fried Oatmeal, 250
My Great-Grandmother's Challah, 316
Pannenkoek, 298
Ricotta and Mascarpone Blueberry Stuffed
    French Toast, 218
Sweet Potato Blintzes, 314

APPETIZERS

Armadillo Eggs, 118
Arrachera Tacos, 330
Karjalan Piirakka, 148
Meat Muffins, 100
Smoked Chicken Wings with Chipotle Ranch
    Dressing, 12
Smoked Whitefish with Pea Pancakes, 134
Spanakopita, 290
Water-Prince Fish Cakes, 70

BURGERS, SANDWICHES, HOTDOGS

Big Poppa Burger, 182
Bombay Talkie Burger, 238
Dangerous Dan's Cereal Killer, 123
Fat City Franks Ukrainian Perogy Hotdog, 258

Grilled Motzy Sandwich, 130
Haddock Burgers with Tartar Sauce, 8
Lamb and Goat Cheese Burger with Stout
    Mustard and Garlic Aïoli, 310
Lobster Roll, 50
Meatball Hero, The, 56
Meatball Sub, 166
Muffuletta Sandwich, 64
Nine-Pound Burger, The, 234
Red Top Burger, 302
Schwartz's Procedure for Smoking Meat, 190
Straight to LHSC Burger, 186
Stromboli, 210
Sumo Dog, 334
TBQ Pulled Pork Sandwiches, 214
Tommy Gun Open-Faced Beef Sandwich, 262
You Gotta Eat This Burger, 178

PASTA AND PIZZAS

Annie's Gnocchi, 206
Bilbao Pizza, 202
Lobster Linguine, 36
Lobster Mac & Cheese, 28
Mafaldine Casarecce, 174
Penne Gorgonzola, 78
Rick's Seafood Pizza, 46
Roast Beef Pizza, 108
Spaghetti and Meatballs, 76

ENTREES

Bacon-Wrapped Pork Tenderloin, 226

Buttermilk Fried Chicken Strips with Spicy Mayonnaise and Popping Candy, 52

Ches's Stuffed Cod, 20

Chicken Bobotie, 198

Chicken Tigania, 194

Duck Confit with Blueberry Gastrique, 224

Elgin Street Diner Meatloaf, 126

Grandma's Cheese and Potato Perogies, 96

Halibut and Chips, 306

Hearty Beef Stew, 254

Kylling with Potato Salad, 230

Landmark Pan-Fried Haddock, 32

Meatloaf with Peppercorn Demi-Glace and Garlic Mashed Potatoes, 140

Moussaka, 154

Paprika Chicken Stew with Potatoes and Kale, 270

Proper Maritime Boiled Lobster with Dinner Rolls, 40

Rouladen, 162

Smoked St. Louis Ribs, 90

Southwestern Meatloaf with Marsala Sauce, 282

Steak and Kidney Pie, 114

Tourtière, 104

Wet Prawn Burritos, 324

SIDES

Beef and Barley Soup, 242

Busters Jalapeño Sausage in Corn Husks, 91

Cachapas, 170

Cold Borscht Soup, 94

Focaccia, 295

Italian Poutine, 82

Potato Salad, 42

Seafood Chowder, 68

DESSERTS

Beeramisu, 60

Bubi's Chocolate Peanut Butter Cheezcake, 86

Bucket of Mud, 16

Cinnamon Sugar Beignets, 274

Coconut Cream Pie, 144

Cranberry and White Chocolate Scones, 255

Deep-Fried Cheesecake Bites, 246

Deep-Fried Chocolate Bar, 122

Diane's German Chocolate Cake, 158

Dottie's Delicious Lemon Tart, 136

Dutch Poffertjes, 338

Mincemeat Pumpkin Pie, 320

Mrs. Riches Monster Mocha Pie, 286

Nenshi Brown Butter Fondant Drizzle, 276

Pagliacci's New York Cheesecake, 294

Tiramisù, 110

EASTERN CANADA

CARAQUET
❏ *déjà BU!*

49A, boulevard Saint-Pierre Ouest
Caraquet, NB E1W 1B6
506-727-7749
www.dejabu.ca

CHARLOTTETOWN
❏ *Water-Prince Corner Shop and Lobster Pound*

141 Water Street
Charlottetown, PEI C1A 1A8
902-368-3212
www.waterprincelobster.ca

HALIFAX
❏ *The Armview Restaurant & Lounge*

7156 Chebucto Road
Halifax, NS B3L 1N4
902-455-4395
www.thearmview.com

❏ *Boneheads BBQ*

1014 Barrington Street
Halifax, NS B3H 2P9
902-407-4100
www.lickthebone.com

❏ *Salvatore's Pizzaiolo Trattoria*

5541 Young Street
Halifax, NS B3K 1Z7
902-455-1133
www.salvatorespizza.ca

INGONISH
❏ *Coastal Waters Restaurant & Pub*

36404 Cabot Trail
Ingonish, NS B0C 1K0
902-285-2526

LUNENBURG
❏ *Magnolia's Grill*

128 Montague Street
Lunenburg, NS B0J 2C0
902-634-3287

MONCTON
❏ *Tide & Boar Gastropub*

700 Main Street
Moncton, NB E1C 1E4
506-857-9118
www.tideandboar.com

NEW GLASGOW
❏ *New Glasgow Lobster Suppers*

604 Route 258
New Glasgow, PEI C0A 1N0
902-964-2870
www.peilobstersuppers.com

SAINT JOHN
❏ *Saint John Ale House*

1 Market Square
Saint John, NB E2L 4Z6
506-657-2337
www.saintjohnalehouse.com

❏ *Urban Deli*

68 King Street
Saint John, NB E2L 1G4
506-652-3354
www.urbandeli.ca

ST. JOHN'S
❏ *Ches's Famous Fish & Chips*
9 Freshwater Road
St. John's, NL A1C 2N1
709-722-4083
www.chessfishandchips.ca

ST. PETER'S BAY
❏ *Rick's Fish 'N' Chips & Seafood House*
5544 Route 2
St. Peter's Bay, PEI C0A 2A0
902-961-3438 (May to September)
902-961-3165 (October to May)
www.ricksfishnchips.com

VICTORIA BY THE SEA
❏ *Landmark Cafe*
12 Main Street
Victoria by the Sea, PEI C0A 2G0
902-685-2286
www.landmarkcafe.ca

WHYCOCOMAGH
❏ *Charlene's Bayside Restaurant and Cafe*
9657 Hwy 105
Whycocomagh, NS B0E 3M0
902-756-8004

CENTRAL CANADA

BOLTON
❏ *Baffo's Pizza & Pasta*
31 Queen Street East
Bolton, ON L7E 1C2
905-857-3444
www.baffos.com

CARLSBAD SPRINGS
❏ *D&S Southern Comfort B.B.Q.*
6501 Russell Road
Carlsbad Springs, ON K0A 1K0
613-822-8652
www.dsbbq.ca

HAMILTON
❏ *Chicago Style Pizza Shack*
534 Upper Sherman Avenue
Hamilton, ON L8V 3M1
905-575-8800

❏ *The Harbour Diner*
486 James Street North
Hamilton, ON L8L 1J1
905-523-7373
www.harbourdiner.com

HUNTSVILLE
❏ *That Little Place by the Lights*
76 Main Street East
Huntsville, ON P1H 2C7
705-789-2536
www.thatlittleplacebythelights.ca

LONDON
❏ *Prince Albert's Diner*
565 Richmond Street
London, ON N6A 3G2
519-432-2835

❏ *Relish the Best in Burgers*
135 Wortley Road
London, ON N6C 3P4
519-667-0606

MONTREAL

❏ *Chez Claudette*

351, avenue Laurier Est
Montreal, QC H2T 1G7
514-279-5173

❏ *The Main Deli Steak House*

3864, boulevard Saint-Laurent
Montreal, QC H2W 1Y2
514-843-8126
www.maindelisteakhouse.com

❏ *Pizzeria Napoletana*

189, rue Dante
Montreal, QC H2S 1K1
514-276-8226
www.napoletana.com

❏ *Schwartz's Deli*

3895, boulevard Saint-Laurent
Montreal, QC H2W 1X9
514-842-4813
www.schwartzsdeli.com

OAKVILLE

❏ *Stoney's Bread Company*

325 Kerr Street
Oakville, ON L6K 3B6
905-849-3627
www.stoneysbreadcompany.com

ORANGEVILLE

❏ *Philadelphia Kitchen*

281 Broadway Avenue
Orangeville, ON L9W 1L2
519-938-8970

ORILLIA

❏ *Tre Sorelle*

133 Mississaga Street East
Orillia, ON L3V 5A9
705-325-8507
www.tresorelleorillia.com

OTTAWA

❏ *Elgin Street Diner*

374 Elgin Street
Ottawa, ON K2P 1N1
613-237-9700
www.elginstreetdiner.com

❏ *Stoneface Dolly's*

416 Preston Street
Ottawa, ON K1S 4M9
613-564-2222
www.stonefacedollys.com

PETERBOROUGH

❏ *Reggie's Hot Grill*

89 Hunter Street East
Peterborough, ON K9H 1G4
www.reggieshotgrill.ca

❏ *Shish-Kabob Hut Greek Restaurant*

220 King Street
Peterborough, ON K9J 2S1
705-745-3260
www.skhpeterborough.com

PORT PERRY

❏ *Haugen's Chicken & Ribs Barbeque*

13801 Highway 12
Port Perry, ON L9L 1A2
905-985-2402
www.haugens.com

ST. CATHARINES

❏ *Joe Feta's Greek Village*

290 Lake Street

St. Catharines, ON L2N 4H2

905-646-3399

www.joefetas.ca

STRATFORD

❏ *Boomers Gourmet Fries*

26 Erie Street

Stratford, ON N5A 2M4

519-275-3147

www.boomersgourmetfries.com

THORNBURY

❏ *The Dam Pub Gastropub*

53 Bruce Street

Thornbury, ON N0H 2P0

519-599-2110

www.thedampub.ca

THUNDER BAY

❏ *Hoito Restaurant*

314 Bay Street

Thunder Bay, ON P7B 1S1

807-344-7081

www.finlandiaclub.ca

TORONTO

❏ *Café Polonez*

195 Roncesvalles Avenue

Toronto, ON M6R 2L5

416-532-8432

www.cafepolonez.ca

❏ *Cardinal Rule*

5 Roncesvalles Avenue

Toronto, ON M6R 2K2

647-352-0202

www.cardinalrulerestaurant.com

❏ *Dangerous Dan's Diner*

714 Queen Street East

Toronto, ON M4M 1H2

416-463-7310

www.dangerousdansdiner.com

❏ *The Grilled Cheese*

66 1/2 Nassau Street

Toronto, ON M5T 1M5

647-347-7062

❏ *Hadley's*

940 College Street

Toronto, ON M6H 1A5

416-588-3113

www.hadleys.ca

❏ *The Musket Restaurant*

40 Advance Road

Toronto, ON M8Z 2T4

416-231-6488

www.musketrestaurant.com

❏ *Phil's Original BBQ*

838 College Street

Toronto, ON M6H 1A2

416-532-8161

www.philsoriginalbbq.com

❏ *Uncle Betty's Diner*
2590 Yonge Street
Toronto, ON M4P 2J3
416-483-2590
www.unclebettys.com

VERMILION BAY
❏ *Busters Barbeque*
177 Highway 17
Vermilion Bay, ON P0V 2V0
807-227-5256
www.bustersbbq.com

WINDSOR
❏ *Bubi's Awesome Eats*
620 University Avenue West
Windsor, ON N9A 5R5
519-252-2001
www.bubis.org

❏ *Tunnel Bar-B-Q*
58 Park Street East
Windsor, ON N9A 3A7
519-258-3663
tunnelbarbq.com

WESTERN CANADA

BURNABY
❏ *Fraser Park Restaurant*
4663 Byrne Road, #103
Burnaby, BC V5J 3H6
604-433-7605

CALGARY
❏ *Diner Deluxe*
804 Edmonton Trail NE
Calgary, AB T2E 3J6
403-276-5499
www.dinerdeluxe.com

❏ *Fat City Franks*
#3 2015 4 Street SW
Calgary, AB T2S 1W6
403-229-3641
www.fatcityfranks.com

❏ *Jelly Modern Doughnuts*
100 1414 8th Street SW
Calgary, AB T2R 1J6
403-453-2053
www.jellymoderndoughnuts.com

❏ *Pfanntastic Pannenkoek Haus*
2439 54th Avenue SW
Calgary, AB T3E 1M4
403-243-7757
www.dutchpancakes.ca

❏ *Tubby Dog*
1022 17th Avenue SW
Calgary, AB T2T 0A5
403-244-0694
www.tubbydog.com

COWICHAN BAY
❏ *Rock Cod Café*
1759 Cowichan Bay Road
Cowichan Bay, BC V0R 1N0
250-746-1550
www.rockcodcafe.com

EDMONTON

Highlands Kitchen
6509 112th Avenue NW
Edmonton, AB T5W 4K3
780-477-2422
www.highlandskitchen.ca

SugarBowl
10922 88th Avenue
Edmonton, AB T6G 0Z1
780-433-8369
www.thesugarbowl.org

Tres Carnales Taqueria
10119 100A Street NW
Edmonton, AB T5J 0R5
780-429-0911
www.trescarnales.com

Urban Diner
12427 102 Avenue NW
Edmonton, AB T5N 0M2
780-488-7274
www.urbandiner.com

HIGH RIVER

Evelyn's Memory Lane Cafe
118 4th Avenue SW
High River, AB T1V 1P7
403-652-1887
www.memorylaneicecream.ca

MOOSE JAW

Deja Vu Cafe
16 High Street East
Moose Jaw, SK S6H 0B7
306-692-6066
www.dejavucafe.ca

NANAIMO

Mrs. Riches Restaurant
199 Fraser Street
Nanaimo, BC V9R 5C1
250-753-8311
www.mrsriches.ca

NORTH VANCOUVER

The Tomahawk Barbecue
1550 Philip Avenue
North Vancouver, BC V7P 2V8
604-988-2612
www.tomahawkrestaurant.com

TURNER VALLEY

Chuckwagon Cafe & Cattle Company
105 Sunset Boulevard
Turner Valley, AB T0L 2A0
403-933-0003
www.chuckwagoncafe.ca

VANCOUVER

Argo Café
1836 Ontario Street
Vancouver, BC V5T 2W6
604-876-3620
www.argocafe.ca

Neighbour's Restaurant
6493 Victoria Drive
Vancouver, BC V5P 3X5
604-327-1456
www.neighboursrestaurant.ca

Topanga Cafe
2904 West 4th Avenue
Vancouver, BC V6K 4A9
604-733-3713
www.topangacafe.com

VICTORIA

❏ *Floyd's Diner*
866 Yates Street
Victoria, BC V8W 1L8
250-381-5114
www.floydsdiner.ca

❏ *John's Place Restaurant*
723 Pandora Avenue
Victoria, BC V8W 1N9
250-389-0711
www.johnsplace.ca

❏ *Pagliacci's*
1011 Broad Street
Victoria, BC V8W 2A1
250-386-1662
www.pagliaccis.ca

WINNIPEG

❏ *Bistro Dansk*
63 Sherbrook Street
Winnipeg, MB R3C 2B2
204-775-5662
www.bistrodansk.com

❏ *Blondies*
1969 Main Street
Winnipeg, MB R2V 2B7
204-338-0185

❏ *Boon Burger Café*
79 Sherbrook Street
Winnipeg, MB R3C 2B2
204-415-1391
www.boonburger.ca

❏ *Red Top Drive-Inn Restaurant*
219 St. Mary's Road
Winnipeg, MB R2H 1J2
204-233-7943

❏ *The Tallest Poppy*
631 Main Street
Winnipeg, MB R3B 1E1
204-957-1708
www.thetallestpoppy.com

John Catucci is an actor, a comedian, and the host of *You Gotta Eat Here!* He may not be a chef, but he knows a great burger when he eats one. John has also been a member of The Second City Touring Company, where he honed the improv skills he now displays in restaurant kitchens across Canada. He lives in Toronto, Ontario. Follow him on Twitter **@johncatucci**.

Michael Vlessides is the bestselling author of *The Ice Pilots* and a freelance writer whose award-winning work has been published in magazines around the world. A graduate of New York University's School of Journalism, Michael lives in Canmore, Alberta, though he has been known to travel farther afield for a plate of poutine, a gourmet hotdog, or a maple bacon doughnut. Follow him on Twitter **@MichaelTextman**.